The Working Population of Manchester, New Hampshire
1840-1886

Studies in
American History and Culture, No. 29

Robert Berkhofer, Series Editor

Director of American Culture Programs
and Richard Hudson Research Professor of History
The University of Michigan

Other Titles in This Series

The Working Population of Manchester, New Hampshire

1840-1886

by
James P. Hanlan

RESEARCH PRESS

Produced and distributed by
UMI Research Press
an imprint of
University Microfilms International
Ann Arbor, Michigan 48106

Library of Congress Cataloging in Publication Data

Hanlan, James P.
The working population of Manchester, New
Hampshire, 1840-1886.

(Studies in American history and culture ; no. 29)
Revision of thesis (Ph.D.)—Clark University, 1979.
Bibliography: p.
Includes index.
1. Textile workers—New Hampshire—Manchester—
History. 2. Amoskeag Manufacturing Company—History.
3. Manchester (N.H.)—Social conditions. 4. Labor and
laboring classes—New Hampshire—Manchester—History.
I. Title. II. Series.

HD6956.T42U647 1981   331.7'677'0097428   81-3355
ISBN 0-8357-1193-5   AACR2

Contents

vi   Contents

Tables

Acknowledgments

I am deeply grateful to the many people who provided assistance, advice, and encouragement in the course of my work.

Virginia Plisko, Elizabeth Lessard, and George Comptois, of the Manchester Historic Association, and Robert Lovett, of the Baker Library, generously assisted me in searching through the resources of their respective institutions. The computer center staffs at Clark University, the College of the Holy Cross, and Worcester Polytechnic Institute helped me to organize and process my data and answered countless questions.

I owe a debt of thanks to Doris Horgan for her careful and excellent job of typing and proofreading. I am grateful to Donald Johnson, Head of the Department of Humanities, and Ray Bolz, Dean of Faculty, at Worcester Polytechnic Institute, for providing financial assistance for research, photocopying, and typing, and, together with my colleagues at W.P.I., for providing encouragement and thought-provoking companionship.

For providing generous financial assistance at a crucial stage of my work, I thank the Merrimack Valley Textile Museum and its director, Tom Leavitt.

I am thankful to Robert Campbell, of Clark University, for his careful reading of my manuscript and to Ron Formisano and Tom Barrow, of Clark, for thorough, frequent, and careful readings and thoughtful suggestions. I owe Ran Langenbach a debt of thanks for providing me with photocopies of Daniel Creamer's WPE notecards. Tamara Hareven, my dissertation advisor, proved herself a friend as well as an advisor. I am deeply grateful for her invaluable comments and assistance.

Most of all, and more than I can possibly express, I thank my wife, Gaye, and my children, George and Janet. They good-naturedly tolerated my absence, my preoccupation, and my lack of attention. I shall never be able to adequately repay them.

Introduction

This study has been undertaken in the spirit of the developing tradition of a new social history. This approach focuses not on the "giants," the elite about whom we often know all too much, but instead focuses upon the experiences of hitherto anonymous people—those men and women who left little in the way of written, formalized records of their lives. There is, in short, a conscious attempt to incorporate into this work those people whom more traditional histories have tended to overlook. Traditional labor histories, for example, have followed the interpretive framework of John R. Commons and associates. The model set out by Commons focused upon workers who belonged to trade unions. To be even more precise, the Commons tradition has tended to place stress upon those men and women who led unions—in this sense, it has been the history of leaders, not of followers or non-members. In spite of its emphasis upon movements that have affected—and been affected by—the common worker, the more traditional approaches have tended to ignore the average man and woman and have remained, in their own ways, elitist works.

Historians writing in this tradition have done a thorough job of studying the process of union growth and development. The problem with this approach is that it has tended to neglect the vast majority of men and women who worked for a wage—non-union workers. Instead of studying workers in the context of their own cultures and their own group and community life, labor historians have tended to study the unionization movement. Until recently, historians have tended to ignore the context of everyday community life within which workers functioned, lived, and formed associations, friendships and values. By placing emphasis upon strikes and similar labor disturbances, historians have tended to ignore the community and cultural context which provided intellectual, emotional and group support for working class people.[1]

In contrast to the older approach, the new social history focuses upon aspects of working class group and community life that have hitherto been either underplayed or ignored. Stress upon group and community life can provide a far clearer picture of life as it was for the majority of nineteenth century working people than could the older emphasis upon the biographies of a small number of working class elites. These shortcomings are now being addressed. Such historians as Herbert Gutman have stressed the cultural dimensions of working class life, while Tamara Hareven has emphasized the role of working class families in the lives of workers in an industrial environment.[2]

Since some of the earliest of the older social history, such as the writings of Caroline and Norman Ware, focused on the milieu of the textile industry, it is perhaps fitting that the new social history is now re-examining the traditional portrait of textile workers and textile towns, and, in the process, discovering much that is new. Thanks to the older history, the patterns of investment, methods of management, wage structure, and technology are well known.[3] Building upon this, the newer scholars have begun to add a richer understanding of the lives of the ordinary people who lived in the textile communities established and, often, run by a few "great men." Hareven, for example, has stressed the centrality of the family in interactions of workers with the workplace and the industrial city.[4] Thomas Dublin's study of pre-1860 Lowell has, likewise, focused upon new themes. Dublin's stress upon the importance of the maintenance of a sense of community as a crucial factor in explaining labor disturbances is a marked departure from the older emphasis upon wages, hours, working conditions, and unionization.[5]

Daniel Walkowitz, in his comparative study of an iron and a textile community, has also stressed the importance of the cultural traditions of workers in explaining the outbreak of worker protest. Walkowitz has emphasized the importance of the immigrant worker as well as the native worker. This is an important theme since the older history tended to dismiss the importance of the period after the coming of the Irish and, later, of other groups, after the mid-1840s.[6] In spite of much work in the area of labor history in textile towns, then, there is much that remains to be done. This study will examine the working population of Manchester, New Hampshire, from 1840 to 1886.

Manchester, New Hampshire, was one of northern New England's major planned textile towns. It was the town which would eventually host the world's largest cotton textile factory, the Amoskeag Manufacturing Company. Those men and women who lived through the "Amoskeag years," whether in the nineteenth century, the focus of this work, or in the twentieth century, the main focus of Hareven's work, were well aware of the paternalistic attitudes and policies of the Amoskeag toward both workers and town.[7] The foundations of the corporation's paternalism were set down, in initial form, in the period from 1840 to 1880. This was a crucial period wherein workers, factory managers, and Boston mill magnates alike sought mutually to explore and, via this exploration, more definitely to establish the parameters of the company's paternalism. This period is, then, essential in understanding the "company town" that Manchester would become.

The years covered by this study witnessed the migration to the city and to the factory of a series of "newcomers." These new workers would have to adjust to industrial life and work discipline and, in the latter years, to a new country as well. As a series of newcomers found their way to the factory, each group would have to find its place not only in the factory but also in the larger society surrounding the factory, the planned company town. Even in the new history, the idea of a "company town" is often taken for granted. Walkowitz suggests, for example, that the paternalistic company towns of Cohoes worked well for the company in suppressing worker discontent (at least until immigrants found their strength in an organized community). Of the recent works on textile towns, only Hareven's has suggested that corporate paternalism may well have been a two-way street, working to benefit worker as well as corporation. It will be one of the contentions of this work that workers were not helpless in the face of an imposed paternalistic schema, but that each group of workers would help to define the "company" plan and to modify it as they adjusted to the corporation and as the corporation and their fellow townsmen adjusted to them.[8]

This study will focus upon the community life of Manchester and upon the process of adaptation and adjustment experienced by varying groups of Manchester's working class population over a 40-year period as they came to settle within, and have an effect upon, the factory-dominated city.

The experiences and adjustments of each of these groups helped to define the parameters of the "company town." The limits, and the limitations, of the Amoskeag's unique corporate paternalism (with which later generations would have to deal, although in altered form) were shaped in the first 40 years of the company's life. The design of the company town proved flexible enough to allow succeeding groups of factory workers to contribute their own input. Just as each new group of migrants to city and factory would have to adjust to new living and working conditions, so the "plan" for the company town would have to prove flexible enough to avoid the social breakdown which an overly rigid planned community might engender.[9]

Adjusting to life in the company town presented major challenges both to workers and to the Amoskeag's resident managers. In Manchester, the early plans of the corporation, as well as the unique geographical limitations of the city, dictated a compact industrial village. The corporation envisioned a series of boardinghouse-like residences, similar to the familiar Lowell model, located in close proximity to the mills.[10] The unique requirements of different groups of workers, and the clashes between the interests of each group as they sought out their own place in both factory and community, led to the eventual modification of the company's original plan. Community development, in short, proceeded not along the lines of the "plan" laid down by the company, but along lines influenced by the cultural backgrounds of the workers, with distinct urban villages gradually growing up along ethnic lines. To be sure, the company boardinghouses and tenements were built, but they fit themselves into a town organized along cultural and ethnic lines rather than on division of work in the factory. One of the guiding hypotheses of this work will be that workers were not entirely passive victims of the industrialization process. Cultural and ethnic background not only served to help workers to adapt to a new industrial invironment but also were crucial factors in influencing the nature of the community that grew up around the factories. In this sense, the workers themselves helped to shape the "planned" community that Manchester would become.[11]

Several other assumptions have also guided this work. The widely accepted model of a "mill town," especially during its early years, is that of a community with a good deal of instability, with rapid and frequent turnover in the town's population.[12] While this may prove true when looking at aggregate data for the town as a whole, it is likely that there is some basis, in a long-lived paternalistic environment, to challenge that view. By looking at different groups of workers, and breaking down the categories that make up aggregate population or in and out migration figures, going beyond the generalized category of "worker," it may be possible to discover that particular groups of workers, by reason of their unique adjustment to the factory and the city, tended to remain in the community long after other industrial workers had moved on. In Manchester, the process of neighborhood formation, particularly for the native born, seems to have provided a small base of a stable population element amidst the shifting mill population.

Neighborhood formation and the institution of the family, particularly among immigrant workers, will be seen as more than vehicles for the transmission of ethnic traditions. Both immigrant and native neighborhoods and the family and community life fostered in those neighborhoods were invaluable resources upon which working class people could draw in times of individual or group need. Without these vital mechanisms, the image of a "mill town" or "company town" population totally at the mercy of an employer who made one-sided decisions might have proven valid. By forming distinct neighborhoods, where cultural reinforcements could provide the various groups that composed the industrial town with reassurance, introductions, advice, and assistance, workers had a crucial edge which allowed them effectively to resist being overwhelmed by the company's planned town. Neighborhoods and families offered Manchester's working population an important alternative to the company sponsored boardinghouses and tenements.[13] Especially for immigrants, the setting of neighborhood, countrymen, and family provided reinforcement for the struggle against a strange environment. The ethnic family provided an alternative to the company boardinghouse milieu. In addition, the boarders provided income that might prove crucial to a household wherein the primary wage earner might not earn sufficient wages to support his family.

Manchester's relative freedom from work stoppages or disruptions will not be seen as resulting from a lack of permanence in the workforce and community among the workers. [14] It will be one of the contentions of this work that Manchester's freedom from work disturbances was related to two factors: the lack of absolute rigidity in the company's paternalism and the rapid development of neighborhoods with their own cultural traditions which would temporarily slow the development of working class consciousness. The company's land sales and distribution system, the flexibility of work rules in the face of workers' pressure, and continuous leadership by one family as the locally-based agent, the chief operating officers of the mills on the local level, will also be seen as helping to prevent serious worker discontent within both factory and city.

Manchester was chosen as the subject of this work for a number of reasons. Almost alone among the major northern New England factory cities, it has not been the subject of serious scholarly investigation. [15] It is almost as if, knowing the pattern that prevailed in Lowell, Chicopee, Holyoke, and similar Boston Associates towns, historians have assumed that Manchester fit the model and was not, therefore, worthy of investigation. With the exception of Langenbach's work on the urban design of the Amoskeag, then, Manchester was seriously overlooked as a subject of historical investigation when this study began. Its unique heritage of corporate paternalism of an exceptionally long standing was completely overlooked. In short, Manchester was seriously miscast in the model applied pro-forma to other textile towns.

Secondly, the choice of Manchester was dictated by the ongoing work of several new social historians who have recently undertaken or completed similar studies. The most obvious and important of these, from the perspective of this work, is the work of Tamara Hareven on Manchester in its later period. It is hoped that this work will provide an important supplement to Hareven's work and that together the two works will provide a social history of Manchester from the foundation of the Amoskeag to its demise in the 1930s. Thus focusing on one community over an unusually long period, the treatment of contrast and long-term adjustment in a factory town over its entire lifespan will be unique. [16] Besides Hareven, other historians have undertaken important work on textile and working class communities recently. This study will serve as an important complement to this body of literature, in some cases reinforcing, by its findings, the hypotheses of others while in other cases modifying or contradicting the findings of these other scholars. Dublin's findings on native born preference for company-owned dwellings, for example, will be confirmed by the data on Manchester. [17] Likewise, Jonathan Prude's contention that workers responded to unpleasant conditions in a variety of ways will be reinforced.

Prude's suggestion that the alternative of leaving the city was one of the key weapons available to early native born factory operatives will be borne out in the Manchester study, but a number of other strategies of workers will also be explored.[18] Walkowitz' suggestion that nineteenth century industrial workers followed a process of "arrival, adaptation, struggle and protest" is borne out in Manchester, but the present study seeks to expand appreciation of the richness and variety of the adaptive mechanisms available to workers in one industrial city while explaining the elements of struggle and protest in a cultural and uniquely paternalistic environment. The paternalism of Manchester, unlike the paternalism of Cohoes, worked for a far longer period of time and to a far greater degree in minimizing the elements of struggle and protest, and did so with similar groups of immigrant and native population.[19]

Lastly, Manchester was chosen because of the unusual richness and variety of the source material available. In addition to the traditional census and city directory materials available for many communitites,[20] a vast array of company records from the Amoskeag Manufacturing Company survive in readily accessible and usable form at both the Manchester Historic Association and the Baker Library. The materials at the Manchester Historic Association were particularly useful for this study and included both quantitative and literary materials. Early company records included contracts with workmen who were to build the company's town, specifying in careful detail the concerns of the company with the minutest detail of life in Manchester. Early payroll records, while sporadic, proved useful in tracing in and out mobility and finding wage information. The company kept complete records of the company sponsored savings plan which survive virtually intact and proved most helpful. Similarly, the company records of the Scots Girls, assisted emigrants, survive at the Manchester Historic Association as do the ledgers listing place of origin for some of the earliest of the mill workers. The extent and variety of the company materials available at the Manchester Historic Association is, practically speaking, far too great to describe fully here.

Company records were supplemented by town records and tax lists at the Manchester City Hall and by city censuses and other materials at the Manchester Historic Association. Joseph Kidder's manuscript diaries, kept on a daily basis from the beginning to the end of the period covered by this work, were unusually complete and proved invaluable.

The New Hampshire Room of the Manchester Public Library contains materials on both the Amoskeag and the development of the city of Manchester. The Manchester Public Library also proved useful in its collection of early local newspapers and local history materials. The New Hampshire State Library at Concord and the New Hampshire Historical Society also proved rich sources of newspaper and quantitative data. The original manuscript returns of the United States Census of population, manufacturing, and agriculture, at the State Library, proved greatly valuable.

This study also benefitted from the official company history as well as several published local histories. Daniel Creamer's W.P.A. study of the closing of the Amoskeag proved useful for historical background. Creamer's note cards, made as part of an intended follow-up study, were generously made available by Randolph Langenbach and added to the rich variety of sources.[21]

This study will attempt to demonstrate the relationship between a paternalistic company, the workers affected by, and in turn affecting, that company, and the city that both working men and women and the founding company helped to shape. The first chapter deals with the transition from old Derryfield to industrial Manchester. It describes the process of the foundation of the company town and analyzes the early social structure of the town, the places of origin of the early work force, and the relationship between newcomers and old residents. Chapters 2 and 3 are both distinct, yet thematically related. Chapter 2 focuses upon the company and its policies both in relationship to the company town and to its workers. Chapter 3 focuses upon the ways in which workers responded, in the 1840s and 1850s, to the company and the reaction of the company and community leadership to the growth of the working class population. Chapter 4 examines the social structure of Manchester prior to 1860 and discusses the place of the textile worker in the social structure of the town. Chapter 5 deals with changes in the social structure, the working population, and the company's policies in the decade following the Civil War. The final chapter includes analysis of a population sample of over 3,600 cases drawn from the manuscript census of 1880. The samples were carefully chosen from three target populations: a native born group, residing in a neighborhood on the outskirts of the industrialized area, but still within the city; an immigrant neighborhood near the industrial area, but not in company owned housing; and lastly, residents of corporation owned boardinghouses and tenements. The contrasts between the groups of working class populations residing in the three sample districts illustrates both the complex makeup of the working population of Manchester and the process of neighborhood formation and differentiation in the industrial city. Together, the complexity of the working population, the ethnic character of neighborhoods within the city, and the past successes of a paternalistic policy helped to convince a new generation of factory managers that the paternalism that had served them well in the past could, with modifications, continue successfully to manage a far more complex working population.

1

Manchester: The Town in Transition

There are turning points in human history, points where the historian can honestly say that what went before is markedly different from what will follow. In the history of Manchester, New Hampshire, such a turning point was 1840. The period of the town life of old Derryfield from its founding in 1751, down through its transformation into the town of Manchester in 1810, and until 1840, is best characterized as one of concord and accommodation. The community was self-consciously secure. Town politics reflected a pattern, long accepted, of leadership by a local elite. Similarly, voter deference was an accepted reality, with the old families serving frequently and repeatedly in what positions of honor and office the town could offer. The Starks, the Moors, the Huses, the Goffes, all were familiar names in Manchester in the 1830s. Men bearing these names, and other equally respected and familiar men, had served repeatedly as selectmen since the founding of the town. On those occasions when these names disappeared from the roles of the town's top elected officials, they most often reappeared in minor town offices. When not serving as selectmen, moderator, or town clerk, these men might well be serving a term as fish wardens, surveyors of lumber, fence viewers, or marshalls.[1]

In the 40-year period from the founding of Derryfield, in 1751, to the genesis of Samuel Blodgett's dream for Derryfield's future, about 1791, the example of the Goffe family serves to illustrate the patterns of community leadership that prevailed. In those years, John Goffe served nine terms as town moderator. He served five terms as town clerk, and five terms as a selectman, as well as holding a number of minor town offices. During those years, as the elder Goffe grew old in town service, his son, John Goffe, Jr., began to serve his first terms of elective office.[2]

With hardly any variation, the first 40 years of the nineteenth century would witness a continuing tradition of social, political, and economic leadership of an elite of older families. Similarly, a pattern of voter deference which allowed these few old families to continue in the honors of local office holding would continue almost unabated for the earliest years of the 1800's.[3]

First in Derryfield and then, afterwards, in Manchester, homogeneity of culture would persist for nearly 100 years. Town affairs were marked for their display of consensus. Not only in the selection of local leaders, but also in the remarkable absence of signs of conflict in the conduct of town affairs, the community was generally in agreement regarding the requirements for a harmonious community life. What little conflict did take place was dealt with swiftly and effectively by the leadership. The leaders of the town could take decisive action secure in the knowledge that their decisions would be upheld by the town meeting and, in a wider sense, supported by the townsmen in their everyday life. Whatever factiousness might be encountered, the town fathers could quickly suppress.

The case of Hannah Farmer represents a concrete illustration of the way in which the town fathers dealt with an obstreperous resident, and also illustrates the support which they were given by the town at large. Hannah Farmer had been a source of contention in the town long before 1799, when the town meeting authorized the selectmen to "deal with" her.[4] Prior to 1799, though, her infractions had been of a minor nature. When she had been delinquent in paying her taxes, her name was posted in public, as it would be for any townsman. When she cut a leaf from the official town record book and destroyed it, though, her behavior called for a far more serious punishment. This sort of behavior was too much for her neighbors to tolerate, and the town meeting faced the problem of Hannah Farmer as one of the matters of official business listed on the warrant. The meeting authorized the selectmen to consider the matter of Hannah Farmer, and to take appropriate action. Thus, when the selectmen decided to "prosecute" her, the entire town stood by their decision. The condemnation of the selectmen was the condemnation of the town.[5]

The selectmen were among the town's most prosperous citizens. They mixed economic well-being with social prominence. The Starks, for example, benefitted from the reputation of their Revolutionary namesake whom townsmen called "Derryfield's man of destiny." The Moors, father and son, by 1835 represented both the town's wealthiest individual and the town's leading merchant. These families were an embodiment of the community's ties with its Puritan past. They embodied the deep roots of the past which held the community together, exemplifying the self-consciousness of the old township. The way in which men lived, their attitudes, their pride, all in the 1830's bore the marks of the past 50 years. If the community's leaders in the 1830's were not the exact same men who comprised the local elite of the late 1700's, then they were the earlier group's sons or grandsons.[6] They had been bred to accept positions of honor, and their fellow townsmen had come to accept that leadership, choosing them time after time.

The selectmen may have been among the more well-to-do of the town residents, and their wealth may have been supplemented by trading, but on the whole they were like their neighbors, farmers serving the interests of an agricultural community. The shared interest of all was land. Land was the basis of the economic and social position of the older families, and land provided the means of a livelihood for the entire community. In a community too small to attract a permanent minister for many years, the older families served as a cohesive force, holding the "respectable" members of the town together. That function was important in early Derryfield. Until the coming of a permanent minister, there would be no regular church services to draw men together. What services there were could generally be held only in summertime in a building that "answered better than a barn." Moral leadership fell to the community's chosen men who saw to it that the strangers (and their liquor) who were attracted by the hunting and fishing at Amoskeag Falls were promptly warned out of town.[7]

Given local tradition, the angry words of Justice John Stark at the 1840 town meeting should be no surprise. Judge Stark posed a question for the town's new industrial residents: "Who are ye that are here to act, and to tread upon us in this manner? I'll tell ye who you are! You're a set of interlopers come here to get a living upon a sand bank, and a damned poor living you will get, let me tell ye!"[8] With those words, the Judge led the old residents out of the town meeting which had seen control of town affairs pass into the hands of the people from the "new village," as townsmen called it, which had grown up suddenly on the East bank of the Merrimack River.

Judge Stark's family had been in Manchester since before the days when the town was incorporated as Derryfield. The Starks had seen the time when the town was, as its name implied, little more than a pasture field for the cattle of Derry and Londonderry. The Judge himself was a descendant of Revolutionary General John Stark, the town's most revered citizen whom local men would regard with the same awe as George Washington inspired. Like the other old families, Stark's had been accustomed to the exercise of leadership in town affairs. The final realization that the "new village" would be more than an across-the-river adjunct of the old town went down hard at that 1840 town meeting.[9]

The older residents had not anticipated that they were on the verge of being caught up in a process that would displace them from traditional relationships to their community and from their agrarian-inspired lifestyles. They had, initially, welcomed the building of factories and boardinghouses. The laying out and sale of lots by the Amoskeag Manufacturing Company in the summer of 1839 had seemed no threat to them. It was assumed that the area surrounding Elm, Amherst, and Hanover Streets, on the opposite bank of the river, would form "an enterprising and thrifty village" which would not only lower their tax rate and provide them with an added source of income, but, additionally, would remain a village.[10]

After the Amoskeag's second land sale, a considerable number of new residents began moving into the town. From 1820 to 1830, Manchester's population had increased by 116, a growth rate of about 15%. During the next ten years, however, the growth rate would be close to 269%, with 2,358 new people in the town. Most of that tremendous increase took place not over the entire ten-year period, moreover, but within the two years before 1840, as the new textile mills were under construction. Never again would the community experience such an expansion. Even the 10,700 increase of the following decade, a growth rate of 330%, would be spread out through a ten-year period (see Table 1.1). Such growth caught the town unprepared, and the entire nature of the community was changed, old residents being overcome and displaced by "newcomers."[11] A contemporary indicated that the townspeople were ". . .unprepared for such progess." The town had made only the usual appropriations for schools, roads, poor relief, and the customary functions of small town governance. They had not foreseen the need for any new town officials, and had appointed none. As the inadequacy of customary arrangements for town affairs became obvious, a special town meeting was called for October 26, 1839, to make provisions for the new village.[12]

The October meeting saw the adoption of a police and fire warden system, modelled on that of New Hampshire's largest city, Portsmouth. A board of health officer was chosen. In distinct contradiction to their tradition of fiscal conservatism which, a few years previously, had seen townsmen wage a 13-year battle against a highway assessment imposed by the state, the town fathers recommended, and the voters approved, $2,000 in loans. This unprecedented sum was to be utilized to construct new roads and to purchase fire equipment for the protection of the new village. In addition, the people of the new village were to be allowed the privilege of nominating their own fire wardens. As the special town meeting adjourned, then, the townsmen were convinced of their liberality in that the "new village was fairly recognized and organized."[13] Having been dealt with generously, what cause would the residents of the new village have for complaint?

The older residents were proud of the just manner in which they had dealt with the creation of the new village. They felt that they had provided everything that could be of use to the newcomers. "Newcomers" was a term used by the older residents to refer to the residents of the new village. While they provided for the new residents' needs, the older group continued to regard them as different, as unwelcome but necessary interlopers who inevitably accompanied each stage of industrial growth and who could, eventually, be assimilated into the patterns of local life. One contemporary observer noted that, in spite of the apparent liberality with which facilities were provided for the newcomers, ". . . so great were their jealousies of them that had they been aware of their prospective power, in spite of their self-interest, it is very doubtful whether the villagers could have got any sort of votes in their favor at this town meeting. These jealousies soon became mutal and produced confirmed opposition which was exhibited in a decided manner on various occasions, soon after."[14]

By the time of the 1840 town meeting, the lines of opposition which would occasion Judge Stark's imprecation had been clearly formed. The latent hostility of the old residents became increasingly open as the "newcomers" began to discuss the possibility that they might control the affairs of the town. The first day of the meeting demonstrated that the people of the new village would not be content to remain passive. On the contrary, they demonstrated their activism when they made a motion to adjourn the meeting and resume the following day on the East bank. To further signify what their intentions were, the new residents suggested that the new townhouse which was to be built (and which would become Manchester's first city hall) should be located in the new village on the East bank, thus permanently removing the seat of local government from the vicinity of the older part of the town. On the pretext of restoring order, which had been seriously disrupted by the newcomers' motion, the moderator, one of the old residents, ordered two lines to be formed outside the meeting house. In this way an orderly count of persons on each side of the issue could be taken. The newcomers, apparently confident of victory, filed out first. After the new residents were outside, those remaining inside made and carried a motion to adjourn to the next day at the usual meeting house.[15]

Not even the 30 special constables chosen the next day to preserve order could save the residents of the old township from losing the reins of community control. Based upon their previous experience, the older residents had assumed that industrial innovation was not inconsistent with the way of life of an agrarian community. Their assumption appeared false only after they had been displaced from control of community affairs by the newer residents.[16]

Derryfield had long cherished control of her own affairs. In 1780, upset at the prospect of being ". . . overpowered by numbers . . . outvoted . . . therefore not fairly represented . . .," the men of Derryfield's 50 families petitioned the New Hampshire legislature. They asked that, when district lines for representation were drawn, Derryfield not be included in the same district with Goffstown, a town ten miles distant with twice as many families.[17]

In addition to a tradition of controlling her own affairs, Manchester had, by 1840, experienced a number of encounters with technology. To each encounter the people of Manchester had made a successful adjustment, but none of those experiences had been on a scale so vast as the building of the Amoskeag New Mills, an enterprise that would eventually become the world's largest

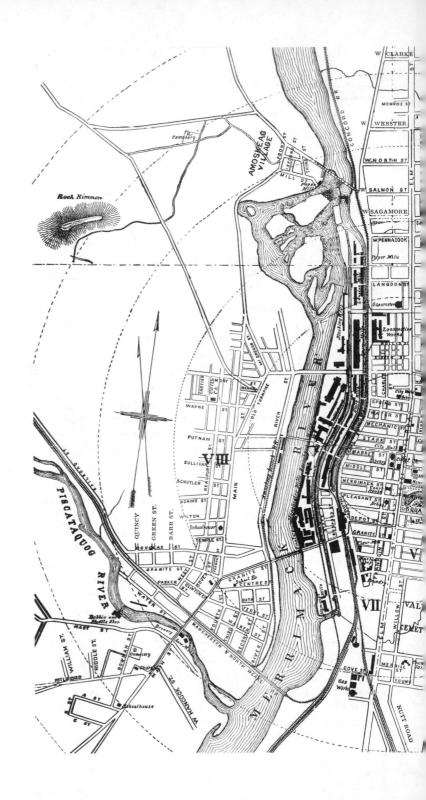

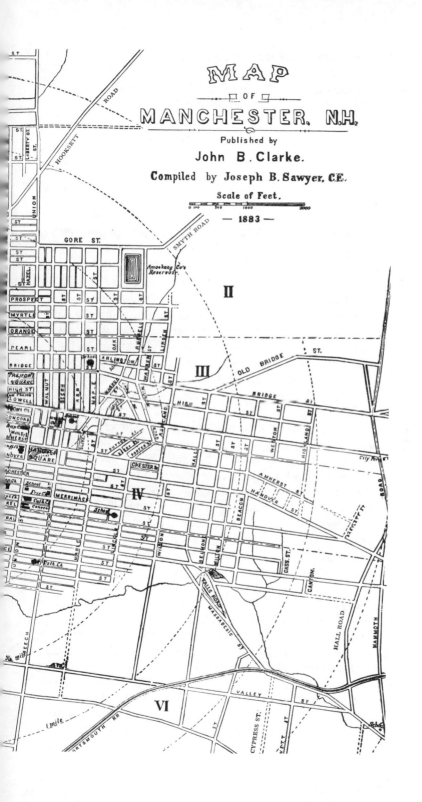

MAP
OF
MANCHESTER, N.H.

Published by

John B. Clarke.

Compiled by Joseph B. Sawyer, C.E.

Scale of Feet.

— 1883 —

cotton textile plant. Recalling the initial disruption of the town's tranquility by technology, Manchester's first Congregational minister would write:

> Some of us remember how very unwillingly the old fishermen, dwelling in the neighborhood of the falls, were to part company with their shad and eels. When dams were thrown across the river to divert its channel, and thus prevent the free passage of the fish, these men felt that their rights were invaded, and, had they possessed the power, they might have felt themselves justified in resorting to almost any measures to restore the ancient order of things, even to the stoppage of every saw and spindle carried by our water falls.[18]

The first man to recognize the importance of Manchester's waters, not only for transport but for power as well, was Samuel Blodgett. In 1793, at the age of 70, Blodgett began the construction of the Amoskeag Canal. He envisioned a canal which would bypass 1/4 mile of rapids at Amoskeag Falls and provide an all-water route from Concord to Boston. Blodgett's canal would be old Derryfield's first encounter with technology. The canal was planned as a five-year project, but his canal would take Blodget 14 years to complete. It cost the old man his entire personal fortune of $35,000-$40,000. Additionally, the canal required the sale of stock and the proceeds from three separate lotteries. In spite of his setbacks, Samuel Blodgett persistently predicted that ". . . despised old Derryfield . . . (was destined) . . . to become the Manchester of America."[19]

Blodgett lived barely long enough to see his canal operate successfully, if not profitably. The opinion held of Blodgett in his own lifetime by his fellow townsmen changed little, though. In 1807, when his canal began operations, there were still those in Derryfield who regarded the man who had introduced forces of innovation to the town as ". . . a demented old man bent upon squandering money in a wild scheme that would profit no one if accomplished."[20] Within three years of the opening of Blodgett's Canal, economic forces would change those opinions. By 1810, Samuel Blodgett's Canal, and the small scale industrial operations that came in its wake, would cause Blodgett's dream for "despised old Derryfield" and her future to approximate reality. The town voted, in that year, officially to change its name to Manchester, acknowledging the dream of an old man who, only three years before, had been regarded as not quite mentally sound. The canal had lowered transportation costs considerably. The pre-canal cost of transporting goods from Concord to Boston was $20 per ton. That cost fell, initially, to $13.50, and then, successively, to $8.50, $5.00, and, by 1838, $4.00 per ton.[21]

It was at about this time, the opening of Blodgett's Canal, that Derryfield's younger sons began to experience the reality of what John Bordon Armstrong called the drawing to a close of the age of self-sufficiency in northern New England.[22] To these younger sons, Derryfield's light sandy soil, poorly adapted to agriculture, was a painful reality. Judge Stark would not have had to remind them that their town was built upon a sandbank. One of them, an only son whose father owned 400 acres, would later recall: ". . . it was not worth ninepence an acre. My father wished me to stay with him; but I told him I could not, —I must go where land was better."[23] Blodgett's Canal provided a solution to young men who found themselves in this position. Townsmen now had a means of supplementing their agriculturally based economy.

Even old Judge Stark, who would later oppose the large mills, would not have to be reminded of the benefits that the Canal had brought to Derryfield. The Stark country store, located on the west bank of the canal, depended on supplying "river men" with food, meals, and lodging. A number of Derryfield families came to be economically dependent upon the river trade. In addition to transients, the canal would bring regular workmen to town. These men were needed to repair, operate, and maintain the canal. They required lodging, meals, and supplies. The canal itself would be largely dependent upon local suppliers for granite, wood, and labor. To satisfy the demand created by the canal and by increased river trade, many Derryfield widows operated boardinghouses long before the mills, with their famous boardinghouses, came to town.

The only discordant note was struck by the boatsmen and raftsmen who came to town for overnight stays. While there is little evidence that these men caused any serious disturbances in the town, their presence was not welcomed by the townspeople. Especially the raftsmen were regarded as men of little or no skill or worthy occupation ". . . a class of common men . . . (who) . . . demanded extravagant wages."[24] These men were paid $2 or $3 for taking freight from Manchester to Litchfield, a distance of about 12 miles. They would then walk back north with their oars, weighing from 12 to 25 pounds, slung over their soulders. The boatsmen seem to have been more welcomed by the townsmen as men of ". . . character, great and good nature . . . (whose) . . . freights were worth hundreds or perhaps thousands of dollars."[25] This initial influx of outsiders was the sole disturbing factor in Manchester's first encounter with technology. In view of the economic relief that the canal and river commerce brought to a distressed farming town, such side effects as undesirable visitors or residents, provided they were few in numbers, could easily be overlooked.

The town could continue to view itself as it was—an agrarian community. Only five years before the coming of large scale industry, the town's self portrait would be that of the old farming town. There would, though, be portents of the future which would grow increasingly disturbing during the coming years. The largest tax in town in 1835 was $72.90. This was paid not by an individual, though, but by a corporation, the proprietors of the Amoskeag

Canal, successors to the dream of Sam Blodgett. The canal company's tax was more than twice the amount of tax paid by the town's wealthiest farmer, Joseph Moor. There was a significant difference in the base of taxation. The canal company's tax, in contrast to Moor's, was based entirely on real estate holdings. Moor, too, owned land. His land was valued at $5,500, but his tax bill for 1835 was based upon more than landholding alone. Moor's tax bill reflected his status as an active farmer, like his neighbors. Besides being taxed for real property, Joseph Moor's tax bill reflected his holdings of horses, oxen, cows, neats and sheep. Unlike most farmers, though, Moor's wealth was visible in the fact that he owned stock, a carriage, and a bank account of some $1,500.[26]

Not only for Moor, the town's wealthiest man, but for all of those among the town's 25 highest ranking individual taxpayers, agriculture would serve as the foundation for prosperity (see Table 1.2). The only valid exception to the generalization was the town's leading merchant; but, then, he was Joseph Moor's son. Another merchant, Frederick Stark, would have $600 in stock, while Gilbert Greeley, the town's fifteenth ranking taxpayer, would value his store's stock at $1,000. Both of these men were farmers first, though, and shopkeepers second. The bulk of their wealth was measured neither in store goods nor cash, but in land, horses, cattle, and sheep.[27]

Of the town's 230 taxpayers in 1835, the majority, some 145 men (and women) owned real property. Only a few less men, 130, owned cows, with oxen and sheep, the next most widely distributed form of wealth, owned by 77 men. By contrast, only 17 townsmen held money at interest, 6 were shopkeepers, and only two reported ownership of bank stock.

The son of the town's most prosperous farmer was among the town's six storekeepers, reporting stock valued at $1,600. His five colleagues ranged from Mark Carr's $400 in stock to Moses Fellows' $1,400. All of these men, with the already noted exceptions of Moor, and Mark Carr who owned only a horse possibly used for deliveries, were farming men as well as tradesmen.[28] Whether, like Abel Corning and Samuel Hall, a townsman owned a single cow or a small dairy herd, he regarded himself as a farmer in a farming town. Even the 77 men who kept sheep did not do so only to sell the wool to factories. Production ranged considerably from David Rowell's single sheep to the flock of Moses Noyes, and was sold to small local manufacturers or kept for home production.[29]

Even at the lower end of the town's economic and social scale, the indication of the nature of the community is that of a farming town. Some men owned so little that they paid poll tax only. Even among those men who owned little or no land, or whose land was worth so little that it was virtually not worth taxing, the main occupation was agriculturally related. Like Theophilus Tilton, whose land was not his own, they had been born and raised in a community where their relatives lived, and where their parents had lived before them. In spite of Tilton's lack of land, he managed to retain his cow, either on rented or on common land.

While at the higher end of the economic spectrum we encounter two merchant-farmers, one industrial company, one woman, and 14 yeoman farmers, at the opposite end, we encounter three women and 54 men. The property values of the men were so small that they paid no tax beyond their poll tax. Eight townsmen were owners of carriages. For the most part, these were among the community's more wealthy members. A carriage was by no means always a sumptuary acquisition, though. Rodnia Nutt, who owned no land, held a carriage valued at $80, the third most valuable vehicular possession in town. Nutt's only other worth was valued in terms of his oxen. This may well indicate that his "carriage" was in fact a wagon or cart used in hauling freight along the mammoth road or for the canal company. Three of the men who owned "carriages" were merchants, and their vehicles may well have been as utilitarian as they were sumptuary. Hauling freight for private purposes and for the canal company was becoming an increasingly important part of the town's economic activity. A farmer's oxen could be used along the canal when they were not being utilized in the fields[30] (see Tables 1.3, 1.4, 1.5).

In view of the town's experience with the Amoskeag Canal, it is hardly surprising that Derryfield's encounter with a small cotton factory, built in 1809 by three local men, had been a relatively pleasant one. The town welcomed the factory more readily than she had welcomed the canal. The small factory would be welcomed as the agent which would fulfill Samuel Blodgett's dream, even though the townspeople would not understand the implications for their community of Blodgett's dream. They viewed the coming of the factory as a convenience which provided a means of supplementing agricultural income. The factory was about 40 feet square and two stories high. Taken together, factory and canal would prompt Derryfield to change its name to Manchester. Initially the Amoskeag Cotton and Wool Factory, as it was known, confined its operations to spinning, with families in the vicinity of the factory providing the labor, in their own homes, for the other necessary processes: ". . . the first step, after cotton was received, was to send it out into families in the neighborhood, in lots of from fifty to one hundred pounds, to be picked . . . four cents a pound was paid for picking cotton."[31]

The success of the Amoskeag Factory prompted new owners to expand from spinning only to weaving, but, as in the processing of picking, to utilize a putting-out system. A local clergyman, describing this welcome innovation by which ". . . a smart weaver . . . (could) . . . earn 30¢ a day . . .," indicated that

. . . some years after the manufacture of yarn was commenced, perhaps because that market was more than supplied, the company introduced the weaving of cloth. It was, however, done not at the mill, but by hand looms, in the families in the neighborhood. Among the most vivid recollections of my childhood, is that of seeing Mr. Jotham Gillis ride up to the house where I then lived, with large bundles of yarn to be woven by the hand-loom process. . . . (Gillis travelled) . . . a distance of five miles (to my house) on horseback, and carried his yarn in bundles tied about his saddle. . . .[32]

Neither the 1809 Amoskeag factory nor its successors, the so-called Bell and Island Mills, built in 1826, caused any considerable unwelcomed disruption in Manchester's lifestyles. Even the incorporation of weaving into the factory itself, which came after the building of the Bell and Island Mills, did not depart from what Manchester had come to expect from industrialization. Neither did the introduction of boarding houses for the workers at the early mill. Boarding houses had been a common local feature since before the opening of the Amoskeag Canal. Moreover, the girls who were to board in the new facilities were often daughters or relatives of local farmers.[33]

Oliver Dean, agent of the Bell and Island Mills, kept a journal in which he recorded what we would refer to today as employment applications. Dean's journal gives evidence of the care with which he "selected" girls "to get an opportunity to come to work in the factory." Notations were made upon the family background and upon the employment history of each applicant. Additionally, such desirable traits as being "acquainted with spinning and weaving" in the home were made note of.[34]

In spite of our modern assumptions about the uniformity of work habits and discipline required by what we have called the factory system, Manchester in her early encounters with the factory seems to have escaped much of the arbitrariness with which modern factories treat their workers. Some of those who came to Manchester's early factories, like Jeremiah Goodenough, 19, and his 17 year old brother, came as apprentices. The Goodenough brothers were apprentice iron workers and were hired ". . . on the same terms as we employ others in similar conditions . . . ." There were those, however, who were allowed to strike their own bargains with Agent Dean, some faring better than others. In December of 1826, for example, Joseph Taylor formally contracted to work in the machine shop for three years. He was to receive $20 for the first year, $40 for the second, and $60 for the third. In addition, he would be allowed to go to school for two months, afternoons, in his second year, provided that he worked mornings and evenings. Not 30 days before, Hiram Bean had struck a similar agreement with the agent. Bean was to be allowed the same salary as Taylor, but he was to be allowed two months of schooling *each* year, and retained the option of working mornings and evenings (for extra pay) in those two months if he wished to do so.[35]

Many workmen who came to Manchester before 1840 retained a measure of independence similar to that described above. They were allowed to strike their own bargains regarding the conditions of their employment, and were not forced either to accept the terms which the company offered or forego working. In 1827 Alfred Hill agreed to work for 7/-per day for a one-month trial period ". . . after which a new bargain is to be made. . . ."[36] There were some men employed by the factory who managed to retain the prerogatives of the individual craftsman. John Langeley, a joiner, was employed in 1826, and ". . . found his own apprentice at $10 per month."[37]

In the late 1820's and throughout the 1830's, Manchester's factories would function as a supplement to the older society and economy. The fledgling factories gave economic opportunities to the farmers' sons, daughters, or brothers who, thanks to the diversity provided by the mills and canals, could find off-the-farm employment. The son who wished to stay at home with his father but, because of the poor quality of the soil, could not, would find, had he been living in the Manchester of the 1820's, an alternative which would enable him to remain in his native community. The farmers themselves saw the value of the factory. Agent Dean often noted particular farmers whom he knew requesting employment for relatives. Not only for relatives, but for the farmers themeselves, the factory could mean the difference between squeezing a living out of the unproductive soil or maintaining the standards of a more comfortable life.[38] The Amoskeag factories had woodlands of their own, and they bought wood from independent farmers. Wood was required for heating, for building, and for machinery. Local farmers would provide the labor which would cut the wood and haul it to the factory. Copies of the relatively elaborate agreements between agent and farmers have been preserved. The agreements specified what work was required, the quantity of wood to be cut or hauled, precisely how many feet from the river it was to be hauled or stored, where and how it was to be delivered, and the amount and type of payment to be made by the factory. Additionally, we might suppose that, given Agent Dean's predilection for oral agreements with his "neighbors," a great deal more work was provided to the local residents than that for which written formal agreements were signed. Not only in terms of providing agricultural and woodland produce for the mills, but in terms of work on the maintenance of equipment, the early mills provided employment to the community. It was not uncommon for the factory to own wagons which it would put out to local farmers to be maintained, repaired, or operated.[39]

The factory complemented agrarian lifestyles by providing the farmer with extra work and income, but, beyond that, the factory also provided a market for the produce of the farm. Workers required foodstuffs. The manufacturing process itself required wool. The machinery required leathers. In addition to buying the products of the farms, the factories sometimes purchased the farms themselves. Prior to the coming of the factory, many of Derryfield's farmers would have been hard pressed to find a buyer. Woodlands that would otherwise have been valueless and, perhaps, fallen into a state of abandonment were offered for sale to the mills. These were the same lands which were the subject of complaint time and again in New Hampshire governors' messages. The governors had lamented the abandonment of the farms and the valuelessness of the lands. Now these lands (or at least those in and near Derryfield) had acquired a buyer. One farmer decided to offer ". . . 100 acres of woodlands commencing about a mile above Martin's Ferry adjoining the river with a large quarry of granite . . . about 10 rods from the river at $10 per acre or will sell his whole farm of 500 acres for $1,000."[40]

Furthermore, there seems to have been little division between factory and farm. Not only did farmers work in and for the factory, but the factory itself, at least in the capacity of landlord, intruded upon the farm. The company rented the old Blodgett Farm, in 1827, to Captain Daniel Farmer. Farmer was to pay a rental of $30 per year. In addition, it was Farmer's obligation to pay the highway tax (or to serve to repair the highways in lieu of taxes), to construct and maintain fences, and in general to "make improvements." Agreements such as those with Daniel Farmer were not unusual. In some cases, agreements were more elaborate, with the factory obtaining, as its rental, a share of the produce of the lands. The mills agreed to rent Daniel Stroney land and a barn

> . . . and for the use of said land he is to give 1/3 of the produce of the same, he to do all the work, and deliver 1/3 of the produce of the same at any part of the village as the company may direct. In case he improves any of the above land for a garden, he is to allow for the same, the same quantity of produce as would have been raised from the same, if planted like the rest of the field.[41]

The incorporation of the Amoskeag Manufacturing company, capitalized at $1 million, in 1831, had little immediate effect on the community. New owners had simply taken over the familiar Bell and Island Mills. Local residents, by now grown used to a gradual process of industrialization, assumed that factories would continue to remain as supplementary to the existing society. They envisioned that society was required to make only minor changes to accommodate industry. So long as the mills had operated in this fashion, complementing local farms, there was no difficulty. Starting about 1840, however, the process began to reverse itself. The older economy and society was becoming increasingly less important than, and supplementary to, the newer order.

By the mid-40's, the Amoskeag Manufacturing Company alone would operate four factories for the production of cloth. The Amoskeag would operate 61,400 spindles and 1,649 looms, employing more than 1,600 men and women in its textile division alone. Moreover, the Amoskeag New Mills, which would eventually buy out the other mills in town, were not alone among the industries coming to Manchester. The Stark Mills, in the mid-'40's, were comparable in size to the Amoskeag, and the Manchester Print Works had begun to introduce still another process—the printing of textiles. The investment of capital was massive, almost unprecedented for the nation, and certainly more than New Hampshire had ever seen. Not only massive, the investment was overwhelming. The growth of industrial operations associated with these investments began to displace the older residents from their customary lifestyles, and to displace the older prestigious families from their positions of leadership in the community. When this process of displacement, particularly of the latter sort, became apparent, conflict erupted and the town was forcefully introduced to the realities of the modern industrial age.[42]

Initially the townsmen's shock and anger at what was happening to their community did not take the form of opposition to industry as such, for in the past industry had proven that it could remain consistent with and subservient to the sort of community that the older residents had inherited and wished to maintain. The older community attributed the evils of industrialism, as they conceived them, not to the factories but to the newcomers—the people—that those factories brought along with them. After losing control at the 1840 town meeting, the older residents would express their opposition to the changes in their town chiefly by attempting to obstruct projects which the new order would find necessary. There would no longer be generosity in providing for roads, poor farms, town buildings and schools. On the contrary, the newer residents could plan on fighting for whatever projects they might want to put through the meeting. The Amoskeag New Mills offered to give the town the land required for a cemetery. No cost to the town was involved, yet the old residents put up a determined opposition to the acceptance of the gift. There was little reason for such intense opposition except the wrath of the older townsmen, and their determination to conduct what obstructionist activities as they could. Contemporary observers correctly attributed this opposition to "the prejudices of the people of the old parts of the town."[43]

In trying to explain their situation, the old residents looked beyond the number of mills, or the size of those mills. They attributed the changes in their town, and the displacement of the older families to the number (and kinds) of people thrust upon them, and the suddenness with which they had come. By the mid-forties, the population of the town would be over 8,000, and by the end of the decade it would approach 14,000. Even in 1844, political rallies were drawing 15 to 20,000 people to Manchester. The growth of the town was awesome to the older residents. They termed it, simply, "unprecedented." In 1835 the town had, roughly, 300 families. Ten years later would witness 300 buildings either in the planning or construction stages. In an effort to establish blame for what was happening in their town, the older residents, confused and frightened, anxious to place "blame," viewed all changes as evils, and attributed these supposed evils to the moral quality (or lack thereof) of the people who came to staff the mills. They assumed that the mill was attracting the worst elements of the larger cities, a people who did not share the local culture—the traditions of the small New England township.[44]

In spite of the prevailing local opinion, the newcomers, for the most part, seem not to have been a culturally different people. On the contrary, the remarkable fact concerning the new industrial resident would seem to have been his small town origin.

Most of the records which could provide evidence of the places from whence migrants came to Manchester in those early years were destroyed in a fire which devastated the newly built town house, which the newcomers had insisted be located upon the East bank. One volume of the city census of 1846 has survived, though. This census required each resident to indicate his name, the town from whence he had come to Manchester, and the year in which he first took up residence in Manchester. Although its pages have been damaged by fire, the census clearly lists 644 men and women. Although not all of the above-listed information is available for each respondent, place of origin was indicated for 324. Of these, well over half, some 189 persons, came from other communities within the state of New Hampshire. Moreover, all but a very few of these came from New Hampshire's small farming towns. They came from rural communitites which must have been culturally very similar to old Derry-field.[45]

Even of those who came to Manchester from outside New Hampshire's borders, few came from large cities. Perhaps two of the largest cities from whence people came to Manchester were Boston and Chicago. Both were aberrations. The 16 men from Boston came from a city much larger than the norm, while the three migrants from Chicago were far outside the usual distance ranges for migrants. Most migrants came from the New England area. Of these, the overwhelming number, 97, came from Massachusetts. While some came from Massachusetts' larger and medium-sized cities such as Boston, Worcester, Springfield, Lowell, and Lawrence, most of those who would leave Massachusetts to work in Manchester's mills would come in dribs and drabs from many of the area's medium-sized cities or small towns.

Moreover, the pattern of migration to Manchester seems to reveal that the further the travelling distance, the fewer the migrants. The myth of wagons sent out by the mills to lure girls from far away, with distance making them captive workers, is given the lie, in the 1840's at least, by the distances, within New

Hampshire, from which workers came to the mills. The nearer the town, the greater the number of people who would come to Manchester to work in the mills. Within a radius of about 25 miles, workers seemed willing to come to the factories. Perhaps they felt secure that, should things go wrong, they could always return home. Whatever the reason, though, the number of migrants seems to drop sharply after a 25-mile radius is reached. Very few girls seem to have come from New Hampshire's northernmost Coos County, for example.

Even among the migrants who came from without the borders of New Hampshire, the number coming from beyond a 56 mile radius drops sharply. To be sure, there were migrants from New York, from Maine, from New Jersey, and even from Wisconsin and Chicago. There was even one man who reported that he had come from the remote and, to the local ear, the esoteric reaches of Boise, Idaho. These were the exception, though. Generally, men were moving from relatively nearby in order to, as Agent Dean would have put it, "get an opportunity to work in the factory." Opportunity for employment seems not to have been inconsistent with relative propinquity to "home."[46]

Although the range of distances within New Hampshire which men were willing to travel varied widely from three miles (from nearby Goffstown) to 103 miles (from Jefferson), a sample of 172 in-state migrants reveals that each travelled an average of 8.9 miles (see Tables 1.6, 1.7, 1.8, 1.9, 1.10).

While the older residents were developing a fear of newcomers, viewing them as outsiders who were alien sorts of human beings, the available evidence would seem to reveal that these fears lacked a basis in fact. The majority of the new population would seem to have been former small town folks, like the men of old Derryfield themselves. Like the people of the older town, the newcomers came from the New England countryside, from communities which must have been culturally very similar to that to which they were migrating. Nevertheless, the impression of the older townsmen was formed not by an analysis of the geographic or social backgrounds or the newer residents, but by the fact that these new residents wanted a voice in the conduct of the town's affairs, and that this meant that older patterns of community leadership would be disrupted. Angry at being displaced from their customary relationships to their community, Manchester's older residents struck out in anger, in whatever ways they could, at the "newcomers."[47]

In 1845, an incident took place which the older residents would view as a symbol of what had happened to their town. They would regard the murder of the town's tax collector, Jonas L. Parker, as the embodiment of the violence, lowering of morals, the disruption of the peacefulness of the countryside which they saw taking place all about them. Parker's murder set off a wave of panic which affected both old and new residents alike. People were urged by the ministers to stay indoors after dark. Wives were told to pray for the safe return of a husband who had to go out at night. Townspeople were urged to keep lanterns burning all night, and to report any noises which they might hear. The panic which seized the town would result in many false accusations against innocent men passing through town, and eventually in the indictment and trial of three brothers who would later be proven innocent. In connection with the tensions between old and new residents, though, the Parker murder takes on its greatest meaning. Not since Judge Stark's outburst at the 1840 meeting had the hostilities which divided the town been so openly expressed.

In one sense the Parker murder should not have been the cause of furor in the town. Men had been murdered in Manchester before. The fishermen at Amoskeag Falls, the rivermen and boatmen, had not been among the gentlest of humans. They had been of some concern to the town fathers. The occasional killings among drunken fishermen had given old Derryfield a somewhat sordid, if undeserved, reputation. Even in terms of conflict between newcomers and settled citizenry, the Parker murder is unique. Only six years before, one of the older residents, Jeremiah Johnson, had been murdered. His killer was proven to be a factory worker, one of the town's newcomers. Coming before the full acceleration of tensions between the two groups, though, the Johnson killing seemed to be accepted without undue alarm by the town. It aroused little interest or concern, beyond the expression of the sentiment that justice should take its course, let alone alarm. It was not only the Parker murder, then, which disturbed the tranquility of the town. Jonas Parker was what disturbed the town. Parker himself had come to symbolize the brash, arrogant newcomer, forcing his way in where he did not belong. He stole (or so old residents would view it) the offices which rightly belonged to the traditional town leadership, not with the intention of settling in the community, but simply as a man passing through. Parker felt little attachment to Manchester, and at the time of his murder was already planning to move on to what he conceived to be greener pastures. For the old residents, Parker embodied the evils that had befallen their town.

Parker had come to Manchester in the 1840's during the initial influx of new residents. He established a bowling alley in the new village which the older residents referred to as Parker's "saloon." Parker's establishment became a gathering place for the men of the new village. The men surrounding Parker, but more especially Parker himself, came to be viewed as typical of the newcomer, men who "lacked finish, stability, and steady going habits . . . they were free and easy . . . bold and adventurous." Parker had taken over a position which traditionally was one of the few honors that a small town could afford. The older residents felt that they alone should hold such positions. Moreover, not just any among the old residents, but especially the leadership elite among those families of the old town were the men for whom such offices were traditionally reserved. Parker's murder served as a reminder to the older community that it was Parker and men like him who had disrupted the tranquility of old Derryfield. Perhaps it was fitting that a man who so symbolized the evils of the new industrial town should be the victim of Manchester's newly discovered violent impulses, but it was also profoundly disturbing.[48]

The Parker murder occasioned a good deal of rhetoric among the older residents. The ministers, too, used the incident to moralize, as not a few of the town's pulpits (and, thanks to the generosity of the mill's owners, Manchester had no lack of pulpits) were used to denounce Parker, and, by implication, all new residents as reaping what they had sown. All of this succeeded in throwing the entire town, old and new residents alike, into a panic which would be remembered for many years to come. Not until the anti-Catholic riot of 1854 would the town again experience so disturbing a reaction as that which the Parker murder had occasioned. Angered and shocked at what had happened to their community during the five years preceding the murder, older residents used the incident as a last ditch protest against newcomers and, more importantly, if unconsciously, against the process of change in which they were caught up, but which they failed to understand.[49]

Unimportant in itself, the Parker murder, combined with the town meeting confrontation of 1840, serves to point out the critical stage of the industrialization of Manchester. For this one town, industrialization was not a process which came abruptly. Instead, it was a long continuing ongoing process. There came a stage in that process, though, when the gradual nature of the changes that had been taking place in the society and economy became cataclysmic. Over the years, the town had come to accept and then to welcome technological innovation. The residents had learned to accomodate harmoniously the changes that accompanied technological innovation.

So long as change came gradually, and so long as it did not displace the older residents (especially the traditional leadership) from customary relationships to their community, it presented few problems. The townspeople had proven themselves able to accept innovation, and demonstrated their willingness to adjust their exclusivistic attitudes to accommodate the newcomers who accompanied change. At that stage where gradualness was abandoned, the older town was overwhelmed by the scale of industry and the suddenness with which it was thrust upon them. It was at this stage that the older social, economic, and political order found change to be unacceptable and determined to resist. The very gradualness of the changes which had taken place in town prior to 1840 had been deceptive. Past experience had allayed the fears and suspicions which had been the town's initial reaction to the modernization that had come with canal building. The town viewed slow-paced changes as no threat to existing lifestyles.

After 1840, townsmen realized that large scale industry could mean that they would be forced to live with a phenomenon which they had never imagined. Large scale industrialization would have implications for the way in which men lived that would be far different from the lesser innovations to which the town had been able to adapt. By the time the town realized what would be the implications of industry on a massive scale, coming on suddenly, it was too late for the townsmen to prevent being displaced from control of the affairs of their own community. They had fought for community control since 1780. Not only would community control not survive the crisis of industrialization, but the community itself, the sense of community prevailing among the old townsmen, would not survive the shock of industrialization. In the brief period between 1840 and 1845, all of the accumulated anger and frustration of the older residents found vent, but by that time it was the anger of a lost cause and a bygone society.[50]

Table 1.1. Manchester, Growth of Population

Census Year	Population	Increase	Percent Increase
1820	761		
1830*	877	116	15.24
1840	3,235	2,358	268.87
1850	13,932	10,697	330.66
1860	20,107	6,175	44.32
1870	23,536	3,429	17.05
1880	32,630	9,049	38.64
1890	44,126	11,496	35.23

*Official local sources set 1835 population at "less than 1,000" (Mayoral address, Moses Fellows)

Source: U.S. Census

Table 1.2. Manchester, 1835, Cross-Tabulations of Inventories of Wealth

	Real Estate	Horses 4 yrs.	Horses 2 yrs.	Oxen	Cows	Neats	Sheep	Stock (Trade)	Bank Stock	Carriages	Money at Interest	No Property This Category
Real Estate	143	63	10	81	107	64	71	4	2	7	8	87
Horses 4 yrs.	63	68	9	54	60	43	49	5	1	6	5	162
Horses 2 yrs.	10	9	10	10	10	10	9	8	0	0	0	220
Oxen	81	54	10	87	81	57	65	2	1	5	5	143
Cows	107	60	10	81	130	65	75	2	1	5	7	100
Neats	64	43	10	57	65	67	53	1	1	3	2	163
Sheep	71	49	9	65	75	53	77	0	1	3	2	153
Stock Trade	4	5	8	2	2	1	0	6	0	2	2	224
Bank St.	2	1	–	1	1	1	1	0	2	1	2	228
Carriages	7	6	–	5	5	3	3	2	1	8	4	222
Money at Interest	8	5	–	5	7	2	2	2	2	4	17	213
No Property This Category	87	162	220	143	100	163	153	224	228	222	213	

N = 230

Source: Town Tax Lists, Manchester City Hall

Table 1.3. Manchester's Merchants, 1835

Name	Value of Stock	Rank in Wealth
Joseph Moor, Jr.	$1,600	38
Moses Fellows	1,400	34
Gilbert Greeley	1,000	15
Frederick G. Stark	600	3
John Gamble	400	23
Mark Carr	400	95

Source: Town Records

Table 1.4. Carriage Owners, 1835

Name	Value of Carriages	Rank in Wealth
Jonas Harvey	$100	6
Israel Merrill	90	10
Rodnia Nutt	80	137
David Webster	75	33
Frederick G. Stark	50	3
Joseph Moor	50	2
John Gamble	40	23
John R. Hall	30	44

Source: Town Records

Table 1.5. Holders of Bank Accounts, 1835

Name	Cash in Bank	Rank in Wealth
Joseph Moor	$1,500	2
Cyrus Moor	1,500	26
Frederick G. Stark	1,400	3
Luther Stowell	1,000	65
Silas Griffin	700	76
Archibald Gamble, Jr.	600	37
Hazen Davis	600	82
William P. Farmer	500	92
Israel Merrill	300	10
Parker Stevens	200	128
Samuel B. Kidder	200	108
Stephen Haseltine	200	101
Samuel Hall, Jr.	200	129
Adam Gilmore	200	126
Josiah Davis	100	147
Alexander Cunningham	100	144
John Gamble	40	23

Source: Town Records

Table 1.6. Places of Origin, 1846 Residents of Manchester

310	No place of origin reported
189	Other New Hampshire cities and towns
145	Migrated to Manchester from outside New Hampshire

N = 644

Source: Register of Residents

Table 1.7. Places of Origin for Migrants from Outside New
            Hampshire

Massachusetts	97
Connecticut	2
Rhode Island	1
New York	6
Vermont	3
Wisconsin	5
Maine	3
Pennsylvania	2
Illinois	6
Michigan	3
California	2
Georgia	2
Florida	1
Idaho	1
Iowa	1
New Jersey	1
Louisiana	1
Missouri	1
Kansas	1
Colorado	1
District of Columbia	2
Minnesota	1
Other	3

Source: Register of Residents

Table 1.8. Migrants to Manchester from Outside New Hampshire,
            1846. (Areas with Three or More Listed Migrants)

City of Origin	Number of Migrants	Distance from Manchester
Boston, Mass.	16	56 miles
Lawrence, Mass.	9	29 "
Dorchester, Mass.	7	56 "
Somerville, Mass.	6	56 "
Lowell, Mass.	5	24 "
Cambridge, Mass.	4	56 "
Methuen, Mass.	4	24 "
Roxbury, Mass.	4	56 "
Chelsea, Mass.	3	48 "
Chicago, Illinois	3	947 "
Haverhill, Mass.	3	24 "
Marlboro, Mass.	3	42 "
Sheldonville, Mass.	3	48 "

Source: Register of Residents

Table 1.9. Migrants to Manchester from Within New Hampshire,
            1846, Nine Towns in Order of Frequency of Migrants

Town of Origin	Number of Migrants	Distance from Manchester
Hooksett	16	8 miles
Auburn	15	8 "
Goffstown	11	10 "
Bedford	10	5 "
Nashua	9	17 "
North Londonderry	7	12 "
New Boston	5	13 "
Pittsfield	5	25 "
Strafford	5	28 "

Source: Register of Residents

Table 1.10. In-State Migration, 1846

1846, Number of Migrants to Manchester	Town Within New Hampshire	Distance from Manchester (miles)
1	Allentown	15
15	Auburn	8
1	Amherst	13
10	Bedford	5
2	Belmont	33
1	Bradford	33
1	Bowcawen	25
3	Candia	12
3	Concord	17
1	Contoocook	22
1	Claremont	55
1	Deering	22
2	Danbury	44
4	Derry	12
3	Dunbarton	12
1	Epping	22
1	Francestown	18
2	Goffes Falls	3
11	Goffstown	10
1	Greenfield	23
1	Henniker	24
1	Hopkinton	18
16	Hookset	8
1	Jefferson	103
1	Jefferson Highlands	100
2	Keene	44
3	Londonderry	12
2	Litchfield	12
1	Loudon	22
1	Mason	24
4	Milford	16
2	Merrimack	10
9	Nashua	17
5	New Boston	13
1	New Ipswich	27

Table 1.10--Continued

1846, Number of Migrants to Manchester	Town Within New Hampshire	Distance from Manchester (miles)
1	Newport	46
1	Northwood	23
7	No. Londonderry	7
2	No. Weare	17
2	Penacook	23
4	Peterborough	27
1	Pembroke	12
5	Pittsfield	25
4	Portsmouth	37
1	Raymond	16
1	Rochester	34
2	Salem Depot	19
2	Sandown	16
5	Strafford	28
3	Suncook	12
2	Tilton	34
1	Wakefield	47
1	Windham	17
1	W. Hopkinton	22
4	Warner	27
1	Winchester	52
1	Wilton	18
1	Lakeport	40
1	Mount Vernon	13
2	Bennington	24
		1,527

Total Number of Migrants: 172

Number of Towns in Sample: 61

Mean Distance Travelled (per person): 8.88 miles

Mean Distance from Manchester of Towns in Sample: 25.03 miles

Sources: 1846 Register of Residents, Manchester
Transportation and Travel Official Table of Distances,
Departments of Army, Navy, Air Force, 1968
Official Map, N. H. Div. of Economic Develop., 1973

2

The Company and the Town

Ever since Louis Wirth dealt with the concept of urbanism as a way of life, over 30 years ago, scholars had been concerned with building models to promote further understanding of urban-industrial society. The very concepts "urban" and "industrial" have been seen as functionally interdependent, with a close relationship being perceived between mechanization and the rise of cities. In dealing with industrialization and urbanization, the tendency has been to regard the two processes as major independent variables. As a consequence of this tendency, other factors—forms of social organization, culture, ethnicity, family, occupation—have been regarded as dependent variables, determined by the technological and economic organization of the society. Writing in the early 1960's, Sidney Greenfield succinctly articulated this viewpoint: "The adoption of the machine resulted in sweeping changes in social organization: factories needed laborers who could be more readily obtained in cities than on farms; urbanism and industrialization worked hand in hand to change the structure of American society; industry needed laborers and the city grew to provide them."[1] Industrialization and urbanization have often been regarded as over-whelming: these were the major independent variables which would transform society, and society, in turn, could only respond to such forces.

This older viewpoint regards workers as but one element—a passive element—in the matrix of urban-industrial society. It is a viewpoint currently undergoing considerable revision. There is an emerging notion that workers did, in fact, have some considerable influence in shaping the urban-industrial society of which, according to an older view, working people constituted almost a passive element—a set of relatively helpless victims. Herbert Gutman has demonstrated that immigrant culture and ethnic traditions can play an important role in the shaping of industrial working conditions and industrial discipline. The worker is no longer seen as a passive element in the social structure. Scholars such as William Goode and Tamara Hareven have suggested that certain aspects of working class lives—institutions such as the family—may be more than simply the creature of urban-industrial society: they may themselves be major independent variables in the forming of that society.

The ways in which groups of workers reacted to their encounter with industrial life may well have had more than incidental influences upon the shape of nineteenth century urban industrial society. By focusing upon individual workers and groups of workers, rather than upon the formal union structures of organized labor, much can be learned about the ways in which working class communities were organized and influenced the lives of their residents and of the larger urban industrial society of which they were a part.[2]

As one of northern New England's major planned textile towns, Manchester, New Hampshire, would eventually host the world's largest cotton textile factory, the Amoskeag Manufacturing Company. Manchester residents who lived through "the Amoskeag years," whether those years be in the nineteenth or twentieth centuries, were well aware of the paternalistic attitudes and policies of the Amoskeag towards both "its" workers and "its" town. Manchester truly was the Amoskeag's town, as Alan Sweezy pointed out in a study of the closing of the mills in the 1930's. He demonstrated that this single company, at one point in time, accounted directly, by itself, for the employment of nearly 60% of the entire work force of Manchester. The foundations of the company's paternalism were set down in the years of initial urban-industrial growth, the period from 1840 to 1880.[3] This was a crucial period wherein both factory and workers would have come to terms with something new—urban-industrial society. It was a period wherein workers, factory overseers, owners' agents, and Boston mill magnates, alike, sought mutually to explore, and via that exploration, more definitely to establish the parameters of the company's paternalism. In this process workers acted to influence the outcome just as surely as they were acted upon by the resultant industrial society. An understanding of this period is essential towards an understanding of the "company town" that Manchester would become. The period cannot be understood without reference to the active part played by the workers in shaping the scociety.

From the time when large-scale textile manufacturing was begun in Manchester, in 1839, and continuing throughout the 1840's, the growth of Manchester was uninterrupted. Both in physical terms—the number of factory buildings, boarding houses, commercial buildings—and in terms of population, the 1840's were years of growth for Manchester. From a town of just over 3,200 in 1840, Manchester increased some 350%, to house over 14,500 people by the end of the decade (see Tables 2.1 and 2.2). Each year the town would accommodate increasing numbers of newcomers.[4]

Not unsurprisingly, more women and "girls" came to Manchester than did men. They came to work in Manchester's mills—a new source of cash income for their labor. By 1849, the imbalance of females was reflected in Manchester's population. There were 45% more women than men in Manchester in that year. Although the extent to which women outnumbered men in Manchester would not continue at the high rate of 1849, there would, throughout the period from 1850 to 1880, be considerably more women than men in the town (see Table 2.3). By 1860, there would be 32% more women than men, while at the end of the period the men were outnumbered by only 22%.[5]

The *work force* of Manchester in 1850 consisted of 5,240 workers in industrial occupations ranging from small cigar making shops—sometimes one-man shops—and tiny "paper staining" shops to the largest of the textile mills, employing thousands of females and hundreds of males.

While women outnumbered men in the general population of the town, they outnumbered them to an even greater extent in the factory work force. 58.6% of the general population of the town were women, but they composed over 64% of the work force of the town. The women who came to Manchester came to go to work, and the work opportunities, in terms of the occupations open to them, were limited.[6] Almost universally, women went to work in the textile mills, while men would have a somewhat wider variety of jobs available to them. This indicates a trend that would continue throughout the period. In 1850, roughly six out of every ten men in Manchester would work directly in cotton mills, while eight out of ten would be employed, in one way or another, by the textile corporations—as machinists, carpenters, maintenance men, etc. With only 20% of the male work force of the town not employed by the textile corporations, occupational choice for men may have seemed limited, but it was even more limited for women. Of every ten women working in industrial occupations in Manchester, in 1850, roughly 9.5 worked directly in cotton textile mills. By 1880, this situation would improve, and there would be a wider variety of occupational opportunities available to both men and women, but, nevertheless, cotton textiles remained predominant. By 1880, cotton goods accounted for 52.9% of the male work force, and 79.5% of the female work force. The improvements in occupational variety available in Manchester are not quite so wide as these figures seem to indicate, for the 1880 figures do not encompass those employed in the dyeing and finishing of textiles, but only in their production. Especially for women, Manchester's mills would remain the only really large scale employer (see Tables 2.4-2.9).[7]

In addition to having a somewhat wider variety of occupations available to them in Manchester, in 1850, men worked in establishments of different size than did women. Men were more able than women to find employment in smaller, more individualized establishments. A woman's occupational opportunities were limited to factories employing 500, 1,000, or 1,500 other people. There were only 18 employers with under 20 female workers, while there were some 47 employers with 20 or fewer male workers. Altogether, small scale employers, with 20 or fewer workers, accounted for 13.6% of Manchester's male work force, but only 2.6% of the town's female work force (Tables 2.10 and 2.11).[8] While wives and daughters went off to the mills, husbands, brothers, and sons could either go to the mills themselves or seek employment in Manchester's machine shops, construction jos, shoe shops, or small service employment—as bakers, confectioners, etc.

The pressure on the town to provide living space for this influx of workers, both male and female, was a constant one, and was often noted with alarm in the local press. Sometimes the spirit of "boosterism," which characterized the growing town, prevailed, and men with money to invest were reminded of the need for housing and of the returns which investment in the housing market promised, especially for the man with just a little accumulation of capital. In 1840, such men were told that "tenements for small families must be in great demand here in the Spring, and it behooves those who have sufficient capital" to jump in and supply the need for such tenements.[9]

Adequate housing, at reasonable rents, was a problem not confined to Manchester's "boom town" period. Rather, it was a persistent problem throughout the period from 1840 to 1880. A labor oriented periodical, *The Manchester Operative,* noted in 1844 that rents were "much too high" for the average working man to be able to afford to live without severely restricting his budget, or, as the writer put it, "living close." On the other hand, for those "men with capital" who had followed the advice offered them in 1840, the housing market, in terms of return on investment, would prove very good indeed. By 1844, men who had invested in housing in 1840 would have achieved a steady return on their investment of 18% per year. The housing problem was particularly severe in terms of "small tenements" since land costs were so high as to be prohibitive, in many cases, for the builder who would supply small, low rent tenements. By the mid-1840's, land for housing was "going for 33 cents a foot, and then it is nothing but frog pond or sand bank," and often located so far from places of industrial employment that a workman did not have "sufficient time to eat his meals" without getting to the shop late and being "docked a quarter" hour.[10]

In part, the scarcity of land and the high cost of private (non-corporation owned) housing was a direct result of the Amoskeag Manufacturing Company's policies. The policies of the Amoskeag in founding Manchester were long-range, well-thought-out, and cautiously exercised. The first stage came when the corporation set about quietly buying up large tracts of land on both sides of the Merrimack River at Amoskeag Falls. After plans for an industrial village were announced, and construction was underway, the company—with near monopolistic landholding power—further revealed its plans for the company town. These plans included the construction of elaborate canals and factory buildings, of course, but they went beyond this.

They included detailed street layouts, "zoning" designations for manufacturing, retail, factory residential, and "well-off" residential sections. As owner of all desirable land, the company was in a position to enforce its "zoning" decisions. Not only in building its own structures, but also in the construction of those buildings which the Land and Water Power Company (an Amoskeag division) built for other industrial and commercial builders, the requirements of the mother company were strictly adhered to. Private developers would have to buy their land from the Amoskeag, and one of the conditions of the sale would commonly be a specific use, and construction of buildings of a specified type. For example, brick structures were specified for certain areas of the town. The first of a series of land auctions to be held by the Amoskeag, wherein land was auctioned off to private developers (bound by the Amoskeag's restrictions), was held in October of 1839. Seventy thousand dollars worth of land was sold to builders who agreed to abide by the corporation's land usage policies.[11]

In the face of continued town growth, the housing situation and the shortage of available land was critical enough, by April 1844, to induce the Amoskeag to offer another land auction. Advertisements of the Land and Water Power Division's land sale, in September, were widely distributed and proclaimed "a great sale of house and store lots . . . very favorably situated in the neighborhood of the Amoskeag and Manchester Mills." The company noted that an unusual opportunity, what they called "a rare chance," was being made available to the general public to share in the growth of the company's prosperity—a prosperity which had seen Manchester grow to a town of 8,000. Manchester would, one day, proclaimed its knowing corporate father, "rival . . . the city of Lowell." One older town newspaper, doubting the 8,000 population estimate of the sale's promoters, expressed skepticism about other aspects of the sale as well. While accepting the Amoskeag's advertisement for publication, the editor felt obliged to warn his readers of the dangers of believing all that was advertised. Appealing to a growing resentment of the corporation, the skeptical editor warned that the chance that was being offered the people of Manchester was the "rare chance . . . to be . . . duped and shaved . . . so close that the beard" might not grow again. The pitch of the corporation was lumped with that of horse jockeys and patent medicine men. As for the optimistic estimates of the town's future, readers were warned that Manchester could rival Lowell only in the speculation and greed on the part of the town's great landholder. In a follow-up story, the editor proclaimed the land sale, "a great humbug," and scoffed at Treasurer Amory's self-proclaimed efforts to keep land prices low enough to enable the small investor to participate.[12]

In spite of the opinion of some in town, exemplified by the skeptical editor cited above, Manchester's growth was almost equal to the claims of the land-sale promoters. By 1850, Manchester's population had increase 74% from what the corporation claimed it to be at the time of its 1844 land sale. Evidence does seem to indicate that, in addition to making a profit, the Amoskeag was concerned with keeping prices within range of the small investor. Participation in town building by the independent builder who was willing to abide by the unique requirements of the company was a part of the overall design for the town. By 1855, the man who had been able to invest some money in land and had heeded the company's 1844 advertisement might well have found himself quite well-off. One local source noted that "most of those we call our rich men made their property by the rise of the real estate—its rise since 1840, '45, and '46." Land that had sold for the outrageous speculative price of 40¢ a foot in 1839 had risen to four dollars. Land which had sold for 45¢ a foot in 1844 had soared to $3.50 a foot. Even the "sand banks" that had commanded only 2-1/2¢ per foot were selling for 20¢.[13] The men who profited from this rise were not, for the most part, outsiders. They were born in New Hampshire and trusted in the growth of Manchester. Some 80% of all property owners in Manchester were New Hampshire natives, with all but a small percentage of the remainder coming from Massachusetts, Vermont, and Maine. Moreover, these were not simply local farmers who had been shrewd enough to hold onto their land, anticipating its rising value with the growth of the factory town. To be sure, there were some farmers, about 14% of the total number of property owners, who profited by the rise in real estate values, but these were not the most numerous group. Far more numerous were the skilled workers. Almost 37% of property owners in Manchester in 1850 were skilled workers, followed in number by merchants and shop keepers (see Tables 2.12-2.15).

New Hampshire natives seem to have done extremely well, both in terms of the percentage of property owners born in New Hampshire and in terms of the amounts of wealth which they were able to accumulate. Of the six men owning property valued in excess of $20,000, five came from New Hampshire by birth. Even among the less well-off, native New Hampshire residents did well, holding about 80% of the wealth of those owning under $10,000. Similarly, skilled workers seem to have done well, owning 39.1% of all property. Property ownership was a male phenomenon (93.4% of all property owners), and was characterized by relative youthfulness, with well near 60% of property owners under 40 years of age. In terms of specific occupational categories, those who did well in acquiring property seem to have been those whose occupations forced them into day-to-day contact with the land. Most noticeably, farmers held more property (14.7%) than any other single occupational group. Next in line on the scale of property owners were shopkeepers, dealers, agents, innkeepers, and stable keepers, but none of these fared so well as the skilled workers. Within the ranks of the skilled workers, carpenters fared best

(10.5% of all property owners). This might be expected, since carpenters would be among those most fully involved on a day-to-day basis with the actual job of building for the town's physical growth. Opportunities for investment in the jobs they were on must have been plentiful—investment in labor, if not in cash. Likewise, it is not surprising that the rate of property ownership was high among construction-related jobs, such as masons and painters. In their daily work these men encountered, far more than the millworker, opportunities for gaining wealth generated by the real estate market in a town with a burgeoning growth rate. What is surprising is the extent to which men in occupations such as machinists (5.6%) and mechanics (4.0%), whose daily concerns were removed from real property, were able to acquire wealth. The number of such men is particularly outstanding when compared to the number of textile operatives able to accumulate holdings worthy of reporting. Only two spinners held reportable property, while only three weavers were reported as property owners. Taken all together, general textile operatives comprised only 2.4% of the property owners in town, while this occupational grouping, as noted earlier, comprised a full 83% of the town's work force at this time. Clearly, in terms of opportunities for property ownership available to them in the 1850's, mill-workers had a sound basis for their feeling, expressed in 1855, that their socio-economic position was declining relative to that of other groups. While textile workers fared poorly in terms of ownership of real property, they did little better, as will be seen later, in terms of accumulating savings. [14]

Throughout the early boom years, the Amoskeag's policy was to make land available for new housing as new factories, machine shops, and businesses came into town. Hence, in 1855, the company held another great land sale in order to provide for the town growth that their soon-to-be-built Number 5 mill would induce, and to fill the growing demand for additional land that had taken place since the last land sale.

The policy of holding periodic land sales enabled the company to benefit from the steady industrial growth of the town. Policy at the land auctions was to sell only if prices fell within certain predetermined limits. Because the company thus controlled the initial stage of construction costs, it had a great influence on the cost of areas of community life such as housing, and this influence extended beyond the company's own housing units. The company's critics would charge that the Amoskeag's land policy was a monopolistic attempt to profiteer. The Amoskeag's view of the situation was markedly different. The company saw itself serving as a stabilizing influence, preventing wild boom-and-bust real estate speculation. The greatest beneficiary of this policy was the company itself, but the company's defenders argued that the town benefitted as well. They argued that the very fact that land, in large quantity, was held in reserve and could, perhaps, be made available for purchase from the company at established prices prevented private land speculators from inflating land values. While the rise in land prices was certain, it was also steady, without wild fluctuations of boom and bust. Those land speculators who did come to Manchester had to be cautious.[15] William Buzzell came from Malden, Massachusetts with the intention of purchasing a large tract of land and subdividing for house lots. Any profits out of reason (as defined by the Land and Water Power Division) that such a speculator might plan on could be wiped out at a moment's notice if the company should announce the sale of similar land at controlled prices. What this meant for men like Buzzell and for the town as well was that, if speculators hoped to be successful, they had to make "improvements" on the land in order to justify the increased prices they would ask. In practical effect, land speculators were compelled to provide such amenities as gravelled streets, landscaping, and a pure spring water supply before they could safely profit from their "development." The company and the town were, thus, relieved from such costs. In spite of bearing these costs, private developers would profit even given the subtle controlling influence of the Amoskeag's huge land reserve. In the mid-1850's, local editors were remarking that "the building of houses had not kept pace with the increase of population, and we judge that it will not for years to come." The housing shortage was so severe that, when one mill burned, throwing hundreds out of work and inducing them to leave the city, the vacant rooms and tenements were immediately filled, and the housing situation was barely affected "so crowded for room were we."[16]

Given the overcrowding of the private housing market, the Amoskeag's policy of requiring workers to live in company housing was regarded by the company's defenders less as a burden placed upon workers than as a service—a benefit—provided for them by their employers. Indeed, the Amoskeag's workers' housing has been long recognized as a model of housing for industrial workers. Company housing was clean, it was rent controlled, reasonable, and, unlike much of the private housing, it was close to the workers' place of employment.[17] There would be no need for rushing out of a tenement without eating a morning meal in order to get to the mill on time. The workers who lived in company housing had only to walk down the street to their jobs. Additionally, there were "moral" benefits of company housing. Workers were frequently reminded that the company rules and regulations were intended for their benefit.

Workers who lived under the protection of the Amoskeag's moral police policy were reminded that they would need not fear the evils of the large boardinghouses which pastors were weekly denouncing from the pulpits. One minister reminded workers that they had come to the city, and "the city . . . organizes evil; evil, that is, becomes a part of the trade and traffic of the city." Another clergyman warned that the large private boardinghouse was "the very hot-bed of . . . temptation,'' where workers would no longer enjoy the protection, ''the restraints, and privileges of the home fireside.'' The boardinghouses, the ministers constantly preached, were not homes.[18] Manchester residents were made aware that they lived in a new form of society—the industrial town—and that special measures were needed to provide surrogate homes for young, impressionable minds. The town's clergy would be among the strongest advocates of the company's paternalism. Libraries, lecture programs, sewing clubs, and any form of organized activity which would channel the workers' off-duty hours into approved ways were welcomed. Recognizing that not all time could be spent in organized activity, the clergy encouraged workers to board in ''respectable'' houses.[19] Nothing was more respectable, in terms of the boarding house, than company housing—whether it be boardinghouse or tenement. A strict, and enforced, set of moral rules governed those who lived in the company's housing. One resident, Gale Stearns, noted that ''. . . most of the help boarded and roomed in the Factory Boarding houses. They had to be in by 10 o'clock at night. If not in at that time they had to give an account of where they had been and with whom. They had to sign a paper that they would attend Divine Worship on Sundays and give two weeks termination notice.''[20]

The land sales policies and the regulatory schema of the company boardinghouse are but two indications of the Amoskeag's larger policy of paternalism. Workers would not only have to adjust to the city and the factory, but they would also have to adjust to larger forces which would, in theory at least, govern their lives. The policies of the Amoskeag did affect workers' lives far beyond the workroom or the millyard gates. Throughout its history, Manchester was very much a ''company'' town; the Amoskeag employed nearly 60% of the town's work force in its closing years, and, together with its associated ''competitors,'' accounted for upwards of 80% of the work force's employment in its earlier years. Such figures regarding employment tell only a part of the story, though.[21]

From the very beginning, even when there were ''competing'' mills, i.e., mills owned by corporations other than the Amoskeag, the policies governing the town's growth and development were the policies established and enforced by the Amoskeag. The Amoskeag's officials would determine what sort of buildings would be erected, where they would be constructed, how much power would be supplied, which industries would be tolerated, which would be encouraged, which forbidden, where locations would be assigned. Official policy between the various textile firms in town was one of ever rivals—never competitors.[22]

The initial drawings for the very physical layout of the town—the streets, parks, squares, zoning for commercial, industrial, and residential districts— was undertaken by the founding company. Canals, churches, and cemeteries alike were allotted space in the town by the original designers. A young junior engineer named Ezekiel Straw drew the initial plans for the physical layout of the town. Straw came to Manchester on what he viewed as a temporary job as a surveyor, and would spend the rest of his life in Manchester, serving as the personification of upward social mobility. Straw became the factory "agent," the chief local operating officer of the Amoskeag New Mills. The agent served as the highest company official in town, in effect the general manager of the company, supervising every aspect of the mills' operations.[23] As agent, Straw was the local court of last resort in regard to company policies, being outranked only by the Boston treasurer of the company with whom he maintained close contact. Not only did Boston assure that competition among Manchester's mills would be in name only, but, by selecting as agent of the most powerful mills a man who had been involved, in detail, in the formation of the company's plans for the town, they assured the continuity of the original intention in building the town. As Straw's son, and eventually his grandson, succeeded him as agent, the family came to represent a concrete manifestation of the company's continuing paternalistic outlook. The social hierarchy of the town was clear even to children. Sons of factory workers would be the playmates of the Straw children, and would be taught by their parents always to refer to their prestigious playmate as "Mr. Straw."[24]

The original "Mr. Straw" was proud of the role that he had played in the establishment of the factory town, and particularly proud of the concepts of paternalism which the Amoskeag embodied. Straw boasted of the company's "liberal policy towards all." In addition to its land sale policy and its policy of providing workers with off-duty amenities while requiring strict moral behavior, the policies of the Amoskeag were evident in many areas of town life. The company boasted of its "courteous treatment on the part of the overseers." This was, in particular, one of E. A. Straw's pet policies. Workers were free to come to the agent directly with grievances against their overseers. On a number of occasions Straw personally investigated workers' grievances and intervened. An old woman named Mary had been fired by her overseer because her age had slowed her down. When it was reported to Straw by her fellow workers, he personally visited Mary, brought her back to the mill, promised a life-long job, and openly rebuked her overseer. For Straw, at least, paternalism was a concrete reality and not simply an abstract ideal hidden somewhere in the midst of the founders' ideology.[25] While the company's land policy may have served to make land, at times, scarce and hence keep rents in the private market high, the Amoskeag's housing was made available, only to its workers and their families, at comparatively attractive prices. Rents on company tenements were kept considerably below the rents charged by the private sector. The company had seen to it that houses were well-designed "for health and privacy." The Amoskeag boasted of its unwillingness to exploit child labor (a policy not always followed by the town's other textile mills). In hard times, the Amoskeag tried to provide alternative employment, and because of the company's size and the number of various divisions—land maintenance, machine tools, locomotive manufacture, housing—layoffs could be partially avoided by providing temporary jobs for workers at other than their regular tasks. Perhaps the alternative work in "hard times" would not be full time or would not pay as well as the worker's regular job, but the worker and his family could stay on in company housing until times improved, and they were sure to note the contrast with some of the other mill towns. Rumors of layoffs and bad times in Nashua, or in Lowell or in Lawrence, were quick to find their way to Manchester, and the seemingly greater reluctance of the Amoskeag to cut back on employment was noted by local workers.[26]

In addition to funding the establishment of libraries, lyceums, discussion groups, and Sunday Schools, the Amoskeag acted in other ways as godfather of the town. Often when a public improvement—better roads, fire protection, water supply, sewage—was planned, the Amoskeag would bear part of the cost —donating land, donating materials and labor, or, sometimes, contributing cash. Some public amenities were paid for almost entirely by the company—a grand hotel, for example, and an improved water supply system was financed by the company. But to imply unfettered altruism or public spirit as the chief motivating factors would be a mistake. Public spirit was tempered by the need to control the course of the public life of the town.[27]

Some idea of the subtlety of the company's mechanisms of control, and of workers reactions, can be gained by examining one aspect of the company's "liberal policy." The Amoskeag's boosters would brag of the "gifts" of land which the company unselfishly bestowed upon town, churches, and civic groups alike for public purposes. The town hall was located on land donated by the company, as were schools, libraries, and churches. The town's parks were laid out, landscaped, and constructed by the company upon company owned land, and donated to the town upon completion. Even the town's cemetery was on land donated by the company. A controversy developed in town over the latter donation which serves to illustrate the mixed reactions with which workers met many company "liberal policies."[28]

The company's donations influenced the town, influenced clergymen grateful for financial help, influenced teachers thankful for classroom heating installed by the boiler works, and tried to influence workers and general public opinion. The workers and general public, though, were more critical of the Amoskeag's liberalism than were town civic leaders. A large group of town residents protested the town's acceptance, with thanks, of a major land donation by the company. The Valley Cemetery was donated to the town, partially improved, with certain conditions—the town was required to maintain it, construct additional pathways through the cemetery as needed, and, in general, be responsible for its maintenance and improvement in the future. Granting of land with conditions attached was standard company policy. It was not unusual to require the recipient of the land, in whatever case, to make such improvements as landscaping, fencing with a wrought iron fence, painted black, and requiring maintenance "forever." Those who objected to the Valley Cemetery donation based their objection on this standard policy. Deeds usually included provisions that land donated could be used only in accordance with the restrictions placed upon it at the time of donation—land must be used only for a park, if donated as parkland. Fences must be built and maintained forever if the original donation so specified. It was well known that the violation of any provision, at any point in time, would mean that the Amoskeag, at its will, could reclaim the land upon demand.[29] Viewing the cemetery donation, town residents and workers grew apprehensive: suppose, at some future date, the Valley Land should become valuable by reason of the growth of the city. The Amoskeag would have escaped paying taxes on the land and could, on some pretext or other, reclaim the land in which relatives, neighbors, or co-workers might lie buried. The possibility of using improper maintenance as a pretext was unsettling for many Manchester residents when it came to the cemetery donation.

The prospect of holding land barely short of freehold seems not to have been overly disturbing in most instances. Over the years, workers who had displeased the company would learn to fight in court the efforts of the Amoskeag, on some pretext, to recover land. Throughout the city, grateful preachers would exhort the gratitude of their congregations for donated land, for help in establishing Sunday schools, religious libraries, sewing and prayer groups. Free, if use-restricted, land was calculated to win public praise. For some residents, though, the prospect of having lived all their lives in a "company" town, residing in a company dwelling, worshiping in a company church, being educated in a company school, was disturbing. But it was not nearly so disturbing as the prospect of, after death, having the company plan a final trick and reclaim "donated" land, and bodily remains along with it. No matter how tenuous the claims of the company might be upon the Valley Cemetery, there was a vocal and considerable group who objected to the town's acceptance of cemetery land with any strings attached. The protest over the Valley Cemetery donation serves as but one example of the force of dissenting public opinion in the company town. In spite of all that the Amoskeag did to assure its influence in Manchester, the company's hold on public favor was often tenuous.

In the interests of maintaining peace and good public relations, it became almost standard practice for the company to overlook many of its conditional requirements. Countless parks never were fenced in with iron fences, went without landscaping and pathways as specified in the original deed, and such requirements were, in practice, unenforced in the interests of prudent town-factory relations.[30] Demands and restrictions, in many cases, were meaningless, and the Amoskeag would bow to the force of public opinion rather than antagonize the townspeople and workers with whom the company would have to live.

The original physical design of the town indicated that the future that was anticipated would be one similar to the model of other "Waltham System" towns. The basic outline of that model is well known. Especially with regard to the work force, it was expected that workers would be drawn from the native farming population. Young women would be especially likely to migrate to the mills, seeking a source of cash income. Likewise in search of a cash income, farming families would tend to abandon farms whose profitability new opportunities in the West and in the industrial towns was rendering increasingly marginal.[31] To attract such a population, prejudices regarding moral decline on the part of the residents of the new factory towns had to be overcome. The company owned boardinghouse and tenement house system, with company-sponsored religious and cultural activities and, in effect, off-time "overseers" to supervise the workers' moral behavior, was specifically designed to overcome the natives' anti-urban and anti-industrial prejudices. The system was reinforced, once workers arrived in town, by sermons, lectures, and discussion groups whose theme was "the moral influence of manufacturing towns."[32]

As a way of furthering this system, one of the express rules of the Amoskeag (and of the other mills because of the Amoskeag's insistence that tenements for workers must be built right along with the construction of mill buildings) was that workers must live in company housing. Official policy was that only those who lived in company housing would be given the privilege of employment in the mills. Those who lived in the housing of the Amoskeag, Stark, and Manchester Mills were required to submit to a system of strict moral supervision. For young women, this meant no male visitors, curfew hours, and compulsory church attendance. Men and heads of households were required to attend church, refrain from drink and strong language, and see to the moral welfare of any boarders or lodgers that they might take in.[33] This system was reinforced not only by company regulations, but by the sermons of Manchester's clergy. Clergymen saw this as one means of providing surrogate families who, in the absence of natural families, would serve to supervise, protect, and guide a young population. Ministers saw the company boardinghouse and the company tenements as one means of overcoming the evils natural to the industrial city. Comparisons were frequently made between the large, private boardinghouse, where moral and physical decay were regarded as a certainty, and the Amoskeag's comparatively small, well supervised resident system.[34]

The idea that company housing policy was easily abandoned or that it was discarded as a foreign born population moved into the mills is a false one. The policy of requiring workers to live in the company's housing (or as an alternative in housing approved by the company) was set out at the very foundation of the factories and enforced (albeit sporadically and unevenly) and reaffirmed throughout much of the nineteenth century, at least down to the late 1870's.[35] In 1870, Agent Straw put the company's policy in this matter in writing. In his own handwriting, Straw sent a memorandum to all overseers. He reminded overseers that all of their workers (and the overseers were responsible for hiring) were required to reside in company housing. As part of their job requirements, overseers were required to ascertain that workers did, in fact, live in company housing. Overseers could, theoretically, grant exceptions individually to this requirement, but it was theoretically expected that, for the most part, the official policy would be enforced. Moreover, all workers, Straw affirmed, were to acknowledge, by their signature or mark, that they recognized and would adhere to the housing and moral guidance policies of the company. They were not to swear, drink, or leave without notice. They were to attend church, arrive at work punctually, see to their proper conduct both in and out of the work place, and, in case of illness or other valid reason for absence from work, send notice to their overseer whose individual workroom rules (made by the overseer) they were to observe. They were not to be put to work without acknowledging, in writing, their willingness to adhere to these rules which were in the form of a "contract." Clearly Ezekiel Straw did not regard the housing and moral supervision policies of the Amoskeag as "paper policy," but rather saw it, in 1870 and down to 1878, when written signatures were not required, as a concrete reality. The overseers were reminded, as if they did not realize, that their own positions were vulnerable and that they were expected to enforce policies, whether they agreed with them or not.[36]

To say that a strict moral paternalism remained official company policy in Manchester throughout the period, though, is not to say that official policy was a reality in the everyday life of the workers. While the paternalistic moralism of the Amoskeag was seemingly unchanging, in practice policy was modified in response to changing times and changing circumstances. The most important factor in changing that policy was the worker who, theoretically, was governed by it. Overseers would find themselves caught between Agent Straw's policies and the realities of the pressures of the workroom. Overseers desiring "good" workers in order to keep up the performance of their rooms would find that

E. A. Straw, Memorandum, 1870. (Courtesy of the Manchester Historic Association).

Regulations for Employees of the Manchester Print Works (Courtesy of the Manchester Historic Association).

REGULATIONS

TO BE OBSERVED BY ALL PERSONS EMPLOYED BY THE PROPRIETORS

OF THE

MILLS OF THE MANCHESTER PRINT WORKS.

THE Overseers are to be punctually in their rooms at the starting of the Mill, and not be absent unnecessarily during working hours. They are to see that all those employed in their rooms are in their places in due season, and keep a correct account of their time and work. They may grant leave of absence to those employed under them, when there are spare hands in the room to supply their places; otherwise they are not to grant leave of absence except in case of absolute necessity.

All persons employed in the Mills of the Manchester Print Works, are required to observe the regulations of the room where they are employed. They are not to be absent from their work without consent, except in case of sickness, and then they are to send information to the overseer of the cause of their absence.

They are to board in one of the boarding-houses belonging to the Company, unless permitted by the Agent to do otherwise, and conform to the regulations of the house where they board.

The Company will not employ any one who is habitually absent from public worship on the Sabbath, or who uses profane and indecent language in the Mills or elswhere, or who uses ardent spirits as a beverage.

All persons entering into the employment of the Company agree to work twelve months; and to consider the usual Mill hours, as heretofore, a day's work.

All persons intending to leave the employment of the Company, are to give two weeks' notice of their intention to their overseer; and their engagement with the Company is not considered fulfilled unless they comply with this regulation, in which case the person well receive an honorable discharge signed by the Agent, if requested.

Payments will be made monthly, including board and wages, which will be made up to and including the last Saturday of each month, and paid in the course of the following week.

☞ Any one who shall take from the Mills or the Yard, Cloth or other Property belonging to the Company, will be prosecuted for every such offence. ☜

These Regulations are considered a part of the contract with all persons employed in the Mills of the Manchester Print Works.

Overseers hiring help are not allowed to set them to work until they produce a copy of these Regulations with the certificate below, signed by the persons hired.

WM. P. NEWELL, AGENT.

Manchester, N. H., ...185

I, the undersigned, of   in the State of

do hereby agree to conform to the foregoing Regulations.

I,   of said

do hereby consent to the above contract.

'they could keep their own jobs only by granting the "occasional" exemptions from company policy as an everyday commonplace.

Not only the overseers, but also the company management, in spite of official failure to recognize reality on paper, perceived the need to be flexible in terms of rule enforcement. As worker hostility to more and more aspects of "big brother" life became vocal, the company became increasingly reluctant to insist on strict enforcement of its "rules," and in practice many rules were allowed to slip into unacknowledged abeyance.[37] As workers came to glory in "independent" newspaper editors' denunciations of corporation policies and corporation officials, the company grew wary of a hostile public opinion and overseers grew wary of a workforce that could, in effect, sabotage a supervisor's career. Workers, through the exercise of informal pressures combined with more formal (newspaper) pressures, would acquire a practical freedom to ignore or modify certain of the mills' regulations.

Table 2.1. Growth of Population, Manchester, 1840's

	Male	Female	Total	% Increase From 1840
1840			3,235	base
1844	2,625	3,531	6,156	90.3
1845	3,595	4,422	8,917	175.6
1846	4,591	5,624	10,125	213.
1847	5,050	7,236	12,286	279.8
1849	5,928	8,614	14,542	349.5

Source: 1850 town report

Table 2.2 Growth of Population, Manchester, at Ten-Year
Intervals, 1840-1880

	Male	Female	Total	% Increase
1840			3,235	
1850	5,765	8,167	13,932	330.7
1860	8,668	11,439	20,107	44.3
1870	10,475	13,061	23,536	17.1
1880	14,698	17,932	32,630	38.6

Source: U.S. Census

Table 2.3. Percentage by which Women Exceed Men, General
Population, 1840-1880

		Percent
1840		
	1844	34.5
	1845	23.0
	1846	22.5
	1847	43.3
	1849	45.3
1850		41.7
1860		32.
1870		24.7
1880		22.

Source: U.S. Census; Town Reports

Table 2.4. Work Force, Amoskeag Manufacturing Company,
1840's, Textiles

	Men	Women
1841	120	560
1848	250	1,400
1850	475	2,100

Source: Amoskeag Material, Manchester Historic Association

Table 2.5. Work Forces of Manchester, 1850, by Industry

Industry	Male	% of all Males	Female	% of all Females	% of Total Work Force
Cotton Cloth	1,152	61.6	3,199	95.1	83.1
Carriages	31	1.7			.6
Harnesses	6	.3			.1
Machine Wks.	370	19.8			7.1
Axe makers	3	.2			.1
Gravel-stone	5	.3			.1
Wood products	31	1.7			.6
Sash-door	31	1.7			.6
Paper stainers	4	.2	1		.1
Masonry	20	1.1			.4
Metalwork	20	1.1			.4
Shoe and boot	164	8.8	95	2.8	4.9
Tailors	12	.6	64	1.9	1.5
Soap-candle	5	.3			.1
Confectioner	3	.2	2	.1	.1
Grist Mill	3	.2			.1
Bakery	10	.5			.2
Cigar makers	1	.1	2	.1	.1

Source: Compiled from manufacturers' returns, Census of Manufactures

Table 2.6. Work Force of Manchester, 1840

Occupation	Number	Percent
Mining		
Agricultural	334	22.5
Commerce	63	4.3
Manufacturing & Trades	1,055	71.0
River Navigation	15	1.0
Professions	18	1.2

Total Population: 3,235; Number of Families: 523

Source: Compiled from Returns, Census of Manufactures

Table 2.7. Work Force of Manchester, 1860

	Male	% of all Males	Female	% of all Females	% of Total Work Force
Textiles	1,593	50.5	3,979	87.4	72.3
Boots + shoes	229	7.3	269	5.9	6.5
Engine works	450	14.3			5.8
Clothing	46	1.5	245	5.4	3.8
Stone works	118	3.7			1.5
Machine tools	97	3.1			1.3
Woodworking	95	3.1			1.2
Leather-harness	47	1.5	20	.4	.9
Publishers	61	1.9	3	.4	.8
Carriage-transport	51	1.6			.7
Bakery-confection	48	1.5	1		.6
Bobbins-text.parts	46	1.5			.6
Misc. mfgrs.	31	1.0	10	.2	.5
Paper mfgrs.	16	.5	19	.4	.5
Mill machinery	35	1.1			.5
Sheet metal	23	.7			.3
Pipe fitters	22	.7			.3
Utilities	20	.6			.3
Bleaching (text.)	16	.5	3	.1	.3
Butchers	17	.5			.2
Cigar mfgrs.	15	.5	1		.2
Misc. service	15	.5			.2
Upholsterers	14	.4			.2
Photographers	12	.4			.2
Blacksmiths	10	.3			.1
Druggists	10	.3			.1
Soap & candle	10	.3			.1
Brewers	9	.3	1		.1
	3,156		4,550		

Source: Compiled from Returns, Census of Manufactures

Table 2.8. Work Force of Manchester, 1870

	Male	% of all Males	Female	% of all Females	Children	% of all Children	% of Total
Textiles	2,517	66.2	3,873	94.5	399	95.0	81.6
Locomotives	400	10.5			7	1.7	4.8
Clothing	42	1.1	136	3.3			2.1
Carpentry	136	3.6					1.6
Marble & stone	74	2.0					.9
Painters	33	.9					.4
Boots and shoes	69	1.8	12	.3	10	2.4	1.1
Furniture	35	1.0	4	.1	1	.2	.5
Metal work	46	1.2					.6
Carriages	36	1.0	1				.4
Blacksmith	13	.3					
Paper mfgrs.	40	1.1	28	.7			.8
Harnesses	22	.6	15	.4			.4
Tools – machinery	117	3.1					1.4
Textile machines	48	1.3	1				.6
Printing	41	1.1	13	.3			.7
Misc. mfgrs.	27	.7	5	.1	3	.7	.4
Utilities	25	.7					.3
Gas fitting	3	.1					
Brewer	25	.7					.3
Cigar mfgrs.	14	.4	1				.2
Photography	5	.1	2	.1			.1
Upholstery	16	.4					.2
Brushes	3	.1	8	.2			.1
Jewelry	7	.2					
Hair works	2	.1	1				.1
Bakery	3	.1					
Winery	1						
	3,800		4,100		420		

Source: Compiled from Returns, Census of Manufactures

Table 2.9. Work Force of Manchester, 1880[38]

	Male	% of all Males	Female	% of all Females	Children	% of all Children	% of Total
All industries	4,632		5,748		458		
Cotton goods	2,450	52.9	4,569	79.5	229	50.0	66.9
Foundry & machine	500	10.8	19	.3	9	2.0	4.9
Carpentry	105	2.3					1.0
Paint & paperhang.	68	1.5					.8
Sash, door, blind	79	1.7	18	.3	3	.7	.8
Carriages, wagons	47	1.0					.4
Marble & stone	36	.8					.3
Plumbing-gasfit.	27	.6					.3
Bread-bakery	20	.4	1				.2
Blacksmith	18	.4					.2
Flour-grist mill	16	.3					.2
Leather	39	.8					.4
Metalwork	15	.3	1				.2
Tobacco	14	.3	3				.2
Photography	4	.2	5	.1			.1
Saddle-harness	7	.2					.1
Other	1,187	25.6	1,132	19.7	217	47.4	23.4

Source: Social Statistics of Cities, U.S. Census

This table was compiled by the Bureau of the Census. Others in this series were compiled by the author from the census returns.

Table 2.10. Number of Employers by Size of Establishment,
1850

Number of Employees	Number of Companies in this Size Category	
	Males Employed	Females Employed
5 or under	30	12
6-12	14	6
13-20	3	
21-50		1
Over 50	6	4

Source: Manuscript Census Returns, Census of Manufactures, 1850

Table 2.11. Number of Persons Employed in Shops, by Size,
1850

Number of Employees	Total Persons Employed in this Size Category	
	Males	Females
5 or under	93	25
6-12	111	64
13-20	51	
21-50		25
Over 50	1,616	3,249
	1,871	3,363

Source: Manuscript Census Returns, Census of Manufactures, 1850

Table 2.12. Nativity of Property Owners, 1850, by State or
             Country

Birthplace	Percent
New Hampshire	80.6
Massachusetts	9.8
Vermont	5.7
Maine	1.3
England	.7
New York	.6
Ireland	.4
Canada	.4
Rhode Island	.3
Connecticut	.1
Virginia	.1

N = 705

Source: Compiled from U.S. Census Sample

Table 2.13. Nativity by Property Accumulation, 1850

	$1,000 or Under	$1,001- 10,000	$10,001- 19,999	$20,000- 30,000	$40,000+
New Hampshire	79.1%	80.0%	94.5%	66.6%	100%
Massachusetts	6.	11.2	2.8	33.3	
Vermont	8.2	5.3	2.8		
Maine	1.5	1.3			
England	2.2	.4			
New York	2.2	.2			
Ireland		.6			
Canada		.6			
Rhode Island		.4			
Connecticut		.2			
Virginia	.7				
N =	134	529	36	3	3

Source: Compiled from U.S. Census Sample

Table 2.14. Occupational Grouping by Property Accumulation, 1850

Occupation	$1,000 or Under	$1,001– 2,000	$2,001– 5,000	$5,001– 51,000	Total
Professional	5	2	12	11	30
Semi-Professional	13	28	39	26	106
Farmers	18	20	49	15	102
White Collar	21	5	9	5	40
Skilled	99	87	50	23	259
Semi-Skilled	19	8	4		31
Unskilled	39	15	7	1	62
Not Known	31	22	15	7	75
Total	245	187	185	88	705

Source: Compiled from U.S. Census Sample

Table 2.15. Percent of Occupation with Property in Each Category

Occupation	$1,000 or Under	$1,001– 2,000	$2,001– 5,000	$5,001– 51,000	Total
Professional	2.0	1.1	6.5	12.5	4.3
Semi-Professional	5.3	15.0	21.1	29.5	15.0
Farmers	7.4	10.7	26.5	17.1	14.5
White Collar	8.6	2.7	4.9	5.7	5.7
Skilled	40.4	46.5	27.0	26.1	36.7
Semi-Skilled	7.8	4.3	2.2		4.4
Unskilled	15.9	8.0	3.8	1.1	8.8
Not Known	12.7	11.8	8.1	7.9	10.6

Source: Compiled from U.S. Census Sample

3

Paternalism's Response: The Workers

There is no doubt that Manchester was a "company town," yet a fact that is well worth remembering is that, in shaping the town, the company did not exist in isolation. The residents of Manchester, the vast majority of whom were textile workers or their families, shaped the community life of Manchester as surely as did its corporate founders. The company desire to influence local affairs meant, in turn, that the Amoskeag would have to display some sensitivity to the sympathies of the local community.

Workers in the 1840's and 1850's used a variety of mechanisms to influence decisions that affected them. They pressured overseers, they used the local press, great in numbers and variety, to voice their concerns, and they formed their own neighborhoods, often apart from the "planned" workers housing, where different groups of workers could maintain their own unique traditions, customs, and cultures. These neighborhoods, where workers spent their outside-of-work lives, served as important sources of unity and reinforcement, especially for the foreign born.

Early neighborhood formation meant that there would be a practicable alternative to the company tenement or boardinghouse. Immigrant families, taking in boarders, could serve as surrogate families for the young men and women of foreign birth whose language, cultural, or religious traditions could make life in the predominately native-born company boardinghouses a traumatic situation.

While there is no doubt that workers were "acted upon," then, it is entirely possible that their abilities to react to industrial situations, to accommodate, and to effect some degree of change in the system in which they found themselves has been seriously underestimated.[1] It will be the task of this chapter to explore the extent to which workers could "maneuver" the larger systems of factory and city in which they found themselves.

A certain amount of maneuverability was built into the way in which certain company policies were designed to be broken or selectively ignored. All workers were supposed to live in company housing—whether boardinghouses or tenements. The company house was an integral part of the Amoskeag's plan

Text of *Regulations for the Boardinghouses and Tenements Belonging to the Amoskeag Manufacturing Company.* (Courtesy of the Manchester Historic Association).

All persons, on taking a tenement, are to sign the lease for the same, and agree, while they occupy the tenement, to conform to the terms of the lease, and abide strictly by such regulations as may have been or shall be established by the Agent of the company for the orderly conducting and management of the tenement.

The tenants of the Boarding Houses will be held answerable for any disorderly or improper conduct on their premises, their doors are to be closed at ten o'clock in the evening, and no person admitted after that time, without some reasonable excuse.

They must not board any persons who are not employed by the Company, unless by special permission from the Agent, and in no case are Males and Females to be allowed to board in the same tenement, and the standard price of board must not be changed by the boarding House keeper, except by consent of the Agent of the Company.

The keepers of boarding houses must give an account of the number, names and employment of their boarders, when required, and report to the Agent the names of such as are guilty of any improper conduct.

The buildings, and yards about them, must be kept clean and in good order; no horses, cattle or swine, are to be kept on the premises, and if they are injured otherwise than from ordinary use, all necessary repairs will be made, and charged to the occupant; also the sidewalks in front of the houses must be kept clean and free from snow. It is desirable that the families of those who live in the houses as well as the boarders, who have not the kin-pox, should be vaccinated immediately, the expense of which will be paid by the company for all who are in their employment.

The habitual use of ARDENT SPIRITS as a beverage, or of Profane or Indecent Language by the keepers of the boarding houses, or permitting others addicted to the use of either to remain in their houses will in all cases be considered a sufficient cause for their discharge, and will be required forthwith to leave the Corporation.

for its town from the very beginning. No large factories would be built, or land sold, to any enterprise that would not build worker housing at the same time. Thus the Stark Mills, the Manchester Mills, and the Print Works, in addition to the Amoskeag Mills and the Amoskeag's machine shop, all had their own workers' housing. All were brick tenement buildings, built close to the mills according to the Amoskeag's design. All companies were to require workers to live in their housing. In the early years of the town, families would be sought out for the number of family members who could work in the mills, and also for their willingness to rent a company tenement, take in boarders, and promise to adhere to company requirements regarding the supervision of those boarders by the head of the household. Supposedly the only variation from the requirement that workers live in company housing was to be allowed by specific and individual permission from the overseer. A valid reason might be, for example, that one had family in Manchester with whom one could live, or that a family from one's native town now lived in Manchester and a worker might choose to live with the home folks. The overseer was the key to the enforcement mechanism, but because of his own vulnerability to the demands, from above, that his room produce, and the pressures, from below, to achieve a workable day-to-day relationship with those whose labor would assure the production and performance that was necessary to his own success, the overseer was reluctant to antagonize his workers. In examining the extent to which the official requirement that workers "board on the corporation" was enforced, one is struck by the exception rather than the rule. In the first 90 days of 1860, for example, 352 workers were hired by the Amoskeag. All of them would acknowledge the fact, in writing, that they were to live in company housing. Only 144, or less than half (40.9%), would do so. By 1870, when Straw reaffirmed company policy with regard to housing, only 23.1% of 660 workers sampled would live in company housing, in spite of the written "contract" which every one of those workers signed acknowledging their obligation to live in company housing.[2]

Of foreign born workers, only 10 out of 43 lived in company housing in 1860, while 134 out of 309 native workers lived in company housing (see Tables 3.1-3.3). In 1870, only 34 out of 229 foreign born workers sampled lived in company housing, while 121 out of 432 native born workers would live in company housing (see Tables 3.1-3.3).[3] By creating a system designed for the exception as well as the rule, the Amoskeag allowed just enough flexibility to prevent its workers from feeling totally dominated by the rules and regulations of life in a company town.

Even in the earliest period, when the factories were just beginning and the moral police force of the factory's paternalism should have been strongest, there is evidence that some workers felt secure enough about the support of the general community to take on the Amoskeag, a formidable adversary. In the early years, one girl, Mary, encountered health problems when she found the work too much for her. She notified her overseer, B. F. Osgood, that she had to leave the mill at once, and that she would live in Manchester with the family of a friend for a while in order to recover her heatlh. Mary's overseer was infuriated because of her violation of her written pledge to give two weeks' notice before quitting. As Mary put it, Osgood "gave me a bill of my time . . . after abusing me with such language as ever polluted the lips of a gentleman . . . (and) . . . ordered me to leave the room."[4]

Not content with firing Mary rather than letting her quit, Mary would find that the Stark's Agent, David Burnham, when informed by Osgood, had exerted other pressures in order that Mary might serve as an example of what would happen to those who violated company rules. Mary found that Burnham had pressured her friend's family, from Mary's native town, not to take her in for fear of losing their own jobs (her friend's father was an overseer). Mary, for violating company rules, found herself out of a job, out of the lodging house where she had lived, and out of the dwellings of a friendly family upon whom she had counted for help. Not broken, though, Mary found others to take her in, and publicized her plight for the whole town to know—and for workers thinking of going to Osgood's room to give thought. Mary's poetry, published in a "neutral" (i.e., not corporation financed and not openly pro-labor) newspaper, denounced both Agent and overseer alike:

> Burnham's mad and Osgood's sad,
> Because I left the mill.
> But how can they (so spruce and gay)
> Always have their will?
> Now be it known throughout the town
> That Burnham is a Hog,*
> And Osgood too, a perfect spew,
> Strut Burnham's barking dog.

*I beg pardon of the poor four legged rooters for this comparison.

Hardly a woman to be broken by an unjust employer, Mary succeeded not only in denouncing overseer and agent, but in her letter, she reminded other workers that there were other rooms besides Mr. Osgood's, and other factories besides Burnham's. If one company, or more specifically, one overseer, would not prove accommodative, then there were others who would.[5]

Mary's encounter with agent and overseer was one manifestation of the factories' larger policy of enforcing and promulgating those rules which they regarded as beneficial to a young work force in need of guidance and supervision. In 1843, alarmed at the extent to which the rule requiring "boarding on the corporation" was being ignored, Burnham determined to enforce it. One town newspaper reported that Burnham ". . . is going to have all of his girls board on the corporation." To this end, Burnham authorized a "Mr. Peavey" to compile lists of girls not presently living in company facilities who would be required to obey regulations and move into a large new tenement that the Stark had just had built. Peavey's overriding concern for the workers' welfare, like Burnham's kind-hearted paternalism, did not go without notice in the local independent press. One mill girl wrote ". . . I do hope that when he opens that large tenement, that little of that hugging and kissing will be dispensed with in the entry, and some other things too ridiculous to appear in print. An old married man had better let the girls alone."[6] Even at this early date, workers' opposition to company policies was growing intense. An editor pointed out that the attitude of agents and mill housing officials was that the corporations had built "great houses down here on purpose to keep boarders, and is it not right that we should have them?" But to the workers the issue was one of personal freedom and not of the financial welfare of a paternalist corporation. One worker protested, "Shall we live in a free land of liberty when that time comes every girl must board on the corporation? No, no, heaven forbid, we never shall see the day. Think of the blood that has been split [sic] for our freedom, and then think (of) the girls being drove in like cattle of the field to eat their victuals, or they cannot have employment. . . ."[7]

Manchester's workers were in a better position, in the early 1840's than those of nearby Hooksett, if the reports from Hooksett can be believed. Reportedly Hooksett workers would return home ". . . after years of toil, changed from healthy, blooming, cheerful youths to sickly sallow, peevish skeletons—their healths and feelings . . . gone to return no more." The workers of Hooksett reportedly had only limited alternatives, for ". . . most of the girls in this mill are from thirty to hundreds (of) miles from home." Manchester's workers came from areas much closer to home than did the workers of Hooksett. The majority of Manchester's work force in 1845, and in 1860 as well, was New Hampshire born. Looking at the 1845 sample, of 172 New Hampshire natives sampled, the average distance of migration to Manchester was 8.88 miles. Even looking at migrants to Manchester from Massachusetts, the average distance travelled was 43.25 miles—hardly so great a distance that workers were trapped far away from home, or at least far away from other cities where industrial employment might be found (see Tables 3.4- 3.6).[8] Moreover, employers and workers alike were aware of job opportunities available to those who felt Manchester's working conditions too severe or her paternalism too constricting. Handbills were plastered throughout town "Factory Girls Wanted at Lawrence, Lowell" and other factory towns. Newspaper advertisements told of opportunities within Manchester, at the Manchester Mills, at John Brugger's hosiery factory, and elsewhere. In some cases, local employers were so hard pressed for experienced workers that they may have modified the work process to some extent, appending the phrase "the work can be done at home" to the bottom of their recruitment posters and advertisements—and this in the 1850's! By the late 1860's, the scarcity of workers was still a continuing problem. Newspapers noted that easily an additional 500 workers could find employment "at higher wages than ever before," if only the men and women could be found to take the jobs. Experienced hands seem to have been particularly sought after.[9]

Throughout Manchester's history, the demand for workers, if at times temporarily slack, rose steadily. By the mid '60's, newspaper editors were declaring

> we have never known such a demand for laborers of all kinds in this city as now, male and female . . . not only . . . old weavers are in demand, but green hands, those that never worked a day in the mills, find steady employment, at an advance of from 25 to 33 percent above former prices. The coveted time when one can 'get a good chance in the mill' has come.[10]

Servants and domestic help had always been scarce in Manchester, for workers had preferred the mill to personal service and, by the late '60's when the demand for mill help had reached remarkable dimensions, men and women, especially women, were abandoning domestic service in cities and towns throughout New England in order to work in Manchester's factories. The complaints of the '40's about blacklisting by employers and the complaints of the overseers—"Oh! They can go where they please; if the mills run too long, the operatives are not obliged to stay!"—disappear in the local press after the mid-1850's. Reality seems to have been that the demand for workers was becoming so intense, as the mills grew, that a worker could protest his or her boredom, weariness, or grievances against overseers or second hands by leaving his or her job, certain that other employment awaited.

As a service to workers seeking out a factory with decent working conditions and fair supervisors, and also as a warning to factory owners and unsympathetic overseers and agents, the town's labor-oriented newspapers regularly published employment information. This information went, in scope, beyond simply telling workers what jobs were available and where the openings were. Letters, bulletins, and travellers' reports all told workers of the conditions in specific factories. Of one factory, workers were advised, ". . . it is no place for anyone to seek employment," not because jobs were not available—they were—but because conditions were not right in the workrooms. The newspaper bulletins warned the factory agents: "How long Mr. Otterson expects to obtain help to work in this mill, if their [sic] is not a change in the managements of one of his overseers, I know not. Until conditions are changed . . . he can but expect that his help worth keeping will leave him."[11]

There were "hard times" when employment was scarce, just as there were boom periods, but in bad times as well as in good, word of mouth, letters, and travellers' accounts, were all reported in the press to inform workers of opportunities and work conditions. News of "the turning of hundreds out of employ, at Lawrence and where other factories are located" travelled fast, and caused "much anxiety among the operatives" about their own jobs. The complaint of the girl who "couldn't get into the mill" but could only hear the overseers' cry "all full!" was heard only temporarily in a town that exhibited the steady growth of Manchester, and full employment was far more common than the turn-out.

There were costs of full employment beyond dollar considerations. Industrial accidents came to be a part of life in Manchester. Men fell from scaffoldings and caught their hands and feet in machinery. Frequent falls and occasional deaths were a reality in the factories. Accidents to men were noted in the press, but much more space was devoted to cases involving children. In spite of the Amoskeag's much proclaimed policy of refusing to exploit child labor, the places where children worked were large and dangerous (see Table 3.7 on places of child employment). One 14 year old boy, Patrick, "was caught in a mule in the Manchester Mills . . . the muscles of his leg were badly torn and his thigh broken." In another instance, "a lad by the name of Arnold, employed by the Manchester Mills, received a severe injury . . . crushing the bone of his arm so as to require amputation." Maiming was a commonplace in this industrial community where workers, unfamiliar with machinery, worked at first with great caution, but, as they became accustomed to routine, grew uncautious as they grew familiar with their tasks. Thus a boy named Patrick Green "had the top of the thumb of the right hand taken off . . . a boy named David . . . got his hand in the machinery . . . a boy named John . . . was . . . caught in the machinery . . . and . . . badly injured in the region of the abdomen." While most were lucky to escape with relatively minor injuries, some young people were not so fortunate. One young man

> lost his life in the performance of his duties in attempting to throw a belt from a pulley with his foot, his leg was caught and he was carried round the revolving shaft with great rapidity, dashing his head against timbers, completely tearing off one leg, and scattering his brains over the machinery. It was a horrid spectacle.[12]

The immediate cause of factory accidents may have been the machinery, the lack of safety devices, or the speed, but eventually workers would argue that the length of the work day, exhausting workers, was the real, if ignored, underlying cause of mill injuries. Hours were too long for Elizabeth who caught her hand in the machinery and had it "severely crushed." One particular incident serves to illustrate the problems involved when a long work day was combined with the employment of children. One local newspaper sought out a story involving the death of an Irish child, Mary Haley, as a result of a mill "accident." The publisher found that no one in the workroom, heavily Irish, would talk about what had happened, and neighbors were similarly hostile: ". . . the facts of this particular accident . . . are studiously kept from the public by Irish families interested, for fear wrong may be suspected, and a girl intending no harm may be arrested for taking the life of another." Mary and another Irish bobbin girl had made their work less tedious by making a contest of it. Contest between one room and another, one building and another, one firm company and another were all part of the pattern of "relaxation." Mary and her co-worker would race to see who could reach the bobbin box first. In the heat of the excitement of one of these contests, Mary was shoved, slipped, and struck her head. Fearful of reporting the accident, she worked the rest of the day through. As Mary left the mill, she collapsed, was carried home by two of the workmen, and died within two hours. Neighbors would tell the newspaperman only that Mary "insisted that the girl who had caused the accident was [sic] should not be punished as it was not intentional." The Irish work force of Mary's room and the neighbors closed ranks to keep the news of what had happened confined, and to protect Mary's work-mate, playmate from punishment. [13]

In addition to ethnic cohesiveness, the story of Mary's plight illustrates another aspect of working life in Manchester's mills. Working close to 12 hours per day, workers had little time left for recreation or relaxation. Thus, they took their games and pastimes to the factory with them. Some workers held contests, pitting work crews against one another in the same room, or individual men against other men. Some workers, especially the younger ones, like Mary Haley and her friend, had difficulty distinguishing between work time and play time, for there was no play time left them. Thus, they took the normal games and excitements of childhood to the factory with them—and the large factories, in spite of Amoskeag's own pattern, were the only practical employers of children (see Table 3.7). [14]

One of the continuing sources of conflict between factory and worker involved the factory's paternalistic attempt to outlaw just such practices— customary pastimes—as had resulted in Mary Haley's death. Whether the primary motive of the agents was to increase production by eliminating distractions or to promote increased safety, the management determined that games, contests, conversation, reading, and so forth, must be put to a stop during work time. In spite of the argument that such policies were in their own best interests, workers, even confronted with the reality of industrial accidents, reacted with anger at the company's attempt to alter traditional practices. One factory girl wrote to a sympathetic local paper,

> during the last three months, I have been spoken to three times, for being seen with a book or paper in my hands, from which I was endeavoring to obtain a little mental food,—Now, why in the name of anything [sic] that's good, can we not have the liberty to read the news when we chance to have a few moments cessation from labor, which I know is not often, and thus enrich our minds as well as the purses of those who employ us?

Anti-corporation feelings such as these, and those expressed in the poem below, indicate that the sentiments of the workers were distinct from those of the "opinion leaders"—clergy, many editors, and professionals—who were more likely than workers to regard the Amoskeag's paternalism as a positive force. By the late '40's and early '50's, the hostility among workers towards the town's corporate founding fathers was building towards the strike of 1855, the one serious labor disturbance in Manchester's early period. One worker spoke for many:

Manchester As It Is

This place is large of great dimensions,
Where demons dwell with bad intention,
Females, incarnate upon its surface crawl,
Steep'd in Hell's dyes and hardened by its laws.
This place is known to the whole nation,
Where devils seek for higher stations,
Fiends, inhuman, make its laws.
Beings created for a more noble cause,
This place has sunk into degradation,
Its victims fallen into confrication,
Burn on, burn up, ye poisonous vipers, burn,
God's name be honored, virtue to its elay return.
This place is meaner in my estimation,
Thank the smallest link in the animal creation,
And could I but paint the lowest gradations,
I would put Manchester lower than the lowest detestation.[15]

Although such sentiments of extreme hostility would seem to portend extensive labor trouble, workers were reluctant to use their ultimate weapon—the walkout—and would resort to such extremes only when the corporation proved particularly obstinate and unresponsive to the other sorts of pressures which workers and town opinion could exercise. In October 1852, one of the Manchester factories learned the dangers of pushing workers too far. A group of workers in the Manchester Corporation's spinning room grew tired of being "subjected to sundry petty annoyances," which they termed "intolerable."

They had accepted a wage reduction, but they were not allowed to see the overseer's time book, so they did not know for how many hours they were being paid, or what their base pay was. More irritating than this, though, was the strictness of the overseer in exercising the company's rules. As the workers put it: "an unusual rigor had been exercised in the police regulations of the department." Employees who protested, objected, or questioned the overseer were dismissed. All of the spinning room workers met and agreed to resign. This was enough to win concessions from the mill, doing away with the more objectionable enforcement of regulations so that the worker "could maintain the dignity of his calling and his own proper self-respect."[16]

Workers insisted on "maintaining their position." One often-expressed fear was that of losing dignity and self-respect as had the workers of Europe. Local newspapers, both corporation sponsored and independent, printed accounts of working conditions elsewhere. While the independent papers reported conditions in other towns, those accused of being pro-corporation often carried stories of the plight of the industrial worker in England. Those cases reported told of the loss of self-esteem and human dignity among British factory operatives. The case of one girl was intended as a lesson to the operatives of Manchester, so that they could see by comparison how truly well-off they were. The girl in question was 17 years old, her father had died, she and her sister were working to support her ailing mother. She "cried many an hour in the factory," and came out at the end of the day so tired that she had to be helped home, pulling her deformed leg along behind her. In spite of ill health, Manchester's workers were told, this British girl had to work, and she did so, "in great pain and misery." Her only consolation was the kindness of her sister who "carried me up to bed many a time." Because she had to stand many hours each day, the doctors had told her that her bones had decayed, and her leg would never again be straight. Compared to this pathetic tale, what, after all, were a few pinched fingers or a little more speed? Stories of crippled children, ruined lives, and utter misery similar to Elisa's, described above, served a deliberate purpose in the press. The image of the foreign worker put before the workmen of Manchester would, it was hoped, teach them to judge their own lot in less harsh terms.[17]

While workers were determined to avoid "Europeanization," they were not content to judge their own position in a favorable light. The two great issues that roused workers' ire seem to have been wage cuts, on the one hand, and the hours of labor on the other. There were ways in which the worker could respond to an overly zealous overseer or agent who insisted upon strict and absolute enforcement of the moral police regulations. Likewise, the boarding-house keeper who kept house by the book might find an empty house as her reward. By workers in effect withholding services, thus assuring that only workers of "poor quality" would work in certain rooms, the overseer could be made painfully aware of his own vulnerability as the man in the middle between workers and agents. Boardinghouse keepers and factory supervisors were vulnerable to pressures from below as well as from above, but the factory agents themselves were, to a lesser degree, vulnerable to pressures. They were charged with maintaining industrial discipline and with adopting and promoting policies that would assure a favorable and peaceful local climate of opinion. In their efforts to persuade clergymen, editors, and merchants to realize the generosity of the Amoskeag and its associated enterprises, the agents saw their own need for a favorable climate of opinion in town. While the mills might have been able to win over preachers and merchants, there were too many men with printing presses to control the entire town, and the press, by publicizing individual cases of oppression, cases of overzealous overseers, abused workmen, and so forth, could, and did, rouse public opinion—so sought after by the agents—in order to affect the degree to which policies that workmen found offensive were either enforced or ignored while allowed to remain officially "on the books." The corporations would even see public officials, fearful of voters' reactions, respond to the Amoskeag's offers to donate lands and services with polite requests for the elimination of certain restrictions or conditions.[18] While living and working conditions, rules enforcement, donations to churches, parks, cemeteries were all subject to a certain amount of local discretion on the part of upper level factory managers in Manchester, the most important issues—perhaps because they were not subject to the local informal accommodative mechanism—were beyond the control of the local agents. Wages and hours, vital concerns to the workers, were not items which a local mill agent could change without approval from Boston, and any such approval would mean not simply a change in Manchester, but an industry-wide adjustment. Industry-wide wage rates were determined in Boston, as was policy on the number of hours the mills (and the workers) would be run, and no amount of local pressure could cause higher local officials to overlook enforcement in this area. One of these issues would fester and lead to unrest unfamiliar to Manchester.

By the time of the 1855 strike, the hours of labor had become a familiar issue to workers. As early as 1844, Manchester's workers would complain of the manipulation of the clock. The morning bell would be ten minutes fast, they would complain, while the evening bell would be ten minutes slow. References to "town time" and "factory time" did not have to be explained to Manchester's residents. The discrepancies were everyday realities to them. If workers were not to be late to work in the morning, they were "compelled to drop their knife and fork and run" to beat the bell. This policy served to aggravate other grievances, and complaints of the speed of the factory's clock eventually worked around to discussions and complaints over other company policies. Without the overriding issue of the hours of labor, other grievances would not have seemed so severe, but taken together with the hours problem, other issues took on a new importance. Workers who complained of the number of hours and who had bought land from the Amoskeag might well find their difficulties compounded. The Amoskeag would "sell land and put restrictions on lots and then you must abide by the restrictions . . . then if the owner of the lot does not happen to think just as they do . . . they will try and pick up a fuss with him, and go to law, and put him to cost, with the pretension that he violated the restrictions."[19]

Built-in inconsistencies in the company designed town (such as the company housing rule and a lack of sufficient company owned housing to enforce the rule) together with the need to cultivate favorable local opinion resulted in a flexible paternalism. There was little flexibility, though, on wages and, especially, on hours. From 1840, the hours of labor appeared as an important grievance. Workers complained, in that year, of being "dragged out of their beds at the ringing of the bell, before five in the morning, allowed some 30 minutes for a lunch, called breakfast and dinner, morn and noon, and not being permitted to leave at night until seven o'clock . . . when they eat . . . a substantial meal cannot be eaten in the time allowed." Workers, unable to change this policy, appealed to farm parents, asking them to consider this before sending their daughters to the factories of Manchester "which should be done only in cases of extreme poverty." The next year, workers complained of having only "a few minutes" for dinner before being "rung in" again. The overseer and the slave driver, parents were warned, were cast from the same mold.[20]

From 1840 through 1855, there were occasional wage cuts which provoked periodic protests, but these protests did not result in industrial disturbances and eventually workers adjusted, however painfully, to changes in wages. The one issue that remained as a consistent grievance, though, was the hours of labor. Informal workers' pressure, the pressure of public opinion, the influence of clergy, the editorials of the press, had, apparently no power to affect this issue. The industrial system that, on many issues, allowed workers to have some input, in informal, unstructured ways, presented at least one issue on which they were helpless. More than other groups, workers would question the well-publicized efforts of the Amoskeag to demonstrate selflessness and community spirit. That questioning would go on in many areas, but in no area such as the hours of labor did the corporation's policy seem so blatantly selfish and at variance with the paternalism which the Amoskeag would have townsmen view as one of their concerns. The number of hours per day and per week which the mills required of the workers would grow as a grievance in Manchester throughout the 1840's and '50's until it came to represent undefended evil.[21] On most other issues, the corporations would find their defenders. Among the press, the opinion leaders, the general public, and even among the workers, the Amoskeag would find advocates for many of its policies. If some workers would denounce the Amoskeag's financing of a town water supply system, for example, seeing in that action only a means of self-protection in case of fire or industrial distrubance, there would be other workers who would disagree, seeing in the provision of such public facilities a laudable example of paternal care in action. Such evidences of concern for the community would be praised by town officials, anxious to supply needed public facilities at low cost. Likewise, shopkeepers and farmers would see, in the Amoskeag's action, a lower tax rate, and the natural reaction among these groups was one of gratitude. The public in general, in an age of boosterism, took pride in "modern facilities," and regarded the company that supplied those facilities with gratitude.

The company's support of temperance speakers, discussions, and anti-drinking campaigns similarly won the gratitude of a town where, in a single year, liquor accounted for over 40% of all arrests (see Table 3.8).[22] While there was another side to the company's concern about the "strong spirits" problem, there was also an aspect of public service. Just as the provision of parks, cemeteries and churches could be regarded as but one of a number of subtle elements of control, so there was a public-spiritedness evident in such policies. For workers, pay intervals of once per month were a hardship. Some workmen in town whose children needed shoes had to make higher cost credit arrangements with merchants. Although not designed to benefit mill workers, there was evidence of careful design in pay policies. Since the various corporations staggered their monthly paydays, the merchants of Manchester did not experience once-monthly buying sprees, but benefitted throughout the month from different groups of workers coming, at different times of the month, to spend their wages. The pay days of the corporations were well known in town. Manchester Mills paid the first week of the month; the Machine Shop the second; and Amoskeag New Mills and Stark paid on the last week. While workers might complain of overly long intervals, there were others in the community who saw the staggered pay schedules as an advantage to them, and thus as evidence that the Amoskeag's policies were designed to benefit the town as a whole.[23]

The one grievance that saw little amelioration, formal or informal, was the one which nearly all of Manchester's residents would recognize as an evil. The hours of labor became a concern not merely of the workers alone, but of the whole community. The issue widened from initial complaints voiced by a few workers to a more general community-wide concern over the length of the work day. Workers' meetings were held to discuss the issue as early as 1844. The early meetings did little more than express their hope that the "ten hour wage system" might be adopted. The workers pointed to the inconsistencies of a self-proclaimed paternalist system where company officials ". . . must have a queer conscience to tell us that their works are a public benefit" while they "compel men to labor fourteen hours" for insufficient wages. In the early years, hours were classified as inseparable from wages as a grievance. It was particularly disturbing to workers' meetings that skilled craftsmen earned "only 7 shillings . . . the laborer only 5 shillings . . . while . . . very many of the bosses who do not touch their fingers to the work get from four to five dollars a day." Eventually wages would stabilize and become a standard matter throughout the industry. While hours also became standard, wage disparities or grievances were less frequently complained of, and hours became the primary grievance of the majority of working men's meetings.[24]

By 1847, the clamor for relief in the total number of hours had grown to such an extent as a grievance that the company did the seemingly impossible—it announced that the working day for the Amoskeag would be shortened by 15 minutes per day in order to allow workers more time to eat their breakfasts. This policy change was preceded by tremendous public agitation—newspaper editorials, letters to editors, mass mettings, petitions to legislators, appeals to conscience, all of which played a part in creating the number of hours as a legitimate grievance. Once again the Amoskeag would display its concern for the workers and the town by acceding to workers' demands. But what the workers had been demanding was a ten-hour day—what they were granted was 15 minutes for breakfast. Within two weeks, workers were denouncing their supposed victory. As a result of the "extra 15 minutes," the machinery was speeded up in order to make up for lost time. Additionally, workers and townsmen alike began to keep a careful eye on the town clock and on the factory clock. The discrepancies between the two began agitation for the ten-hour day all over again. Factory clocks were fast in the morning, slowed during the day, and were behind at night, so that exactly 15 minutes was added to the length of the day by "faulty clocks." A local editor railed at the corporations who "make their operatives labor as long as before, and work harder at the same time, and all the time talking about their generosity in giving them fifteen minutes for breakfast."[25]

From 1844 onward, the demand for the ten-hour system became increasingly popular in Manchester. Local labor-oriented newspapers printed success stories of the efforts of the mechanics of Fall River and New Bedford, and of organizing of workers in Worcester and Lowell in their demands for the Ten Hour Day. By 1847, the wider circulation papers had picked up the call of the labor papers for the ten-hour day, arguing in editorials that what had once been regarded as a complaint by a narrow group of radicals had become a wide and respected movement. There were even some corporation officials who would recognize that the movement for a ten-hour day was a widespread phenomenon and not the cause of "a few hair-brained fanaticks." The neutral press, religious leaders and publications, governmental resolutions—all joined workers in calling for a ten-hour work day and in adding respectability to the Ten Hour Movement. With widening local support, the ten-hour day created problems for the Amoskeag management. It had, throughout the controversy over the ten-hour day, been the position of the management that if such demands should come from their own workers rather than from wild-eyed agitators, then the agents would listen. In spite of the extra 15 minutes supposedly granted workers, the ten-hour movement continued to gain in strength. One local editor saw the extra 15 minutes as specifically designed to stave off investigation by the New Hampshire legislature. Such tactics might work in Massachusetts, he noted, but would "run aground on the solid good sense of the people of New Hampshire."[26]

Even with the passage of a ten-hour day law in New Hampshire, the battle was far from won since the law was so weak as to be practically meaningless. Throughout Manchester the Amoskeag and the other mills (particularly those employing children) attempted to force employees to sign special "contracts" giving up their "rights." One mill girl wrote to a "neutral" local paper:

> We are about to leave each other, to seek different homes. We have been discharged because we would not sign away what was made for our benefit; some whose hearts were with us were obliged to sign it for they had mothers here to maintain; others because they lived near their home. . . .

Not only letters to newspapers, but also petitions to stockholders and managers were among the tactics employed by workers anxious to have the new Ten Hour Law implemented and strengthened. In 1847, the men of the Amoskeag Machine Shop drew up the following petition:

> To the Stockholders of the Amoskeag Manufacturing Company, at Manchester, New Hampshire:
>
> The undersigned would most respectfully represent, that they are operatives in the Machine Shop of said company, and that they would gladly be governed by the beneficent principle of the Law of the last legislature of this state, which recognized Ten Hours of continuous labor as a DAY'S WORK: believing, as we do, that it would be for the interest of all concerned in the labor of this establishment,—the employers, as well as the employed—that this principle should prevail:—We therefore would most earnestly request that you would so act in the premises,—that your operatives in this shop be required to labor Ten Hours only on each day.[27]

The position of the agents had consistently been that demands for the ten-hour day had no support among their workers. If workers in Manchester should have such demands then, of course, the mill management held that they would be considered by a company that had always had the workers' welfare as one of their primary considerations. The demands of outsiders, though, of radical labor organizers come to Manchester to foment trouble, could not and would not be considered.

While insisting on their willingness to listen to the grievances of their workers, the agents transmitted instructions to overseers that the petition above, and any like it, were not to be circulated in the rooms, millyard, or residences. Once again the overseer was the man in the middle. Although they were required by those above them to enforce such policies, many overseers harbored secret sympathies with the workers. One overseer wrote in fear that "I may have my head struck off by the guilotine of factory rules and regulations, yet I feel it my duty to speak on behalf of the workers." Workers were told by overseers that, in spite of the overseers' function as rules enforcer, they were as anxious as the workers to see the ten-hour day, and they were even more fearful of discharge, and in a more open, exposed position than were the workers. One Manchester overseer put it bluntly:

> . . . although the overseers seem to favor the company to their efforts to work you the usual number of hours, yet depend upon it, they are with you for the short-hour system, and when they say to you, sign this, or you will be dismissed, they say to themselves, I hope she won't sign it. I will venture to say, that there is not an overseer in Manchester whose feelings are not of this character. . .[28]

Throughout 1847, mass meetings at City Hall, newspaper editorials, demonstrations, and worker demands filled the public life of Manchester. One set of resolutions was modelled after the Declaration of Independence, and concluded with the pledge of "our lives and our sacred honor" in support of the Ten Hour Day.

In spite of the resolutions and demonstrations of workers, there was no reduction in the hours of labor until 1853, after public agitation had calmed. The Amoskeag proved far less flexible on the hours of labor than it had been on a score of other, earlier issues. In 1853, the Amoskeag, followed by the other mills, announced an 11-hour work day, from 7 A.M. to 7 P.M., with one hour off for dinner. By 1853, agitation had subsided, and the company could claim to have responded to no outside pressure, but only to "manifest propriety." The problem with a policy instituted because of manifest propriety was that, just as the Amoskeag had unilaterally shortened the working day, so it could lengthen the day. It was the Amoskeag's effort to restore an 11-3/4 hour day which led, in 1855, to Manchester's first serious widescale labor disturbance.[29]

The announcement of the lengthened work day caused some confusion among workers and townspeople, for the hours of work varied with the calendar. During the summer months, when daylight was longest, work would be longest—12-1/2 hours per day from late April to late August. During winter, the day ranged from 11-1/2 to 11-3/4 hours (see Table 3.9). By announcing the policy changes at an advantageous time, the Amoskeag could make it appear to be only a 30 minute increase in the work day. It was not long, through, before workers and the general community realized that the claims to only a short increase were deceptive. The new policy represented, in effect, a return to the 11-3/4 hour day. Early in March 1855, local papers publicized the true hours arrangement. The 12-hour day, denounced in 1847, was again a reality in Manchester in 1855, and, one after another, newspapers, clergymen, and politicians denounced the policy as one "of very great and very just complaint among the operatives." Even moderate editors realized that the 11-hour day, let alone the 12-hour day, was too long, and urged that "this increase should be resisted by every fair and legitimate means." Corporation-sponsored papers stood alone in giving the arguments of the management that, since farmers and storekeepers worked long days, the position of the mill operative was relatively fortunate.[30]

The corporation-sponsored press would argue that the action was unfortunate, but that it was not the choice of either agents or owners, but was dictated by economic necessity. Official policy was that there were only two alternatives—reducing wages or increasing hours—and that the company had demonstrated its concern for both workers and town by choosing not to "cut down" wages. The choice was presented by the company as a necessity, and the alternative chosen as one which displayed concern and responsibility. Not only workers, but all town residents were incredulous: "when the corporations . . . present these alternatives as an imperative necessity of the times, the people don't believe them."[31]

In choosing between alternatives, it was noted throughout town, that there was one other alternative never considered. There could be no reduction in company dividends. This the agents called "prerequisite." In choosing to lengthen hours rather than cut wages or pass dividends, the Amoskeag seems to have chosen unwisely. Workers expressed their willingness to take a slight cut in wages rather than a lengthening of hours. The 11-hour day, only recently adopted, was a grudging compromise to the demand for a ten-hour day. Emotion regarding the Ten Hour System lingered in town, and the Amoskeag's announcement that hours would be increased gave fresh impetus to the Ten Hour Movement. One local man pointed out that there was a certain amount of logic in the Amoskeag's arguments, but that there was also fault: ". . . since prices are regulated by . . . supply and demand . . . it cannot be insisted that the price of labor shall be entirely exempt from these . . . but the period of labor involved so many great and vital considerations connected with the well-being of the human race" that it should not be subject to economic laws. The laws governing the hours of labor, it was argued, were not economic but physical: "ten hours of labor per day, especially within doors, is as long a period as is compatible with a prudent regard for . . . comfort and health."[32]

With the announcement, in February 1855, that the 11-hour day would be abandoned in favor of longer hours, the working men and women of Manchester held meetings, parades, and rallies and pledged to resist the reinstitution of "the old system . . . to the bitter end." The announcement was particularly disturbing to workers since the 11-hour work day, instituted only one year earlier, had seemed to herald the coming of further reforms. Indeed, some of the agents of Mancheser's mills had endorsed the ten-hour work day in principle, and had publicly urged corporation-backed candidates for public office to support it. Workers and voters alike were angered, for they had associated the triumph of the ten-hour day with the election of corporation-sponsored office seekers. One week after election, the increase in hours, with the resumption of the 11-3/4 hour day, was announced.[33]

Since all of the informal pressures which had, in the past, been effective against the implementation of unpopular measures had failed to prevent the Amoskeag from lengthening the work day, workers had only one alternative left. The women of the Manchester Mills walked out first. The agent of the Manchester Mills, David Gillis, had seemingly supported the ten-hour day by supporting politicians who favored the ten-hour movement. On an early Tuesday morning in March, several hundred women took to parading in the streets. They were joined, after lunch, by large numbers from other mills—the Stark and Amoskeag—who responded to the bell calling them back from lunch by taking to the streets. Led by a band, the workers marched through the streets of Manchester, carrying banners, cheering, and singing.

Mass meetings were held on that first afternoon and evening as well as on the next day. Some of the town's prominent middle-class business leaders and politicians acted as go-between, carrying communications and information between agents and workers. By the second day, the walkout was nearly universal as those shops and factories that had not yet been affected took to the streets to demonstrate their support of the mill workers. The only response which workers consistently drew from agents was that they should "adhere to their regulations."

The following day, Manchester's newly elected mayor demonstrated that he was "more partial to law and order than to music" when he took the side of the factory managers, and followed the instructions of the agents that he "disperse the mob." David Gillis insisted that Mayor Abbott read the riot act.

The mayor's reading was met with good natured shouts and cheers as well as with shouted comparisons between Mayor Abbott at Canal Street and Major Pitcairn at Lexington. The workers took Abbott's act all in good spirit, even his display of temper at the band whose humor Abbott failed to appreciate. Each of Abbott's sentences was interspersed with the beat of drums, bugle, flourishes and "appropriate" music. Abbott's threat to arrest the band was met with a challenge to him—produce a statute against music, said the crowd. All went well until the mayor reminded the workers of how good the Amoskeag had been to the town, to the public welfare, and to each of them individually. He reminded them of their own ingratitude and moralized on what they "ought" to do. Abbott's remarks called to mind the grievances against the company—not simply on the question of hours, but grievances against the whole system and discipline under which workers lived. The mood of the crowd changed. One angry mechanic opened his dinner pail and threw the contents at the mayor, missing him but hitting David Gillis on the head with a donut, sending the crowd into fits of laughter, and causing visiting company officials from Boston to flee for fear of their lives. With mayor and company officials departed, the workers marched through the streets voicing their grievances and demands for ten hours in song:

> Gillis and Adams may rave,
> And Smith may tear his hair.
> The Boston men may come to town,
> For them we do not care.
> So go for the Ten Hours,
> Then go for the Ten Hours,
> For we know that is right.[34]

For over three weeks, men and women marched through the streets of Manchester, shutting down much of the town's industry. It was a shutdown supported overwhelmingly by the people of the town. In spite of the mayor's being in service to the corporations, the entire city fire department turned out as an escort for the strikers, marching and carrying banners themselves. Newspaper editors assured "young ladies" that they were no less lady-like for their conduct. Indeed, they were assured, their conduct was in keeping with what would be expected of "5000 sons and daughters of the Pilgrims." Townspeople took up public collections for those in need, and paid the fare home of those who chose to leave town. The Town Hall was the site of daily meetings and rallies as the mills began, increasingly, to feel the pinch. Within three days, the Manchester and Stark Corporations had closed up completely, and the Amoskeag continued in a vain attempt to run some of its machinery with a few remaining hands. All of the agents except the intransigent David Gillis realized that a shutdown of several months duration seemed a reality.

Tempers rose as pressure to accede to workers' demands was met with agents' refusal and the Amoskeag's determination to keep at least a token force in the factories to add to attempts to dispirit the strikers. Unusual pressure was put upon the overseers at the beginning of the strike to see that the workers in their rooms stayed in line and did not join the walkout. One overseer for the Stark Corporation, George Hancock, was so pressured by management on the one hand and workers on the other, that he allegedly assaulted one of his workers. A girl named Mary Hinman went to Hancock and indicated that she would join the strikers, asking Hancock to give her a bill of her time so that she might receive her pay. Mary had planned to return to her home in Concord, Vermont. Witnesses testified that, upon being told by Mary that she would join the strike, Hancock "caught her and kicked her, without provocation." The courtroom was jammed with strikers as Mary's lawyer told magistrate and onlookers that ". . . He who lays his hand upon a woman, other than in blessing, is a wretch, whom 'twere base flattery to call other than a coward." Hancock was fined court costs of $4.85 and paid a fine of $10, and was required to post $100 bond for his future good behavior. Even if Mary had been successful in getting a bill of her time from Hancock, she might still not have left the mill unharmed. One girl who took a bill of her time, given her by her overseer, to paymaster William Webster was assaulted, as Mary had been. Being higher up in the corporation, Webster was fined only $6.

Given incidents like the above, the corporations found that their usual defenders were either quiet or in the ranks of the opposition. On most issues of controversy in which the mills were involved, there were those in town who would vocally take the factory's part, honestly feeling that the Amoskeag felt a genuine concern not only for its workers but for the well-being of the town as well. In this instance, though, there were no defenders of the corporation at all. Used to at least mixed praise, the Amoskeag found itself denounced as having "as little regard for the comfort, wishes and health of their operatives as we should expect to find on a sugar plantation." No one stepped forward after Mayor Abbott to defend the Amoskeag's generosity and wisdom, for the issue of the hours of labor showed, as no other question had, the falseness of pretensions of corporate paternalism.[35]

Only the corporation-sponsored newspaper took a position that could be interpreted as favoring the mills, and even then there was no all-out support, but simply a voicing of the corporation's position. Workers read the paper regularly in order to gauge the feelings of the corporation agents, managers, and owners. Within a few weeks, the corporation's proclamations that economic necessity had forced a wage cut or an increase in hours became less frequently expressed. Likewise, the claim to have acted in the best interests of those people dependent upon the corporations—Manchester's workers and residents—disappeared as the climate of opinion that would sustain such sentiments evaporated in all-out support of the strikers' human exigencies. The corporations' initial bluster and harangues against outside agitators and ungrateful workers were gradually replaced—first by hints in the corporation paper that the factories might "forgive" those who returned to work, and then by "propositions of amnesty semi-officially circulated throughout the city."

By early April, the problem of factory owners and agents was one of how to save face. It was unthinkable that agents should accede to the demands of operatives and thus lose face. It was likewise unthinkable that the Ten Hour Day should be recognized, either officially or unofficially. Such recognition would have implications that would affect far more than just the workers of Manchester.

The most that could be conceded, and the workers, in spite of pledges to enforce a ten-hour day recognized this, was a rescinding of the added "15 minutes," that is, a return to the 11-hour work day. To prepare the way for this settlement, the factory press began reporting "rumors" that the 11-hour work day would be re-established shortly "because of changed (economic) circumstances (in the industry.)" With the unacknowledged surrender to rescind the lengthened day, it was widely recognized in town that the strike had been won, in spite of the fact that "the agents made no formal surrender to the refractory operatives, but it is well understood that they have agreed to return to the old time table as soon as they can with a decent show of self-respect."[36]

The "rumor" was that by the twentieth of April, self-respect's demands would be satisfied. In the meantime, the factories were the losers. Some workers chose to return to work in early April, satisfied that the companies would make good, and their hours would be reduced by the end of the month. Others chose to wait until the official announcement was made. Still, the factories were the losers, for they now faced an unprecedented labor shortage especially among the experienced help, hands whose presence could help assure smooth operations. Within three weeks, thousands of workers had packed their bags and left town. Managers had good cause to lament the departure of "the more experienced help" and of the skilled workers. Within "a single day" the jeers of agents had been ". . . turned to terror" as they saw their factories closed and their carefully cultivated public support evaporate. One local editor called "this demonstration . . . not a mere protest of an empty stomach, but of a sensitive mind." A "neutral" commentator, assessing the strike in terms of city, workers, and corporations, suggested that, where paternalism was unbending to popular will, the factories would be the ultimate losers. He argued that the problem of the scarcity of trained and skilled help which the strike had done much to aggravate would not be soon remedied.[37]

Even if the problem of manning the factories was solved following the strike, there was a more important aspect to the strike. It demonstrated that, while paternalist actions had gained the mills some local supporters, the day-to-day identification, in a working town, would be with the workers and not with the owners, in spite of their library endowments, public projects, parks, and all similar programs calculated to win the support of the residents. One of the town's articulate leaders upon whose support the Amoskeag had counted argued that the strike ". . . will suggest to the agents and directors the propriety of recognizing the right of the operatives to be consulted when it is proposed to make changes in either the time or the price of labor. Had this been done . . . this excitement would have been avoided." He warned the corporations that workers did, indeed, have rights, and that they were not without "homes to shelter them from oppression" in spite of the fact that they might reside in factory-owned dwellings.[38]

Local residents realized that the workers had won (in spite of their failure to achieve the 10-hour day). The official corporation version of the strike, circulated throughout New England, was that the strike had been lost, that workers had returned to the mills on the company's terms, without any concessions whatsoever. In truth, though, the agents pledged personally to civic leaders and to clergymen, and even spoke to individual experienced hands about to leave the city, that "it will be all right in a few days." Meanwhile the overseers were openly lobbying among workers, promising a return to 11 hours. Local clergymen were urged by corporation officials to preach "from the pulpit" that a settlement based on a return to the old hours was a certainty. All of the informal means of communication that had been fostered by the Amoskeag were utilized to assure that a favorable settlement would follow, even while the official version remained one of uncompromising rigidity. These were not false assurances, and by the twenty-eighth of Apirl the old hours—11 hours per day—were back into effect.[39]

While the strike failed to achieve the ten-hour day, an issue that would remain hotly argued for years to follow, it did succeed in providing a demonstration of the informal mechanisms operating to limit a corporation that was apparently all-powerful. Just as decrees regulating where workers would live, when they would worship, and how they would account for their time both in and out of the workroom were modified in practice by the workers' day-to-day patterns of exerting pressure to modify or abolish the enforcement of unpopular rules, so even wages and hours—theoretically governed by harsh economic realities—were not matters for absolute unilateral decision. In spite of the fact that they lacked a formal union structure, workers could, and did, voice their needs. In spite of a potentially overwhelming paternalism, Manchester's working population played a crucial role in shaping the community life and community attitudes and managed to affect the policies of their employers.[40]

Workers who found themselves able to affect the shape of their community life and influence the policies of their employers found themselves powerless to affect wages and hours. As the price of cotton goods rose, as dividends paid to stockholders rose, and, at the same time, wages and hours remained substantially unchanged and unaffected by either worker discontent or hostile public opinion, workers found new ways to protest. One of the more controversial methods that workers employed to supplement low wages was pilferage—the companies' phrase for this practice was "larceny on a grand scale—the stealing of cloth." Unable to bring about an increase in wages, some more daring workers set about finding more novel alternative solutions to their problems. One editor's question was an everyday reality to the mill workers of Manchester: "when the poor man pays sixty centers per yard for his wife's dress, and the laboring man works twelve hours per day for a bare subsistence, while the corporation for which he works, and which gets such prices for its goods, divide forty percent, per annum of clear profit—What's the remedy?"[41]

Lucia, who worked in the Amoskeag's Upper Weave Room #5, found her own answer to the high cost of workers' clothing. Miss A. made a cloak and a fancy skirt for Lucia with cloth that Lucia provided. Miss A. took her pay in cloth. Mrs. G. made Lucia a dress on the same terms. Lucia was convicted on two counts, fined $20 plus $8.62 in court costs, and ordered to pay the Amoskeag $32 in reparations for what, by her estimates, was under 15 yards of cloth.

Lucretia had come to Manchester from Vermont only one year before being apprehended stealing cloth by Mr. Justin Spear, a name the operatives came to know well. One month Lucretia took some cloth "under my skirts . . . I took one piece at a time . . . this was the first time I ever stole." Mr. Spear pursued Lucretia to Vermont. She was 12 years old.[42]

Bertha, 19, lived in the same boarding house as Lucretia. Like Lucretia, she would bring gifts of cloth to the boardinghouse keeper. She exchanged cloth with other girls, including her sister, Fanny, also 19, "because it was thicker than hers" and better suited to the garments she desired to make. She was apprehended by Mr. Spear. One woman was arraigned for being present in a house where stolen cloth was found, while another protested to the constable that "you must not take that for I have worked hard for it." In some cases "bonds" of $500 were ordered posted for future good behavior, and fines far exceeded the market value of the missing cloth. It was fortunate, perhaps, that none of the girls had been so injudicious as to "catch and kick" their overseers—who would guess what their fines might have been then?

Officer Justin Spear was the man in charge of investigating and prosecuting cloth thefts. The Amoskeag and other mills give publicity to Mr. Spear's successes and to the fines imposed by the courts. Using corporation-sponsored newspapers, they attempted to convey the lesson that "it is of no use for any of the operatives in the mills to steal from their employers with the idea that they can escape from the clutches of Mr. Spear. 'It just can't be did.' " Mr. Spear's successes were noted in finding and pursuing girls who had left the mill, returning to their homes with gifts of cloth for family and friends. For stealing 25 yards of cotton cloth, Anne D. was pursued and fined $33. For stealing 3 pounds of woolen yarn, Annie S. was fined $37. Jane was fined $7, ordered to pay court costs and the cost of pursuit, $19, ordered to make restitution to the Amoskeag for $8.75, and to pay the Amoskeag's costs of prosecution and investigation of $7. All together $8.75 worth of cloth, at retail selling price, cost this one former mill girl $41.75, plus the incalculable cost of humiliation. This latter penalty was a lesson the mills tried to drive home—was the cloth worth the cost of the community's knowing that a girl was a thief? The corporation's pet newspaper recounted a case similar to Jane's. The amount of cloth stolen was allegedly 100 yards, while costs and fines totalled over $80, "rather dear cloth even in these times."[43]

The matter of corporate profits, the rise in the price of cotton goods, and the stability of wages and hours were important issues in the public life of Mancester by the mid-1860's. A Manchester "neutral" paper reported that "the manufacturers are selling goods at a clear profit of one hundred percent . . . yet these manufacturers are about everywhere trying to keep . . . the thirteen hour day . . . and yield to the eleven hours in a very few instances." While operatives were still working an 11-hour day 10 years after they struck for 10 hours, manufacturers declared 40% dividends. Local opinion pointed out the inconsistency of a paternalist employer quick to ask workers and townsmen to shoulder the burden of "hard times" by taking longer hours, shorter wages, or half-time employment, yet quicker to share the benefits of prosperity in good times only with the stockholders. The issues behind the 1855 strike did not fade from local minds, but lingered on to emerge frequently. If a girl could not afford a dress because the cloth that she had manufactured reflected a 100% markup on the part of the manufacturers, distributors, and retailers combined, then who was to blame her if she took her wages in kind, unknown to the "lords of the loom?" One editor indicated that townspeople were not unreasonable. They expected the stockholders to get a fair return, but, as well, "we like to get goods . . . at a reasonable price, and to see labor rewarded in some reasonable proportion." Others argued that there was "something wrong . . . when stockholders . . . have . . . had four semi-annual dividends of twenty percent, besides many of the usual size" while those who worked for them could not afford the high costs of the goods they labored to produce. The

Amoskeag's vigorous anti-theft campaign is indicative of the seriousness and extent of the problem. Again workers found an informal way around the company's policies. Many workers were willing to risk apprehension and public humiliation in order to find an alternative to an insufficient wage structure.

While paternalism was calculated to win local support, it was not entirely successful. Editor after editor, clergymen, politicians, and workingmen's groups all joined in deploring the wages and hours of the mills. On other aspects, paternalism, when willing to bend, might have held its own, but on the issues of wages and hours, the town was nearly unanimous in seeing "something wrong." The same arguments, the same figures, were cited repeatedly by diverse persons and groups: something was wrong "when the poor man pays sixty cents per yard for his wife's dress, and the laboring man works twelve hours per day for a bare subsistence, while the corporation for which he works . . . divides forty percent . . . clear profit." The surest remedy was felt to be for "the laboring men and women in our shops and mills . . . to entrench himself [sic] securely behind a sound public sentiment and protect himself." The idea that public pressure had affected other aspects of company policy and would eventually affect this issue as well was adhered to firmly.[44]

If public sentiment in Manchester's early years, partaking of the spirit of boosterism, viewed the Amoskeag and associated mills in the light of a caring father to the town, then this ceased to be true certainly by the early '50's. By the time of the 1855 strike, public pretensions of paternalism were demonstratedly false as the overriding issue came to be the hours of labor. More than any other issue, this showed the faults in corporate paternalism and led townsmen almost universally to denounce their "founding fathers." After 1855, denunciation of the corporation became *de rigeur*. While the corporation might enjoy praise for particular actions, it would not enjoy the widespread public acclaim that it had seen in its earlier years. Candidates for public office, mindful of Mayor Abbott's encounter with angry townsmen, did well to avoid any hint of being corporate puppets. It was mandatory to appear as a candidate of the people even before 1855. Between 1845 and 1851, 44 men of identifiable occupation served on the Common Council (see Table 3.10). For the most part, they were solid working men. Seven were professionals, but 18 were clearly working men—carpenters, farmers, stable keepers. Even the most numerous occupational grouping to serve—overseer (11)—had either risen from the ranks of workers or were men who, as the 1855 strike sympathies of many overseers demonstrated, could understand an operative's position. They were also, of course, capable of being pressured by the factory management, and hence represented a kind of political compromise—they were capable of perceiving the worker's situation, but presented no distinct threat to Amoskeag control.[45]

By the 1860's, the ethnic composiiton of the town had changed, but the flavor of Manchester as a solid, working-class town had become even more dominant than in the early years. Even as Irish and French-Canadian immigrants arrived and began to take their places in factory and town, the worker-oriented sympathies of Manchester's residents, viewing the corporation with sometimes thinly disguised suspicion, became dominant. As, and when, new groups won acceptance in Manchester, they did so because, like the native Yankee men and women who preceded them, they worked long and hard.

Table 3.1. Birthplaces, Amoskeag Work Force

	1860	1870
New Hampshire	195 (55.4%)	293 (44.3%)
Other U. S.	114 (32.4%)	139 (21.0%)
Foreign	43 (12.2%)	229 (34.6%)
N =	352	661

Source: Compiled from Amoskeag Material, M.H.A.

Table 3.2. Place of Birth by Residence in Company Housing,
            1860

Nativity	Percent of Work Force	Percent of Company Housing
New Hampshire	55.4	59.7
Massachusetts	16.8	11.1
Ireland	6.8	2.1
Vermont	6.5	11.1
New York	4.0	7.6
Maine	2.3	.7
Germany	2.3	.7
Canada	2.3	3.5
Rhode Island	.6	.7
Pennsylvania	.6	.7
Connecticut	.3	.7
Midwest	.6	.7
Other U. S.	.9	.7
Other Foreign	.9	.7
N =	352	144

Source: Compiled from Amoskeag Material, M.H.A.

Table 3.3. Place of Birth by Residence in Company Housing, 1870

Nativity	Percent of Work Force	Percent of Company Housing
New Hampshire	44.3	42.9
Canada	24.8	14.1
Massachusetts	6.8	7.1
Vermont	6.7	13.5
Ireland	5.1	1.9
New York	3.3	5.8
Maine	3.2	6.4
Scotland	2.1	3.8
England	1.7	1.3
Germany	.6	—
Connecticut	.3	.6
Rhode Island	.2	.6
Other U.S.	.6	1.3
Other Foreign	.3	.6
N =	661	156

Source: Compiled from Amoskeag Material, M.H.A.

Table 3.4. Work Force Nativity, Manchester

	1845	1860	1870
New Hampshire	56.6%	49.3%	32.9%
Other U. S.	43.3	39.7	41.3
Foreign	--	10.8	25.7

Source: 1846 City Census; U.S. Census, 1860, 1870

Table 3.5.   Ethnicity—Manchester—1850

Country	% of Total	% of Foreign Born
Native U. S.	85.4	--
Ireland	9.5	65.3
England	1.5	10.3
Canada	3.3	22.3
Scotland	.3	1.7
Swiss		.2

Source: U.S. Census

Table 3.6.   Nativity, Amoskeag Work Force

	1860	1870
New Hampshire	55.4%	44.3%
Massachusetts	16.8	6.8
Ireland	6.8	5.1
Vermont	6.5	6.7
New York	3.9	3.3
Maine	2.3	3.2
Germany	2.3	-
Canada	2.3	24.7

Source: Census of Manufactures; Amoskeag Material

Table 3.7.   Employers of Child Labor, Manchester, 1870

Size	Number of Establishments	Percent of Child Work Force Involved
Under 6 child workers	2	1.0
6-12	2	4.0
13-20	-	-
21-50	2	15.5
Over 50	2	79.5

Table 3.8. Manchester Arrest Record, 1851

Crime	Percent of All Arrests
Found drunk	43.2
Noise, brawl, tumult	16.3
Assault	13.7
Larceny	7.9
Common drunkards	7.4
Gambling	6.3
Disorderly conduct	5.3

Source: Town Records, M.H.A.

Table 3.9. Amoskeag Hours Schedule, Announced for 1855

Date	Days	Hours per Day	Total Hours
Feb. 20-Mar. 19	24	11.75	282
Mar. 20-Apr. 19	27	12	324
Apr. 20-Aug. 19	104	12.5	1300
Aug. 20-Sept. 19	27	12	324
Sept. 20-Oct. 19	26	11.75	305.5
Oct. 20 -Feb. 19	105	11.5	1207.5
	313		3743

3743 hours
  53 less time lost for not running a full day Saturdays
3690 hours

Average work day = 11.79 hours

Source: Amoskeag Materials, M.H.A.

Table 3.10. Occupations of Common Council Officeholders,
            1846-51

Professionals	7
Clergy	2
Entrepreneurs + High White Collar	3
Merchant	4
Overseers	11
Manual Workers-- Skilled + Unskilled	17

Source: City Directories, Town Records

4

Social Structure to 1860

In a re-introduction to Margaret Byington's 1910 study of the households of Homestead, Pennsylvania, Samuel Hays stressed the importance of dealing with the multi-dimensional elements of a mill community. Hays' emphasis on the complexity of working-class communities underscored the importance of analyzing relationships between work, home, and community. Preoccupation with one element of working-class life—such as Byington's detailed study of family budgets to the exclusion of other aspects of community life—ignores the multi-dimensional aspect of the human past. Any study of an industrial population must deal with the larger community beyond the factory, for the worker finds himself in the community as well as in the work place.[1]

The distribution of wealth in the larger community, the composition of property holding and propertyless groups, and the existence of a relatively stable population group are all factors which must be considered when studying a factory working population. The social and economic hierarchy of the factory town affected the way in which the worker was judged by his fellow townsmen, status-wise, as well as how he may have regarded himself and his own position in the social and economic hierarchy of the factory town.[2] It will be the task of this chapter to explore the social structure of Manchester in the years prior to the Civil War. This will provide a backdrop against which later (1860-1880) factors such as household composition, household income, number of household members in the factory, and the policies of the corporation can be set.

In the years prior to the Civil War, the single most significant change that took place in Manchester as reflected in the town's quantifiable records, came with the initial influx of factory workers. This broke down the old town's social structure, revolutionized its economic structure, and necessitated the overhaul of the town's school system, its method of taxation, and a whole range of other town functions—from birth records to burial space. Some understanding of the scope of the change involved can be gleaned from the town's tax records for 1835, five years prior to the introduction of large-scale enterprise. When set against the records for 1845—five years following industrialization—town records reveal some of the changes that took place in Manchester's social structure.

In 1835, Manchester was a small town. Almost every aspect of its life was dictated by the pursuit of agriculture. It was a town on a small scale. Two hundred and thirty-six taxpayers composed the entire tax paying population; of these, 216 were individuals and 20 were partnerships in small business pursuits such as storekeepers or haulers or small-scale manufacturers. The aspirations of the residents in 1835 were closely related to farming. Just as had generations before them, Manchester farmers sought to enlarge their landholdings, to buy another cow, more sheep, more pigs, to plant more fruit-bearing trees, in short to expand their social and economic standing in the community by increasing the productivity of their farms.[3]

Within this agrarian community there was a fairly wide dispersal of land ownership (see Tables 4.1, 4.2). 57.4% of all individual male heads of households owned some land, while 42.6% owned no land.[4] Whether he owned a $20 plot or a $5,000 farm, the man who had succeeded in acquiring land in an agrarian community had secured a place for himself in the social hierarchy of the town that was denied to over one-third of his counterparts.

If real property was important, it was by no means the only form of material acquisition for Manchester's citizens. Even more widespread than land ownership was the ownership of cows, pigs, sheep, or other farm animals. Some 61.5% of all individual taxpayers owned one or more animals. 38.4% of the population had no agriculturally-related possessions. Taking into account factors such as money in the bank and other forms of wealth, 30.7% of Manchester's population in 1835 was totally without possessions of any sort—agricultural lands, animals, money, or any other form of property.

How could the landless survive in a farming community? How could those who owned animals, whether a $10 cow or $384 in stock, but held no land, exist in such a community? Some of Manchester's propertyless 30% no doubt got by as farm laborers; still others were able to find work in the construction of the textile mills. Still, these two factors together would not account for nearly one-third of the adult male heads of household who had no real property. Those who owned animals but no land were required to come to some sort of understanding—land rental, farm labor, or domestic service—with a land owner to enable them to live and to raise their modest herds. Those without either lands or animals would be dependent upon others in town in ways that the 1835 tax records do not enable us to discover. It is important, though, to note the existence of a large percentage of the propertyless in pre-industrial Manchester. Later and more complete records will suggest propinquity to family members, and hence the probability of strong family ties at this earlier period as well, as a factor enabling the apparently propertyless or landless to live near wealthier family members.[5]

More important than the mere fact of land ownership or holdings of other sorts of property was the amount—the value—of a man's holdings (see Tables 4.3, 4.4). Individual land holdings in pre-industrial Manchester ranged from one man's $20 plot to another's $5,500 farm. Similarly, there was a wide disparity in the value of farm animals, ranging from a $10 cow (cows were by far the most popular animal, owned by 119 different men) to a $384 herd.

The average landowner, then, was neither a poor nor a wealthy man, and the average owner of farm animals was neither the owner of a single cow nor of a large herd. For the 27.8% who owned less than $35 in animal stock, Israel Merrill's $210 herd of cows must have seemed like the most a man could achieve. Likewise Ross Barrett, owning only a $20 plot of land, must have envied Joseph Moor or Frederick Stark, with their $5,500 and $3,500 farms. Stark, although owning less land than Moor, was a particularly impressive citizen. There was not a man in town who failed to recognize him as a descendent of the hero of Bennington, and accord him the respect that his wealth and family demanded.[6]

Land ownership was an individual and a family affair. Of 144 land owners, 124 (68.1%) were individuals, while 20 (13.8%) were small business partnerships or corporate land owners. Hidden in this apparent egalitarianism is the scale of corporate holdings, even at this early date, as compared to the holdings of individuals. All property in town valued above $5,500 was owned by corporations associated with the Amoskeag. Of the non-individual owners, 16 were small businesses or partnerships with holdings of under $1,000. The average (mean) valuation for these businesses was $443.75. The mean for all businesses, small or large excluding only one, was $1,068.75, an amount only slightly above the figures previously cited for individual land owners.

Looming over all, though, was one huge land owner. By 1835 the Amoskeag Locks and Canals held Manchester real estate valued at $18,000. This disparity presaged Manchester's future growth.

The extent to which the Amoskeag's investment in pre-industrial Manchester dwarfed every other business in town can be illustrated by examining the operating scale of other local businesses. The town had 7 storekeepers in 1835. All were individually owned, family operated enterprises, sometimes with two local families combining to operate a "large" store. The owners had investments in their businesses ranging from $400 to $1,600. The average store keeper held $828.57 in stock, while as many invested over $600 as invested under that amount. These small stores re-emphasize the tone of life of the small farming community. What the tax data does not make apparent is the fact that the older farming group had been undermined by land sales to the Amoskeag, and would shortly be visibly overwhelmed by the scale of the Amoskeag's investment. Part of the story of Manchester's industrialization that has remained hidden is the persistence of a comparatively large number of pre-industrial families throughout industrialization and rapid population turn-over. In spite of the impact of industrialization on the agrarian community, members of that older community or their descendents remained in Manchester in spite of physical dislocation and the shunting-off of farming as the town's primary activity.[7]

To say that the town was divided into 8 political districts in 1835 is to mislead, for politics was not the basis for Manchester's eight "districts." The district division was based on the support of school houses, although the same district structure would carry over into the industrial town and become the basis for political ward organization (see Table 4.5). In 1835, the 8 districts ranged in size from District 6's six households to District 4's 57 households. The smaller districts were also the more isolated and poorer. District 6, for example, had no property valued at over $1,000, and 71.4% of all land holdings in the district were valued at $500 or less. For this isolated area, support of a school house was a real burden. By contrast, District 4, the location of the industrial village, was more fortunate in having 18.3% of its property valued over $1,000. The existence of a small group of large taxpayers made the support of a school considerably less of a burden for the 68.3% in the district who owned less than $500 in property. Much of the town's school business in 1835 consisted of bickering between one school district and another over the distribution of town revenues from one or two more fortunate areas to the less well-off areas in town. The school district system was changed with the introduction of large scale factory operations, but the future political ward divisions would be based on the original school district lines.[8]

A dramatic change in volume of record-keeping, in categories of taxable wealth, and in simply keeping track of all persons required to pay taxes is evident within ten years. By 1845, the town tax collector's job had become full-time, professionalized, and politically controversial (one tax collector was murdered in the intervening years, and older residents refused to accept minor robbery as a motive, some of them feeling that Jonas Parker's refusal to favor corporate taxpayers played a role in his death). In 1835, 236 taxpayers composed the entire town tax list. For 1845, surviving records, which are incomplete, exist for 1,518 taxpayers. This represents an increase of 543%—an increase that could not be dealt with by a part-time town clerk. Surviving data remains for 1,365 households and 146 businesses (partnerships and corporations). This represents an increase of 532% for households and 2,000% for businesses. Manchester was no longer a town of a few small store keepers. Tax revenues generated from manufacturing and commercial growth would end the petty bickering of the local school districts; industrialization began new quarrels, but the tax revenues generated each year solved the older financial woes of the town.[9]

The crude egalitarianism that had prevailed in the distribution of wealth ten years earlier was no more. Previously, some might have been better off than others, but no one in town was wealthy. In 1845, though, the disparity between rich and poor was much greater. Real property values now ranged from a $50 plot to $172,000. Ten years before, even including the property of the Amoskeag, mean value and median value figures were within a few hundred dollars. This was so no longer. In 1845, the mean property value was $2,117.56, but the median was $901.44, indicating the extent to which the value held by a few large owners towered above the property held by lesser men (see Table 4.6).

Excluding all business and corporate taxpayers, as in Table 4.6, helps to put this data into a perspective that gives a realistic picture of the distribution of wealth in the town. In terms of individual wealth, there had not been really significant change since 1835 (see Tables 4.7, 4.8). The amount of taxable property in town and its average value had increased, but the value of business, commercial, and corporation property was where the most significant increases had been!

By 1845, the poorest land owner in town would be only $30 better off than his counterpart of ten years before, while the poorest store keeper would actually be worse off—owning $50 in land as opposed to the $150 held by his counterpart of ten years before. This does not reflect a deterioration on the part of the business owner, but is a result of a proliferation of small shop owners, come to town to serve a growing mill population. Overall, the individual owner benefited less from the town's growth than did the business, manufacturing, and commercial sector of the town.

Although some men gained materially from industrial growth, the majority failed to do so (see Table 4.9). In 1835, approximately 43% of Manchester's adult males were propertyless. Ten years later, 72.3% of the town's men were without property, and the 1845 data includes categories other than merely real property. It seems ironic to refer to a society in which only 57% of the population owned property as egalitarian, yet, in comparison to the 1845 situation, the earlier town did have an egalitarian distribution of property. It is also clear that even for those individuals who did own property, they did not, for the most part, share in the phenomenal growth of the town as did manufacturers, storekeepers, and other businessmen.

In 1845, for the first time since Derryfield was founded, the town's method of taxation broke down. The town found that it was not possible to tax equitably in an industrial community without totally revising the method of taxation, the method of tax collection (to post delinquents' names, relying on the pressure of public disgrace to bring payment, would no longer suffice), and the categories by which a man's wealth could be measured. For the first time, the value of a man's land was not measured by the richness or rockiness of his soil, but by proximity to the industrial growth area of the town. The value of sheep, cows, and oxen were categories that were becoming increasingly meaningless for large numbers of townsmen. For those who remained in the more isolated sections of town, clinging to farming as their main occupation, these categories did as well as they had in the past; but for the greater segment of the population, new ways of assessing a man's material worth and levying taxes had to be arrived at. The town added entirely new categories to its tax lists, categories designed to measure the changing nature of the industrial prosperity that Manchester had witnessed in a brief time span. Now that the town had banks, bank deposits were added as a means of assessing worth. Likewise, securities (stocks) were taxed, as was available cash, the value of buildings in addition to the value of land, the value of bridges, ferries (private bridges and ferries by this time were all owned by the Amoskeag), locks and canals, and mills and factories. In these early years, mills and factories seemed very much the same things, but later factories would be developed as a separate category to apply to non-textile manufacturing. Three of these new categories, in practice, applied to only one class of taxpayer, although many different company names appeared separately. Only the town's textile mills—the Amoskeag and Stark Mills—paid taxes for wealth determined by the categories: mills and factories; toll bridges; locks and canals. Understandably, these were the largest taxpayers in town. The true scope of the Amoskeag's wealth was somewhat hidden by its organization of numerous operating companies—land and water power; locks and canals; textile operations.[10]

There were 73 stores and shops in Manchester in 1845 compared to 7 in 1835. Of these, 47 (64.4%) were individual or family operations, while 26 (35.6%) were partnerships or companies. The size of the individual store keepers' investment was relatively small (see Table 4.10). The smallest store keepers, men like Dan Bartlett, owned nothing but the stock in their rented store, and this was worth only $100. The better-off merchants, like Artemas Russell, owned a small ($250) shop well-stocked with merchandise ($1,200). Russell was exceptional, though, for 80.9% of all individual merchants in town failed to have stock worth over $1,000 in their shops. The "average" individual merchant had invested only $616 in his wares. There was ample room in the new residential districts for the small store keeper who could scrape together a few hundred dollars or less. As the non-Amoskeag tenements grew, and as first the Irish and later other ethnic groups came to Manchester, the small neighborhood store would continue to grow, even if the owners cannot be said to have prospered.

The 26 partnerships or corporations that kept stores and shops invested on a far larger scale than did individual entrepreneurs. The average partnership or corporation in retail business held $3,500 in stock, while the median figure for such operations was $600, indicating that many such enterprises were run by men with limited resources who had combined forces. The figures for company and partnership retail stores are misleading, though, since the town did not know how to tax the finished product of the textile mills that was waiting for shipment out of town. There was no category developed for taxing finished manufactured goods, so the products of the Stark and Amoskeag Mills were taxed as if they were sitting on the shelf of a small local store keeper. This explains the existence of three "wealthy" shopkeepers, with "stores" stocked with from $20,000 to over $26,000 in "goods." In reality, these were not stores at all, but textile goods finished with production. When these "shops" were disallowed, a different picture of the retail sector operated by partners and companies emerges (see Table 4.11). Partnerships which comprise most of the 26 non-independent retailers, account for an average of only $397 more in investment than the average individual shop keeper. Joseph Kidder regarded himself as typifying Manchester's store keepers and small businessmen. Clearly, at least in financial terms, Kidder stood above those whom he regarded as his colleagues. Kidder's store, with $5,000 in merchandise, may not have been far above "average" according to tax lists, but when viewed according to the amount of investment in retail shops of his fellow store keepers, Kidder, who also owned a delivery horse and wagon, another factor making him exceptional, was among the most prosperous merchants in the early industrial town. The advantages of partnerships were for the wealthier of the town's merchants.[11]

There were other signs of prestige in the town's hierarchy besides commercial wealth. Nine men were proud owners of private carriages, although there was a wide gap between Nathan Parker's $50 vehicle and the "average" $285.56 carriage. At least one of the older farming group felt the need to butress his standing in the community's eyes with the purchase of a fancy carriage. Nehemiah Chase, with $4,500 in real estate and cattle, stood apart from the average farmer. What truly made Chase stand out, though, was his investment in carriages. His $850 investment marked him as a man of unusual wealth.[12]

In 1835, the basis for wealth and prestige was ownership of farm land and livestock. By 1845, ownership of land had come to be regarded as an investment in real estate and this, along with business and manufacturing, was the new basis for community standing. Only ten years earlier, men had judged their wealth and their standing in the community largely in terms of the number of acres they cultivated and the number of farm animals they acquired. In 1835, 55.1% of the town's heads of households owned at least one cow. In 1845, only 4.7% of the population did so. This not only reflects the existence of a large, landless factory population, it also helps to explain how some men, such as

Nehemiah Chase, could successfully acquire a large dairy herd—a phenomenon unheard of ten years earlier. When the next door neighbor owned cows, it was not necessary to buy milk from a dairy (see Table 4.12). Just as a few of the factory workers would prosper, so a few of the old farming community would make a commercially successful transition, either to large-scale commercial agriculture, as Chase did, or to profitable real estate dealership, as did Frederick Stark.

The town's new tax system provided for the computation of the total wealth of taxpayers, whether from real estate, farm animals, investments, bank accounts, or other unlisted categories. The tax collector did not always compute this figure, though. It was not needed for those at the lower end of the tax scale—they owned no property worth taxing, and sometimes paid only the school tax, or the poll tax. Total value figures were reported for 514 taxpayers (see Table 4.13), 368 of these being private individuals. The wealth of a few at the upper end of the spectrum mirrors the awesome investment of the Amoskeag Manufacturing Company. In truth, though, the figures mask the influence of the Amoskeag more than they reveal it. Every taxpayer in town owning over $10,000 in any sort of property was either a direct subsidiary of the Amoskeag, such as the Locks & Canals Co. or the Land & Water Power Co., or they were dependent upon and informally associated with the Amoskeag, such as the Stark and Manchester Mills. Of six such companies, four were Amoskeag subsidiaries holding from $15,000 to $450,000. In terms of the Amoskeag being the only significant holder of large amounts of property of whatever form, Manchester was very much a company town. Individual owners held all of the lesser-valued property and much property of middle value, but no one and no independent business can be said to have been wealthy. The company's vast wealth overshadowed all else in town.

In 1835, there had been a close relationship between the value of a man's land holdings and the value of his other holdings. Large land holders had also owned the largest herds, and the most productive orchards (see Table 4.14). By 1845, it was no longer valid to equate the largest land owners in town with the most prosperous farmers. New factors determined a man's standing in the community: his place in the manufacturing hierarchy (agent, overseer, second hand, loom-fixer); his place in the commercial hierarchy (Joseph Kidder's comments to the contrary, certain moderately successful merchants clearly saw a special place reserved for themselves in the community, and many sought political office); real estate speculation (land as a speculative commodity, rather than the slow acquisition of additional farm land, became a factor).

For many men, non-agricultural investments in land were the main form of "savings." Yet 30% of private land owners owned less than $600 worth of real estate, while 59.3% owned under $1,000.

The value of land holdings is less significant than is the question of who property owners were—what groups in the population tended to acquire property. The 1850 manuscript census provides some picture of the pre-Civil War patterns of property ownership in Manchester, and allows comparisons between occupational groupings and property accumulation.

Those who did best, in terms of absolute numbers of property owners, were native New Hampshire men. Of 691 people reporting property holdings, 559, or 80.9%, were New Hampshire natives (see Table 4.15). Next in line were other New Englanders, comprising together 17.1% of all property owners. Bringing up the rear were the foreign born. Taken together, all foreign born comprised only 1.5% of all property owners. In addition to being the numerically greatest category of property owners, New Hampshire natives did better than non-natives in terms of acquiring property of greater value (see Table 4.16). They comprised, for example, almost 91% of all owners of $5,000 or more in property. All holders of over $5,000 were New Englanders. Natives were familiar with the market in real estate, and they were better able than outsiders to take advantage of personal contacts with fellow New Englanders. At all levels, New Hampshire born men predominated, although "outsiders" did managed to acquire lesser values of property.

In terms of occupational groupings of property owners, more skilled workers owned property than did the members of any other group. Textile operatives ranked with the semi-skilled as the least frequent owners of property (see Table 4.17). Professionals comprised only 4.8% of property owners, but there were few professionals in town, and as little as five years previously, it had been regarded as a family disgrace to have a son so "impractical" as to have to send him off to college. Given this climate, it was little wonder that there were relatively few professionals in town to join the ranks of property holders.

In terms of the relationship of occupation to the value of property held, as opposed to the number of property holders, semi-professionals fared best, comprising 31.3% of all men holding over $5,000 in property. Skilled workers were next in line, comprising 28.8% of those holding over $5,000 in property (see Tables 4.18, 4.19).

Certain levels of property ownership seem to have been more open to some groups than to others. Among professionals, for example, although they comprised only 4.8% of all property owners, it was clearly more likely that a professional would hold more than $3,000 in property than it was that he would hold a lesser amount. Of all professionals holding property, 63.4% owned more than $3,000, while no semi-skilled or general textile operatives achieved this level of property accumulation, and only a small number (6.4%) of the unskilled did so (see Table 4.20).

The semi-skilled, unskilled, and textile workers fared poorest. Of all textile workers owning property, 52.9% held small amounts—under $1,000—while 69.2% of the semi-skilled and 62.9% of the unskilled fell into the under $1,000 groupings. This was in marked contrast to the professionals and semi-professionals. As has been shown, these two groups were not numerically large in terms of the total number of property owners. Those professionals and semi-professionals who did hold property, though, tended to hold over $3,000 worth of value. 63.4% of all professionals who owned property owned in excess of $3,000, while 46.1% of semi-professionals who owned property held over $3,000.

It is not surprising that those expected to have larger incomes—professionals, for example—tended to hold property of the higher value groups, nor is it surprising that the lower paid—unskilled workers, for example—tended to own little or no property in the upper range of the scale, but remained predominately holders of lesser amounts. Farmers, many of them having held onto once valueless farm lands, found the worth of their lands fairly well spread throughout the range of values. What is remarkable is the extent to which skilled workers participated in property ownership—and at all levels. Skilled workers composed 43.7% of all property owners. Although they tended to own property of lesser value, they did own property in the upper ranges of the scale as well. They were not excluded from the higher categories of wealth as were the semi-skilled and textile workers. The question of what "skills" were represented among these property owning workers is important in determining whether their skills gave them advantages in the acquisition of wealth. Building tradesmen, for example, would be in a better position than, say, machinists to witness and take advantage of the physical growth of the town. This holds to some degree, for carpenters and stone masons were represented heavily among skilled property owners, but a surprising number of other tradesmen owned property as well. The major occupations represented are illustrated in Table 4.21. These occupations account for 84.7% of all skilled property owners. The remaining 15.3% is composed of a few men in many different trades: harness makers, wheelwrights, metal workers, brick layers, carriage makers, watch makers, bakers, cigar makers, printers, and others. All felt land to be a good investment or a necessity for raising their families, and they put their resources into property ownership.

Textile operatives were by far the largest single occupational grouping among the working population of Manchester, yet they were among those groups least likely to own property (comprising 2.7% of all property owners). The few textile operatives who did own property found themselves among the groups whose valuations were concentrated among the lowest categories. With 52.9% of textile workers owning property holding under $1,000 in valuation, it would seem that the textile workers, comprising the largest single group of workers in town, and the group upon whose efforts the success of the town was based, found themselves close to the bottom of the town's economic hierarchy.[13]

The most popular contemporary explanation for the failure of textile workers to acquire property was that the factory work force was not stable enough—textile workers did not stay in Manchester long enough—to develop any significant degree of ownership of real estate. The Amoskeag's explanation, the arguments of "booster" literature, and the explanation of contemporary histories was that textile workers, knowing they would not form any permanent attachment to Manchester (one observer compared the mill workers to school children at a boarding school), chose to keep the material assets that they were able to accumulate in more liquid forms than those measured and counted by tax collectors and census takers. The corporation was proud of its savings bank for workers, and city directories, histories, and Amoskeag literature stressed the number of workers who chose to participate in the company's "savings bank experiment."[14]

Amoskeag workers opened 4,387 separate savings accounts with the corporation over the life of the savings bank, officially five years, but unofficially, like so much else that the Amoskeag chose not to acknowledge, about ten years. Of 879 accounts analyzed from the Amoskeag's savings bank records, the average (mean) opening amount was $81.49. Amounts of initial deposits ranged from $1 deposited by a lowly female operative to $700 deposited, in violation of the company's own extensive rules, by a male overseer. If such large deposits are disallowed, a different picture of the average opening value of workers' savings accounts emerges. It is fair to disallow such deposits, for they were either made by supervisory help (which was not the intention of the savings bank—nor was its intention to accept large amounts), or they were representatives of merely a temporary "holding place" for a large amount of cash, not being used as an opportunity to build savings, but merely to arrange for temporary safekeeping. Discounting large deposits, and looking only at the accounts of workers who participated regularly and used the savings bank as its founders maintained it was intended to be used, the average worker who opened an account did so with $32.32, and kept his or her account active for 8.9 months.[15]

Textile workers may have used the company's savings bank as an alternative to other forms of property accumulation, but over their account's nine-month average lifespan, 75% failed to accumulate over $100. The whole savings bank experiment points again to the issue of the corporation's paternalism and the workers' reactions to it. Contemporary critics of the Amoskeag pointed out that the mill was gaining the use of workers' savings for investment purposes. The Amoskeag countered that it paid the prevailing interest rate and that its primary motive was to encourage workers' thrift by providing a service that no bank in town was willing to undertake.

There was no bank in Manchester, in 1841, willing to accept savings. In providing such a bank, the Amoskeag was fulfilling its self-defined role of corporate paternalist. Until 1846, the Amoskeag allowed workers at the Stark and Manchester Mills to save with the Amoskeag's employee savings bank. In looking out for the welfare of its workers' savings, the corporation acted on the direct instructions of its board of directors, some of whom had been involved in the savings bank movement in Massachusetts.[16]

Whether philanthropically motivated or not, the Amoskeag's savings bank experiment inspired protests almost from the beginning. Over a period of five years, the protests grew in intensity to the point where the corporation would announce its abandonment. One of the local press' most popular themes had become the control of corporations. In Manchester, this sometimes meant reform of railroad abuses in their land acquisition policies, it sometimes meant no more than Democratic political rhetoric, but, as resentment of the Amoskeag's policies grew, general denunciations of "corporations" were interpreted by many as direct references to the Amoskeag. The corporation's critics raised disturbing questions: could a manufacturing company carry on a land sale business? Could it engage in the construction business? Were there to be no limits to its activities? Could it ally with the railroads? Could it operate the banks? Petitions to the legislature, newspaper articles, letters to the editors and rebuttals, and mass protest meetings were based on these themes. By reference to "the corporations," those who were disaffected by the Amoskeag's paternalist policies could appeal to a large number of persons disturbed by various large business practices.[17]

The issue to which the Amoskeag was most vulnerable was the charge of having exceeded the limits of its corporate charter by openly engaging in a general banking business. Rather than see this issue unite all anti-Amoskeag sentiment in Manchester with other anti-corporation feeling, the company announced, in 1846, that, since the Manchester Savings Bank had been formed to deal with small depositors, the company would abandon its own savings bank. The company's control over the new bank was by no means as thorough as had been its own in-house operation, but one of the overseers was on the bank's board of directors, and others on the new bank's board had close ties to the Amoskeag. The company did not openly acknowledge its sensitivity to criticism of its involvement in wider community activities, but it effectively took the offensive away from its critics by abandoning, at least in theory, its savings bank operation.[18]

The company regarded saving face in the matter of the savings bank discontinuance as important, just as it regarded it as important in quietly granting workers' wage and hour demands without ever publicly acknowledging recognition of grievances. It could abandon the savings bank experiment because its interest in maintaining a facility for workers' savings would be carried out. It could afford to acknowledge publicly the bank's discontinuance because, in practice, the savings bank's operation continued without much change almost down to the Civil War.[19]

Ann B. Osgood came to work in the Amoskeag's mills in 1846. The following year, a full year after public announcement of the company's discontinuance of its savings bank had been made, Ann Osgood opened a savings account with the factory agent for $36.61. The agent continued to open new accounts after 1845, and accepted deposits, although discontinuing opening new accounts, through the end of the 1850's. When Ann Osgood left the mills on April 30, 1857, she closed her ten-year old savings account and took her final payment of $69.70. Over a decade when the Amoskeag, to all public appearances, and according to its public statements, was out of the banking business, Ann Osgood had deposited $216.41. Like other workers, most of whom remained in the savings bank and in the mills for much shorter periods of time than she, Ann Osgood made regular yearly deposits, made few withdrawals, and carefully saved her receipts. She would need them in 1857 when she accused the clerk of a $60 error made three years before. Without her receipts and her passbook, Ann Osgood would have had little chance of the Amoskeag's acknowledging its error.[20]

While Ann Osgood's longevity in the mills and in the savings bank is notable because it is the exception rather than the rule, the amount of Miss Osgood's treasure trove is not exceptional. Over her working career in Manchester's textile mills, Ann Osgood had put aside only $22 per year, average. When this figure is compared to the amount of property held by those in other, non-textile, occupational categories it is striking that, in a textile town, the textile worker ranked among the least well-off. Even considering "hidden" forms of wealth such as savings, the textile worker fared poorly in the accumulation of wealth, and this in spite of Joseph Kidder's self-consciously middle class remarks about the prosperity of the average worker in the Amoskeag's mills. Perhaps what Kidder meant was that the mill workers paid their bills at his store. In the years before the Civil War, the textile worker's place in the textile town's hierarchy of status and wealth was close to the bottom in spite of company rhetoric and the impressions left by middle class observers.[21]

In the 1840's, one of Manchester's clergymen suggested how difficult it would be to trace the mill population from year to year when he referred to Manchester as a vast boarding school. The entire mill population, including males, he estimated, would stay in town only three years—four years at most—

and then move on. Recent historians have described similar populations as a society of "men in motion." The difficulties normally encountered in tracing a working population are compounded when that population is a long-acknow-ledged group of "movers." In spite of the difficulties, it is important to learn who stayed put in pre-Civil War Manchester and who moved on. The 1835 and 1845 tax lists can be used to determine what segments of the older pre-industrial community stayed on in the new industrial town, and what the characteristics were of those who tended to move on.[22]

Pre-industrial Manchester had 220 heads of households (1835). Ten years later, following industrialization of the town, records survive for 1,365 heads of households. In the 1845 records, 50 men can be located who lived in Man-chester in 1835. Only 22.7% of Manchester's pre-industrial heads of household remained in town five years after the opening of the factories. The fabled instability of the population of textile towns, it would seem, applies to more than just mill workers. Virtually all of the 1835 population in the tax records had been farmers or had been engaged in farm-related activities. Some would have been displaced by the Amoskeag's construction, records may not survive for some others, but these factors alone do not account for the disappearance of 77.3% of Manchester's pre-industrial population in a ten-year period.[23]

What about the 50 men and their families who remained? Some remained because of tradition. The Stark family was well-known and respected. There was not a man in town who did not recognize the descendents of the Hero of Bennington. Four Stark families stayed put in Manchester following industri-alization. John Stark, Jr. had held onto his family's farm, valued at $2,000, and was operating it. John, Sr., who had owned $2,200 on the earlier records, retained only a small plot of land worth $150 in 1845. He lived near his son and other family members, though. Robert Stark lived nearby, but, like some other members of the family who would appear in 1845 but who had not been recorded ten years earlier, he owned no land. His total worth was represented by one cow, value $12. The last Stark was also the one who had fared best (see Table 4.22). Frederick G. Stark was one of the town's wealthiest men in 1835. He owned a $3,500 farm, livestock valued at $148, and had $600 in the bank. Ten years later, Frederick Stark had "sold out" his farm to the Amoskeag Manufacturing Company. He retained only a house and a small plot of land, located near other family members, valued at $500. To say that Frederick Stark did not retain the old family farm is not to say that he was landless in 1845, though.

He invested the proceeds from the sale of his farm in land, scattered throughout the city, and was one of the largest private land holders in town in 1845. He had served as selectman numerous times and he had served as town moderator, but, after he sold his farm to the Amoskeag in 1836-37, he seems to have spent most of his efforts on admistering his properties.[24]

What is notable about the Starks is that some disappear from 1835 to 1845 —Samuel, Albert, John II, Grardus—while others appear for the first time—like Benjamin and Campbell. The $2,000 farm that John Stark, Jr. owned was the focal point for the settlement of the Starks who appear in 1845. Settlement in clusters around family-owned land helps to explain how some family members owned livestock yet had no land of their own to raise it on. It explains why John, Jr.'s livestock disappeared from 1835 to 1845 while his farm remained the same size—he had relinquished ownership of his animals to his sons, but held on to his land. The large plot of land owned by John, Jr. was the nucleus for the family settlement. All of the Starks settled near John, Jr. Family ties persisted even after the size of the old Stark lands had been considerably reduced in scope. Even Frederick G. Stark, owning well over $11,000 in real estate in 1845, chose to live on a small plot of land which he retained from his sale to the Amoskeag because it was located near other family land. With the amount of property Frederick Stark owned, he could have lived anywhere in town.[25]

The Kimball family represents another illustration of persistence and interdependence. Four Kimball households persist from 1835 to 1845 in two distinct branches. One settlement of Kimballs clustered around Amos Kimball, the other around Frederick Kimball. The Kimballs shared in the material growth of the town. Total family land values rose from $4,830 in 1835 to $10,000 in 1845. Like the Starks, though, not all of the Kimballs were well-off. Some were seemingly propertyless. This was the case for Jonathan Kimball in 1835 and for Benjamin, Henry and John S. in 1845. Some, like Amhers, owned no land, but had 2 cows. For the propertyless Kimballs, as for the poorer Starks, settlement in family clusters around land owned by a well-to-do family member was essential. The exact terms on which family patriarchs allowed their lands to be utilized by family members will probably remain unknown. The very fact of contiguous settlement by poor and wealthy family members does indicate, though, that material acquisition was not the only factor influencing persistence. Family ties were important in determining whether or not a man would remain in town.[26]

Of the 50 households traced from 1835 to 1845, 42 (85%) were located within areas contiguous to relatives. Websters, Pierces, Fellowses, Huses, and others lived either next to or nearby other members of their families.[27]

The 50 households have one other shared characteristic besides nearby residing kin. That factor is land ownership by one of more members of the family settlement cluster. Frederick Stark's pattern of living near the family farm, yet engaging in commercial activity is an aberration. Few men owned over 15 scattered real estate investments in town, as Stark did. For most, family ties were also ties to the soil. These were families that retained an active interest in farming, in spite of their life amongst industrial growth. Manchester was surely a "mill town," but a significant number of the more stable population elements were farming households. Some members of those households would eventually (demonstrably by 1880) go to work in the factory in order to supplement farm income. The biographical sketches of the prominent members of the stable population group presented in contemporary sources, such as Clarke's history, are pictures of commercial men—men of the middle class, merchants like Joseph Kidder, lawyers, and physicians. While men like Kidder do compose one segment of the town's stable population base, another segment of the population that remained in town for relatively long periods of time came from the agriculturally-oriented households of the town. This group is important in itself and important because of contiguous family settlement, providing a base for the comings and goings of other family members, some of whom would eventually find their way into the factory work force, providing a group of textile workers with local family ties. The early factory work force (pre-1860) had few ties to Manchester, and did, indeed, reflect the truth of a boarding school-like population with rapid turnover.[28]

One test of the extent to which the older farming group contributed towards a stable population can be made using the 1850 census of agriculture. There were 199 farming families in Manchester in 1850. How many can be located 5 years earlier? Fifteen years earlier? It can be shown that a relatively high percentage of this population had remained in town for these fairly considerable periods. Manchester's pro-labor sense of "community" with the textile workers cannot be explained only by the sympathy of "prominent" middle class shopkeepers, lawyers, and physicians. Although not textile workers themselves, Manchester's farming families were accustomed to hard work, and they were more likely to have family members working in the mills than were recently arrived professionals or semi-professionals. This group had not been taken into account in commercial histories and directories, but the very fact of their persistence gave them weight in the community.

Of 199 households in 1850, 92 (46.2%) had been in Manchester five years before. The significance of this group can be gauged when comparing similar efforts to trace textile workers. Using city directories, only about 6% of textile operatives can be traced back 5 years. Even using company payrolls, efforts to trace at five-year intervals in the 1840's are condemned to failure (see Table 4.24).

Of the 199 households, 54 (27.1%) can be located in Manchester in 1835—15 years previously. Comparing these long-term residents' wealth to the wealth of the general property owning population, it is apparent that long-term residents fared better than average (see Table 4.23). Longevity in the community meant that this group not only had money, but the prestige of "old family names" as well. Not all were reluctant to engage in the politics of the new town as Frederick Stark had been. Kimballs, Huses, Moores, and others would run for office along with more recently arrived commercial men, and a number of the older residents would succeed in holding office in the industrial town. Those who stayed in town for 15 years fared better than most (see Table 4.25). They weathered the transition to the industrial town, holding onto, and sometimes enlarging, their holdings. The "average" 15-year resident actively farmed 46 acres, held another 66 acres in reserve, and owned $284 in animal stock on his farm. They did well for themselves and they formed a base for the settlement of other members of their family.[29]

The persistence encountered among the farm-based population of Manchester is striking when contrasted with similar efforts to trace the general working population of the mills (see Table 4.26). Of 284 such mill workers located in 1844, only 42 (14.8%) remained in town four years later while only 17 (5.9%) can be located five years later. Similar efforts among the general working population of the town reveal how unusual it was for a man to remain in town even as long as five years. Looking at the prevailing wage rates in Manchester in 1850, it is understandable why the unskilled or those who started out without the benefit of local family land failed to join the ranks of the property holders. Average wage for a day laborer, without board, was $1.25 per day, for a carpenter, $1.50. Prevailing board costs per week averaged $2.00.[30]

Although Manchester was a "mill town," mill workers did not participate in the economic growth of the town. They were excluded from the town's social and economic hierarchy. The sympathetic attitude of much of the town's press towards textile workers may be explained in part by the presence of large numbers of skilled workers among the property owning group, and by the persistence of another "working" group—older farming residents—who sympathized with the factory workers, and would increasingly do so as their landless relatives joined the factory work force.[31] In view of their failure to share proportionately in Manchester's prosperity, it is hardly surprising that Manchester's workers turned inward to their neighborhoods, their churches, their countrymen, and their families.

Table 4.1. 1835 Real Property Ownership (As Percent of
            Total Population) [32]

	%	N =
Propertyless	42.6	92
Property Holders	57.4	124

Table 4.2. 1835 Owners of Farm Animals (As Percent of
            Total Population) [33]

	%	N =
Owns 1 or More Animals	61.5	133
Owns No Animal Stock	38.5	83

Table 4.3. Wealth Ranges, 1835 [34]

1835 Land Values		1835 Animal Values	
Range:	$20-$5,000	Range:	$10-$384
Median:	$ 795.91	Median:	$ 78.25
Mean:	$1,048.31	Mean:	$106.91
Std. Dev.:	$1,067.09	Std. Dev.:	$ 93.46

Table 4.4. 1835 Real Property Values[35]

	Amoskeag Excluded	Amoskeag Included
Range:	$20-$5,600	$20-$18,000
Median:	$ 703.33	$ 705.00
Mean:	$1,028.60	$1,146.45
Std. Dev.:		$1,786.46

Table 4.5 Political Subdivisions, 1835

District	No. Households	No. Taxpayers
1	30	36
2	41	41
3	40	44
4	57	60
5	8	9
6	6	7
7	18	21
8	16	18

Source: Town Records

Table 4.6. 1845 Real Property Values[36]

	Individual Property Owners	Corporate and Business Owners
Range	$50-$6,800	$50-$172,000
Median	$1,171.74	$ 4,081.78
Mean	$ 900.53	$ 1,000.00
Std. Dev.:	$1,077.66	$16,749.40

Table 4.7.   1835-1845 Comparison of Individual Real Wealth[37]

	1835	1845
Range:	$20-$5,500	$50-$6,800
Median:	$ 795.90	$ 900.53
Mean:	$1,048.30	$1,171.74
Std. Dev.:	$1,067.09	$1,077.66
	N=124	N=241

Table 4.8.   1835-1845 Comparison of Business-Commercial Real
            Wealth[38]

	1835	1845
Range:	$150-$18,000	$50-$172,000
Median:	$ 425.00	$ 1,000.00
Mean:	$1,755.00	$ 4,081.78
Std. Dev.:	$4,024.39	$16,749.40
	N=20	N=118

Table 4.9.   1835-1845 Property Ownership (As Percent of Total
            Population)[39]

	1835*	1845
Propertyless	42.6	72.3
Property Holders	57.4	27.7
N =	216	1,363

*Real property only; 1845 data for all reported categories

Table 4.10.   Individual Mercantile Wealth[40]

Independent Shopkeepers' Investment in Wares		
Range:	$100-$1,800	
Median:	$496.66	
Mean:	$616.27	
Std. Dev.:	$496.94	N=47

Table 4.11. Joint Mercantile Wealth[41]

Partnership & Companies' Investment in Wares		
	Includes All Categories	Excludes Finished Production
Range:	$200-$26,111	$200-$5,000
Median:	$ 600.00	
Mean:	$3,500.42	$995.65
Std. Dev.:	$7,204.32	

Table 4.12. 1835-1845 Comparative (Land-Animal) Ownership*[42]

	1835	1845
Land Owners	124 (57.4%)	241 (17.7%)
Animal Owners	133 (61.6%)	113 (8.2%)
Mean Land Value	1048.30	1171.74
Mean Animal Value	106.91	89.46

*Excludes businesses

Table 4.13. 1845, Total Valued Wealth[43]

	All Taxpayers	Individuals	Businesses
Range:	$10-$450,200	$10-$6,800	$50-$450,000
Median:	$ 800.07	$ 710.50	$ 996.89
Mean:	$ 3,271.92	$ 967.46	$ 9,203.78
Std. Dev.:	$25,918.35	$1,047.01	$48,557.58
N =	514	368	144

Table 4.14. 1835 Land-Animal Value Range[44]

Land Value	Under $100 Animal Value	$101-200 Animal Value	Over $100 Animal Value	Total
To $500	39 (32.7)	3 (2.5)		42 (35.2)
501-1,000	17 (14.3)	15 (12.6)	3 (2.5)	35 (29.4)
1,001-2,000	4 (3.4)	9 (7.6)	10 (8.4)	23 (19.4)
Over 2,000		7 (5.9)	12 (10.1)	19 (16.0)

Table 4.15. Nativity of Property Owners, 1850 [45]

New Hampshire	559 (80.9)
Massachusetts	66 (9.6)
Vermont	40 (5.8)
Maine	9 (1.3)
Other New England	3 (.4)
Other U. S.	3 (.4)
Foreign	11 (1.5)

Table 4.16. Level of Wealth by Nativity, 1850* [46]

Wealth Level	Nativity				
	New Hampshire	Mass.	Other New Eng.	Other U.S.	Foreign
Over $5,000	79 (90.8)	7 (8.1)	1 (1.1)		
$2,001–5,000	150 (83.3)	19 (10.6)	7 (3.9)		4 (2.2)
$1,001–2,000	143 (77.3)	20 (10.8)	20 (10.8)		2 (1.1)
$ 501–1,000	142 (81.1)	14 (8.0)	14 (8.0)	2 (1.1)	3 (1.7)
$ 500 or under	45 (70.3)	6 (9.4)	10 (15.6)	1 (1.6)	2 (3.1)

*Percentages are % of given wealth level

Table 4.17. Occupational Groupings of Property Owners, 1850 [47]

Skilled	271 (43.7)
Semi-Professional	102 (16.5)
Farmer	102 (16.5)
Unskilled	62 (10.0)
Professional	30 (4.8)
White Collar	23 (3.7)
General Textile Operative	17 (2.7)
Semi-skilled	13 (2.1)

Table 4.18. Occupational Groupings Owning Over $5,000 [48]

Semi-Professional	31.3%	
Skilled Workers	28.8	
Farmers	18.8	
Professionals	13.8	
White Collar	6.3	
Unskilled	1.3	
Textile Operatives	--	
Semi-Skilled	--	N = 80

Table 4.19. Occupational Grouping by Level of Wealth, 1850[49]

Occupational Level	Property Value					
	Under $500	501–1000	1001–1500	1501–2000	2001–3000	3001–5000
Skilled	63.0	50.6	63.5	43.3	32.5	26.7
Professional	3.7	1.9	1.4	1.1	5.0	9.3
Semi-Profess.	1.9	7.1	5.4	26.7	18.8	25.6
Farm	7.4	9.0	9.5	14.4	28.8	30.2
White Collar		3.2	6.8		5.0	4.7
Semi-Skilled	3.7	4.5	1.4	2.2	1.3	
Textile	5.6	3.8	1.4	4.4	3.8	
Unskilled	14.8	19.9	10.8	7.8	5.0	3.5
N =	54	156	74	90	80	86

Table 4.20. Percent of Occupation Group at Each Property Level, 1850[50]

Occupation	Property						
	$500 or Under	$501–1000	$1001–1500	$1501–2000	$2001–3000	$3001–5000	Over $5000
Professional	6.7	10.0	3.3	3.3	13.3	26.7	36.7
Semi-Prof.	1.0	10.8	3.9	23.5	14.7	21.6	24.5
Farm	3.9	13.7	6.9	12.7	22.5	25.5	14.7
White Collar		21.7	21.7		17.4	17.4	21.7
Skilled	12.5	29.2	17.3	14.4	9.6	8.5	8.5
Semi-Skilled	15.4	53.8	7.7	15.4	7.7		
Textile	17.6	35.3	5.9	23.5	17.6		
Unskilled	12.9	50.0	12.9	11.3	6.5	4.8	1.6

N = Professional 30; Semi-Prof. 102; Farm 102; White Collar 23;
Skilled 271; Semi-Skilled 13; Textile 17; Unskilled 62

Table 4.21. Skilled Property Owners, 1850[51]

Carpenters	73	(26.9)
Machinists	39	(14.4)
Stone Masons	27	(9.9)
Mechanics	28	(10.3)
Shoemakers (Cordwainers)	25	(9.2)
Butchers	14	(5.2)
Blacksmiths	12	(4.4)
Painters	12	(4.4)

Table 4.22. Value Stark Family Lands, 1835-1845[52]

	1835	1845
Total Value, all Family Owned Land	$10,800*	$10,750** $11,100***

   *Includes all family members
  **Excludes Frederick G
***Property held by Frederick G. Stark alone

Table 4.23. Property Values, 15 Year Residents, 1850[53]

	Range	Mean	Median
15-Year Residents	$200-15,000	$3,694.44	$3,466.67
General Property Value*	$300-15,000	$2,739.76	

*Excludes 7 largest taxpayers (all corporations)

Table 4.24. Trace Results, 1850[54]

1850 Population	Located, 1845	Located, 1835
199 (100%)	92 (46.2%)	54 (27.1%)

Table 4.25. 1850 Property Values by Length of Residence[55]

	Range	Mean	Median
5-Year Residents	$200-15,000	$3,284.44	$2,600.00
15-Year Residents	$200-15,000	$3,694.44	$3,466.67
General Population	$300-15,000	$2,739.76	$2,000.00

Table 4.26.   Trace Results, 1844-1852[56]

Mill Workers Trace Results, 1844-1849		
1844 Population	Located, 1848	Located, 1849
284 (100%)	42 (14.8%)	17 (5.9%)

General Working Population Trace Results, 1848-1852		
1848 Population	Located, 1850	Located, 1852
181 (100%)	38 (20.9%) 102 (100%)	11 (10.8%)

Total working population, 1850 = 5,240 (1877 male; 3363 female)

5

The Rise of the Foreign Born

The 1860's presented Manchester with more than her share of problems and challenges. In addition to the challenge of facing the Civil War, Manchester would face the temporary shut-down of the textile mills, the town's *raison d'être*. After the war, Manchester faced a new industrial situation and the mills of post-Civil War Manchester were different, in many ways, from those of the pre-Civil War years. Perhaps one of the most significant changes was the predominance of a foreign born (or second generation) work force which would be commonplace in many factories after the war.[1]

The Civil War years present a problem for the historian who would deal with a textile community. These are towns that are expected, in normal times, to be areas of higher than "normal" population turnover. Now that we realize that "normal" turnover itself can be larger than previously imagined, the problems of dealing with a community with a long-acknowledged tradition of population turbulence seem even more formidable. Given normal circumstances, some modest success might be achieved in tracing the careers of mill workers over, let us say, 10-year intervals. Given the wartime disruption of Manchester's industrial establishment that took place for a considerable time during the Civil War, added to the problem of young men joining up and marching off to war, the effort to trace a usually mobile population in unusually mobile times becomes overwhelming. Given these obstacles, what can be done is to compare the nature of the post-Civil War textile community in Manchester, and the position of the worker in that community, with that existing in pre-Civil War years.[2]

1860 began ominously for Manchester, and other northern New England textile towns, with the collapse of the Pemberton Mill in Lawrence. Other historians have pointed to the Pemberton Mill disaster as symbolic of the changing times through which the textile towns had gone, but it seems worthwhile to reinforce the impact that the Pemberton Mill had, not for academics studying these towns years later, but for contemporaries. It is worth remembering that Manchester was linked to Lawrence, and to other towns, via the absentee ownership of the mills. For people in Manchester, especially for those who went to work daily in mill buildings virtually identical in style, if not in function, to the Pemberton Mill, the collapse was not something that happened to people somewhere else, but seemed as real as if it had happened in town. It caused workers to question the purpose of their labor and of their existence, to speculate on the futility of their lives, and, for some, to doubt the existence of a providential God. The Pemberton disaster was dealt with in sermons, in editorials, and in public talks and prayer meetings. One of the "leading citizens" who participated in the public reflection on the Pemberton Mill was editor-merchant Joseph Kidder.

Kidder usually saved his moralizing for Odd Fellow Addresses, "talks" to young men at the YMCA, fraternal groups or other public occasions. Usually, Kidder's diary was a personal-business document of few words confined to business notations or extremely concise spiritual "notes." When it came to the Pemberton Mills collapse, though, the usually terse Kidder filled the space for five days, January 11 to 15, confiding to his diary:

> Yesterday I went to Boston. On my return to Lawrence I learned the particulars of the most awful and thrilling occurrence that has ever taken place. A brick mill containing six, or eight hundred operatives fell while all the hands were engaged in their work. Hundreds are killed in the most horrible manner. The scene is awful, and beyond the power of the human pen to describe so an eye witness told me. The whole town is in mourning, and the whole community in the deepest sorrow. Indeed so appalling an affair has never occurred in this or any other country that I am aware of. The particulars—at least some of them I will give at another time. How unaccountable are the events that occur to men! At Lawrence there were six or eight hundred men, women and children engaged honestly and industriously to gain a livelihood and in a moment, without the shadow of warning, they are killed amidst falling timbers to instant death, or those who were not instantly killed only dragged out a more lingering and miserable death—by fire and water. Now how can this be accounted for? Has the Providence of God so called any thing to do with it? It is perhaps a hard question to answer—for we are told, and we all believe it—that not a sparrow falls without the notice of the good God. For one I am free to admit that I do not believe in the doctrine of God's special providences as some people do. I am satisfied that He governs by laws—by general and not by special laws. If these laws are violated no matter when, nor where, nor how, the consequences of such violation will surely follow and no power can avert it. The weight broke down the Pemberton Mills, not the house of God.[3]

Self-consciously a spokesman for Manchester's middle class business community, Kidder reflected the growing uncertainty of a group that had not seen anything, locally, so suddenly dramatic as the collapse of the Pemberton Mill. What Kidder and his peers had witnessed, though, was the gradual transformation of what had once been an almost exclusively native-born society. When Kidder confided the remarks above to his diary, Manchester was still a "native's" town: workers were predominantly Yankees, and control of the town was clearly in native hands and would remain so for years. The perceptive, though, would look toward Lawrence not only for what examples could be drawn from the Pemberton Mill, but for what the changing nature of an increasingly immigrant work force could imply.[4]

Already there were signs that Manchester was headed for drastic changes in the composition of the work force. Since 1844, there had been a Catholic population in Manchester. The occasion of the building of the first Catholic church, in that year, had set off civil disturbances as a nativist mob had attempted to demolish the building. By 1860, the Catholics had church seating capacity for 3,000 and property (schools, orphanages, and churches) officially valued at $40,000. All of the 16 Protestant churches in town, together, sat 8,975 and held property valued at $96,200. The Catholic population was foreign born (mostly Irish and French Canadian), but in terms of numbers, resources, and, perhaps, influence, natives could sense their growing importance. The native households, dominant in the 1860 census, would be dominant for the last time, for post-Civil War changes would change the shape of Manchester's work force.[5]

A sample of 61 households in Manchester's industrial district drawn from the 1860 manuscript census returns reveals a majority of native born house-holders living side by side with Irish and French Canadian immigrants. Forty-one of the households sampled (67%) lived in detached, single family dwellings, while 20 households lived in two-family dwellings. As in earlier years, the single family house remained the expected dwelling arrangements for most households. The households in the sample ranged in size from a single person household to a household of 43 persons, mean size being 8.7 persons (see Table 5.1).

The sample revealed a considerable number of larger households—those with eight or more residents. In part, this was an accommodation to the company's boardinghouse policy. All of the large, businesslike boardinghouses were family-run operations and were not, in this sample anyway, "corporation housing." Clearly, large numbers of workers chose not to "board on the cor-poration," but preferred to retain some measure of control over their lives outside of the work place, even if that meant accommodating themselves to the whims of a boardinghouse keeper. There were six houses in the sample that were "land lady" run operations, but interestingly enough only one of these was exclusively for women, with no men being allowed to board or live in the house. All of 68 year old Esther Parker's boarders were women, and all were textile mill workers except for her own daughter and the Irish domestic, both of whom were kept busy caring for some 26 boarders. Mrs. Parker's predilection in favor of women boarders also extended to nativity—all but one of her boarders was native born. Mrs. Parker ran the kind of boardinghouse that was idealized in the "Lowell System" myth—all women—and advocated locally as the second-best alternative for a girl new to the city (the preferred alternative advocated by local civic leaders and clergy was that the girl live in company-supervised dwellings). In practice, though, the "mixed" boardinghouse seems to have been the preferred alternative of the workers themselves. The other five boardinghouses in the sample, while mostly "female," were not segregated on the basis of sex nor, exclusively, on the basis of nationality, although there was a clear differentiation in status between some.[6]

The boardinghouse of Lucy Ainsworth, 64, and her daughter Charlotte, 30, housed 32 boarders, 2 of whom were adult males, 1 youth, and 29 female textile workers. The unusual thing about Mrs. Ainsworth's boarders was that 4 of them had accumulated significant amounts of property, ranging from $500 to $1,500. A more "typical" house, though, and more family-oriented, was that kept by Sophronia Lamridge, 32. The two men in the Lamridge household were both relatives of the boardinghouse mistress, while the 25 young women textile workers all paid their room and board. The boardinghouse mistress was Canadian-born, and her house attracted Irish, Canadian, Scots, and native-born young women. Seven of her boarders were illiterate and one was "idiotic."

Two working men and their wives supplemented the family income by keeping boardinghouses. John Doland, 57, worked as a watchman while his wife, Elizabeth, 46, kept more than busy at home by maintaining a home for her 6 children, ranging in age from 7 to 28, and 35 boarders in addition to herself, her husband, and the children. While most of the Doland's boarders were women, they did have some male boarders. Mrs. Doland's youngest boarder was Mary Atherton, 14, who worked every day in the cotton mill, while her oldest was Carrie Fuller, 33, a spinner. The Doland household reflected the comparative youthfulness of Manchester's working population (see Table 5.20). There are two striking things about the Doland household. Every boarder was, like the Dolands themselves, native born. Clearly Manchester's growing foreign born population would not have been made to feel welcome at the Dolands' house. In contrast to some of the boarders, the Doland children remained in school and out of the world of work outside the home until at least age 19. Only the two eldest Doland children, Susan, 28, and Martha, 25, were in the work place. The other Doland children, ages 7, 12, 15, and 19, all were in school. In contrast, the household was home to 7 other young people, boarders under 19 years of age, who went to work daily in the cotton mills. Elizabeth Doland kept house for 43 people with no domestic help other than the help which her own children surely must have given her; her "wages" were the rewards of seeing her own children remain in school when so many other young people went into the working world at a young age.[7]

Other boardinghouse families were not so fortunate as the Dolands.

William George and his wife, Sally, kept a boarding house, but, of their 3 school-age children, only 1, Clara, 9, remained in school. Perhaps it was necessary for the George children to go to work at an earlier age since their father did not work outside the home, perhaps an indication of some physical disability. Certainly without an outside income, this boardinghouse keeper and his wife would have been hard pressed to keep three children in school with only the income from one 22 year old child to support the family. Another case of a worker whose wife kept a boardinghouse while he worked was that of Calvin Corliss. Corliss worked as a laborer while his wife, Caroline, kept house for the 3 children, aged 2 to 15, and 27 boarders, one of whom was a domestic servant, helping Caroline Corliss to tend to the family "business." The Corliss' 2 older children, including 16 year old Ellen, were in school, while 2 other 16 year olds in the Corliss household, boarders, both went off to work daily as weavers in the mills. Again, here was a worker's family whose "supplementary" income from the family boardinghouse allowed the children the luxury of remaining in school until their late teens. Having young people their own ages, or younger, in the same house who went off to work daily in the mills must have reinforced awareness of the fortunate position of such children.[8]

Some farmers found, in large old farmhouses, a readymade supplemental business. Allen Nutting and his wife held farmland, a working farm, valued at $1,500. Nutting worked hard on the farm and was assisted by his 5 younger children, aged 4 to 16. His eldest two children, Eben, 16, who had just left school, and his older sister went off to work every day in the mill as weavers. In addition to the part-time work of his children, performing chores around the farm, Nutting had other help. Myron Bailey and Calvin Richardson both worked for Nutting as farm laborers and boarded with him. Both men had wives living with them in the Nutting household, and both of these farm laborers' wives went off to work daily as weavers. In addition to working in the mill, Mary Richardson had to care for her son, Edward, 9, who, like the younger Nutting children, went to school during the day and helped out with "chores" after school. In addition to her own family of 9, the Richardson family of 3, and the Bailey family of 2, Mary Nutting had 15 boarders to look after—a major task, but also a major contribution to the family budget. Other farmers, like Asa Libby, 62, either found boarders a useful way to supplement farmland that was increasingly less profitable or found the income from boarders a welcome way of supplementing their estates in their old age. Libby lived with his daughter Lucy, 21, who worked for the mills as a dresser and helped her father keep house for 7 boarders, all of them, like the Libbys, native born.[9]

Three industrial workers (a master mechanic, a dyer, and a weaver) kept small boarding houses, while a much more common occurrence was boarding within a family. Fourteen households in the sample took in boarders, but did not run a "boardinghouse." That is, 14 families took in from 1 to 4 boarders as a means of supplementing the family income, but did not run large-scale boardinghouse operations. Silas Hamilton's practice was common. Hamilton, a master mechanic, born in Maine, had come to Manchester to work for the Amoskeag shops. In Manchester, he met and married his wife Emily, 2 years younger than himself, and purchased a small home where he lived with his young wife and 1 year old son and took in 1 boarder, a 39 year old dresser for the Amoskeag. Levi Watermann, likewise a master mechanic, bought a small home where he, his wife and daughter, and one boarder, a young woman who was a weaver in the mills, lived. A sign of affluence was the single family, living in a separate single family dwelling without boarders or lodgers. A sure sign of affluence was the household that could afford to live in this way while maintaining a domestic servant. One such household was that of Charles S. Richardson. Richardson was 33 years old in 1860. He lived in a house valued at $2,500 with his wife Mary, 31, his sister Mary, 24, a school teacher, and his daughter Maggie, 2 years old. In addition, the Richardsons had a maid, Johanna A. Keefe, 27, an Irish servant who lived in the household. Richardson could well afford to have a servant. He began work for the Amoskeag as a youth and, from 1841 to 1854, he benefitted from contracts with his uncle who was the paymaster and cashier for the company, handling huge sums of cash and being well rewarded for his services, both in terms of salary and in terms of prestige and power. Richardson was so well-regarded by his employers that he was able to name his own successor, and appointed his nephew who served for 45 years. His neighbors and associates would refer to him as "Mr. Richardson;" only E. A. Straw, who would be his only local superior, would dare to call him "Charles." It is worth noting, though, that the things that set Richardson apart from his fellow townsmen were as much attitudinal as material. Richardson did not use his superior income to set himself off from the workers of the town, and his neighborhood included the very households that have been thus far discussed. The number two official of the Amoskeag lived alongside mechanics, watchmen, weavers, machinists, and seamstresses. While none of his immediate neighbors kept large boardinghouses, there were such houses literally within a stone's throw of Richardson's home. For Richardson, it was a decided advantage to live in close proximity to the company's counting house, and if that meant living among the factory workers, then there seems to have been no stigma attached, at least not in 1860 or previously. It should be noted, though, that most of Richardson's neighbors were native born. Two householders were born in England, one in Germany, and one in Canada, although the Canadian household was located at some distance from Richardson's and the larger boardinghouses, some of which were run by French Canadians, were some distance away from the Richardson household. Richardson's immediate neighbors were good, solid, skilled workmen including master mechanics who lived on either side of Richardson. One can well imagine the deference that would be accorded young Maggie Richardson as she grew older. It would be a safe bet that her playmates treated her with the same deference accorded E. A. Straw's son, Herman.[10]

Those of Charles Richardson's working neighbors who did not take in boarders most often made ends meet by living in two-family housing. Ten such multiple family houses existed in the Richardson neighborhood, and firemen, mechanics, master mechanics, carders, and general "operatives" lived in such houses. Usually those who lived in two-family houses did not take in boarders and generally had smaller households, most consisting of husband, wife, and 2 or 3 children. Even here, there was no hard and fast rule, though, and occasionally a master mechanic, like Daniel Pulsifer, could be found living with his family of 4 in the larger part of a two-family dwelling and taking in a temporary boarder. When this did occur, though, there were never more than one or two boarders, probably either because space limitations dictated that the number of boarders in such housing would be limited or because, paying a lower rental, families living in multiple dwellings were not compelled by economic necessity to take in boarders. It is worth noting that, in 1860 as previously, the single family house prevailed outside of the company-owned boardinghouse district. Such houses may have been adapted to meet the large demand for workers' housing and the financial compunctions urging householders to take in boarders, but it is worth recognizing that there was a wide variety of different types of housing, and not all conformed to the "system" advocated by the mill operators.[11]

If the existence of non-company owned housing for workers on a wide scale indicates that the officially proclaimed "system" had many holes in it, then there are other such indications as well. Fire companies were voluntary and, theoretically, exclusive. A man applied for membership in the volunteer companies, was investigated by fire officials, and had to serve an apprenticeship. The greatest honor that the fire companies could bestow upon a member was allowing him to pull the hand-tubs to the fires. In practice, though, social control broke down. There were two bells in town used to alert fire company members of a fire. The problem with this system was that all of the town's residents were alerted, and not all were content to remain in their places. In fact, when an alarm was sounded, the ancient "honor" of pulling the ropes of the pumpers fell to whoever grabbed the ropes first, and the men and boys of the town, fire company members or not, fought for control of the ropes, leaving their places in the factories and mills to rush to join the "exclusive" membership of the official volunteer fire companies.[12]

The older social order had broken down in other ways, too, and in spite of family-centered boarding where, theoretically, the head of a family would oversee the boarders in his household, Manchester in the 1840's and throughout the 1850's sometimes seemed much like the popular image of the wild west. Clergymen of all denominations were concerned with the atmosphere of saloons, gambling halls, bowling alleys, and dance halls. One Catholic clergyman made a practice of patrolling the town regularly once a week looking for "the Saturday night dance," and, upon finding it, broke in with his walking stick swinging, preaching damnation to all. Although not so "activist" in opposition to such activities, Congregational clergymen regularly warned their flocks of the consequence of dancing, portraying in vividly realistic terms the torments of hell that awaited those of the congregation who frequented dance halls, pool halls, or saloons.[13]

By 1860, there was a good deal of evidence to indicate that the older social controls had indeed broken down in spite of the noble efforts of both Protestant and Catholic clergy and civic leaders. The U.S. Census for 1860 revealed more than one "house of ill fame" practicing openly and prospering. In the house kept by Lucy T., 29, there were 7 prostitutes, all younger than Lucy. The significant thing about these women, ranging in age from 18 to 28, is that all except the two youngest reported substantial property accumulations, ranging from $200 for one girl who called herself a "fancy woman" to $5,400, which had been accumulated by one of the older women. They practiced their trade openly and prospered in a town that still officially preached and tried to enforce a stringent morality. There is other evidence, too, of the behavior that so alarmed the clergy and corporate officials. In 1855, Manchester's volunteer fire companies had sponsored a regional fireman's muster. The fire companies were manned by men who were given "an honor reserved for men of proven leadership in the community." Several hundred of the visiting "community leaders" rioted in Manchester after having been cheated at cards in one of Manchester's gambling saloons. Contemporary descriptions of the firemen's riot resemble popular television images of the wild west. There were gunshots in the street, drinking, looting, and saloon keepers defending their "hotels" with loaded shotguns. This certainly was a far cry from the "official" portrait of the factory town portrayed by the corporate officials. Behind the concern of the clergy there lurked the real problem of a high rate of illegitimacy, gambling, heavy drinking, and the resultant perception of moral decline. The Amoskeag did not give up the fight. Its introduction of steam fire engines (which it manufactured and sold to the town) in 1859 was probably aimed as much at reducing the need for large volunteer fire companies as it was at increased efficiency. The new equipment required fewer men, since no hand pumping was involved, and men with greater skills operated the specialized equipment, thus preparing the way for professional, paid fire fighters.[14]

If the Amoskeag intended to continue to fight what it regarded as a loosening of the official "system," there were others who preferred to give up the fight and acknowledge that times had changed and moral standards appropriate for an earlier age might best be surrendered. The local YMCA, a group originally dedicated to fighting gambling, drinking, non-corporate boarding, and "idle time" for workers, dissolved in 1860, apparently feeling that its efforts were in vain. When reformed, years later, the "Y" would have slightly altered goals. The voluntary societies that would emerge in increasing numbers during the late 1860's and early 1870's would have a different focus: status preservation or improvement for the middle class, recreation and self-improvement for the middle class and the more skilled or favored workers, and help for the deserving poor. The post-Civil War constituencies served by voluntary organizations would change drastically. [15]

Before the war, the native born unquestionably dominated the town. Some extent of the power of the native born in Manchester can be gleaned by the formation of a separate "Irish Regiment" from Manchester to fight in the Civil War. While local histories make a point of praising the commander of the Irish Regiment and noting his military promotions, most "heroes" were native born. After the war, the importance of the foreign born would change. Because of sheer numbers, foreign born residents would change the nature of the town in the late 1860's and early 1870's. But, as of 1860, the foreign born composed only 6.1% of the population, statewide. Their weight locally was much greater, though. The foreign born composed over 27% of Manchester's population on the eve of the Civil War, and most of Manchester's foreign-born were of one background: the Irish represented the greatest number of foreign-born residents by far (see Table 5.2). [16]

While the shutdown of textile operations during the Civil War was a disaster in some respects, it was an innovating force in other ways. Pressed to look toward new means of keeping their investment productive, the factory owners sought out all possibilities and some of the options considered involved greater use of European raw materials, European methods of production, and European workers. The Amoskeag sent agents to Europe to seek out alternatives to cotton and to some limited extent these agents were successful. They were more successful in finding skilled workers, though, who could be induced to come to Manchester to utilize their specialized knowledge. Some English woolen workers were brought to Manchester during the war as were highly skilled German gunsmiths. This latter group was a particularly valued immigrant group since the Amoskeag received a major rifle contract shortly after the outbreak of hostilities. This enabled the company to remain in operation, although on a different basis and with a different group of workers. The skilled machinists who were not of military age were, of course, retained and to some degree augmented by similar men who were transferred from the textile mills to the machine shops. The women workers and unskilled men were not so fortunate: for them there could be no substitute for the shutdown of the cotton mills. In 1860, on the eve of the war, textile operations accounted for 72.3% of Manchester's work force of 7,707, employing 50.5% of all male workers and 87.4% of all women (see Table 5.3). There was no other single industry that could possibly absorb the numbers of workers thrown out of work by the closing of the textile mills, although the official company history of the Amoskeag boasted of the extent to which workers could be shifted from textiles to machine shop operations. This policy applied only to men, and even then it was severely limited. For many native born women, the alternative to working in the mill remained returning home, and the likelihood that such women would return to the mills once the supply of cotton was refurbished after the war was extremely small. Many of the native born who left town either to return home or to fight in the war did not return, and when the mills started up again, they would rely on foreign born help. The experience with foreign born workers, particularly with the German gunsmiths, encouraged the Amoskeag to seek out more foreign born help.[17]

The best single example of the company's policy of encouraging foreign born workers came immediately after the war. Having had good luck with the English skilled textile workers and with the Germans, the Amoskeag decided that it would rely on skilled Scots weavers as the spearhead of its efforts to diversify its product line and introduce a wider variety of high quality textiles. In 1868 and again in 1870, the Amoskeag sent an agent to Glasgow and other areas in Scotland to recruit "girls" to come to Manchester. On the whole, the Amoskeag's experience with the Scots weavers would be a good one, and, by 1880, many of the original group remained in the employment of the company, having induced some of their fellow countrymen to come on their own. By 1880, over 90% of Scotland-born workers in Manchester were engaged in textile employment.

In seeking out the "Scots girls," though, experience was not the only criterion that the company applied. Embued with the company's continuing sense of paternalism, the Amoskeag agents in Europe insisted on references regarding each girl's employment record, her moral character, her belief in God, and her reputation in the community. Letters from pastors, neighbors, and employers were gathered for all prospective employees. Those "Scots girls" who were selected for employment were advanced their passage to America, and, in 1868, sometimes a clothing allowance or, in rare cases, money for personal expenses. E. A. Straw and other local leaders regarded themselves as the descendants of the Scots-Irish settlers of old Derryfield. If the future held a labor force of immigrant workers, they would have preferred these Scots workers.

Paternalism, though, was not charity, and the Amoskeag competed in a market with other firms. Once working in the factory, the Scots girls would be required to pay the Amoskeag back for the amounts "advanced" to them for their passage and expenses. The company calculated that the girls owed $2,106.45 collectively from the 1868 recruitment and $1,409.36 from the 1870 group. In some cases, the girls paid the company back by cash (deducted from their wages each month for up to 11 months), and in other instances payment was "by allowance"—a certain portion of their debt being cancelled for each month that they remained with the Amoskeag. Clearly, the Amoskeag wanted to encourage the Scots back home in Scotland who might be tempted to come to America to follow their fellow countrymen to Manchester. Business was business, though, and the company did not always recover the amounts advanced, a fact which caused the company to tighten up regulations for the second group, the girls who came in 1870, and eventually to abandon sponsored migration as a company policy.

Of the 44 girls brought over in 1868, the company recovered costs in full for 34. For ten others there was a loss. Dorothea M. had received her passage and an allowance for four yards of cloth. In spite of the carefully gathered references, character checks, and interviews, Dorothea never paid back a cent of the $51.30 that she owed. Mary B. had received passage and 30 yards of cloth. For Mary, the company had advanced $58.79, perhaps an index of her desirability as a worker, but it recovered only $5.25. Undoubtedly, Mary found her skills in demand at other companies as well, or perhaps, once in America, she chose to live with relatives, to marry, to move to a larger city, or to pursue whatever she wished. For other girls, the company I.O.U.'s also proved insufficient inducement to stay in the factory. Agnes R. had been advanced passage, cloth, and ready made clothing, incurring a debt of $51, but she stayed in the factory only long enough to repay $15. Similarly, Agnes D. worked during July and August of 1868, paying back $10 of her $45 debt and then she left the factory (and probably the city). All in all, the Amoskeag lost slightly over $300 on the 1868 "girls." The reasons as to why those who left chose to do so were not recorded. Some few seem to have had little intention of remaining in the factory at all, while others lasted a few months before leaving, thus perhaps indicating that the work was more than they could take. Surely no girls would have defaulted on a debt to the Amoskeag and remained in the town that was dominated by the company.

In spite of a few bad experiences, the company was pleased enough with the 1868 migrants to sponsor a second recruitment expedition to Scotland. But the company had learned something from its first "generous" approach, and probably from the large number of non-Scots immigrants who were pouring into town in the late 1860's. The 1870 recruitment effort followed the careful screening process in Glasgow just as had the effort of two years previously. The 41 "Scots girls" who came in 1870, though, were each advanced exactly $37.25 in passage and cloth allowance. The 1868 recruitment had witnessed 10 girls who defaulted on repayments. The 1870 recruitment showed only three reported defaults. One of these, Margaret M., complained personally to E. A. Straw, the final authority in the Amoskeag's world, that she had been unjustly charged by having her passage deducted from her wages when, in fact, she had prepaid her own passage in Scotland. Upon investigation, Margaret's claim was upheld and deductions from her pay were halted. Hence, there were actually only two defaults among the 1870 workers. Clearly, the company had learned a lesson from its first encounter with the problems of the "labor agent" and kept more careful control over both its advances and its collections. Having once been burned, the agent sent to Scotland was careful to inquire into the credit reliability of each "sponsored" migrant.

Two years earlier, some of the girls had been able to drive a hard bargain. Two of them, indeed, had insisted on passage being advanced for a "companion," presumably a relative, as well as for themselves. In 1868, the company felt that it so sorely needed these workers that it went along with such terms. By 1870, while still encouraging Scots' migration, the company was less willing to pay the price asked by the girls and was more insistent upon its own terms. Each girl was advanced her passage, and her passage only. No longer could a particularly desirable worker drive a hard bargain to obtain supplies or clothing and passage was certainly not to be advanced for a companion![18]

By 1870, the Scots girls could not bargain with the company because it was becoming clear that the company could get all of the workers it needed, skilled or otherwise, from other groups and it would not be necessary to send special agents to induce foreign workers to emigrate. The ethnicization of Manchester was underway. Within another ten years, the city census takers would make marginal notes designating certain streets by ethnic inhabitants. For Manchester's foreign born, residence in their new city home was to be in "urban villages," with large clusterings, by ethnic group, in certain sections (see Tables 5.4-5.7).

Both native born areas and the newer immigrant neighborhoods experienced substantial growth rates during the late 1860's and early 1870's. As the foreign born moved into an area, it would seem that the native born moved out, while the influx of foreign born workers into the city accounted for much of the growth in immigrant neighborhoods. By 1870, 30.4% of the city's total population was of foreign birth. Considering that many "natives," though, were the sons and daughters of the foreign born, the true influence of this group was far in excess of what the statistical data reveal. As the Amoskeag's management had anticipated, immigrants composed a significant part of the factory work force after the re-opening of the mills. Most of these workers were, as later tables will show, Irish, but French Canadians would begin migrating to Manchester in numbers about 1868, and by 1871, there would be 2,500 French Canadians in the town. Large numbers of foreign-born workers enabled the mills to grow even further as the overwhelmingly dominant employer. For both men and women there were fewer non-textile jobs after the mid-1860's. For women, the situation was particularly dismal, since 94.5% of Manchester's 4,100 working women, in 1870, worked in the textile mills. Things had not been that much better in terms of employment opportunities ten years earlier, but by 1870 it was a fairly sure bet that, if a woman worked outside the home, she worked in the cotton mill. In 1860, a woman might work in a shoe factory or stitching ready-made clothing, but these markets for the work of women had either shrunk or failed to grow at a rate corresponding to that of the cotton factories. The story was much the same for men. Of all other available work opportunities for men, not a single one grew in the decade of the 1860's, while the textile factories experienced great expansion. In 1869, the Amoskeag, assured of success in its new markets, opened another major mill building—mill number 7. This prosperity would continue during the 1870's, and the Amoskeag would erect another two major mill buildings in that decade. In addition, the Amoskeag had begun to divest itself of non-textile subsidiaries such as the locomotive works that had grown out of its machine shops, and concentrated increasingly on textiles alone. The company also began to employ children workers in spite of its earlier stance against such a practice (see Table 5.8).[19]

With a drastic population turnover, a concentration on a new textile market, the consolidation of the Amoskeag into a textile manufacturing company and the divestiture of machine tools, locomotives, and engine works, plus the new immigrant work force, Mancheser was a very different town after the mid-1860's. It is important to learn how Manchester's new immigrant workers affected the distribution of wealth and power in the town. To what extent did this new group of workers share in property ownership? To what extent did they participate in "higher level" jobs? To what extent did the company alter its earlier tradition of paternalist supervision? The U.S. manuscript census returns for 1870 and 1880 provide one of the best resources for the exploration of some of these questions. For 1870, the city's most heavily "immigrant" section will be chosen for computer analysis of the census returns. For 1880, such an area, consisting of industrial workers of first and second generation immigrant background will be contrasted with a heavily "native born" section. The 1880 data, being more complete and enabling the researcher to ask questions about longer range processes, will be considerably larger than the 1870 data. It will be the task of the remainder of this chapter to analyze the

1870 data. This data was drawn from the heavily immigrant neighborhood surrounding St. Anne's Church, Manchester's first Catholic church and, until the year after this sample, Mancheser's only Catholic church. At St. Anne's, the older Irish and the newly arriving French Canadians temporarily subsumed the differences that would eventually break out into open hostilities, causing the French Canadians to form their own church in 1871 and eventually to move into their own neighborhood on the opposite bank of the Merrimack. In 1870, though, French Canadians, Irish, and other immigrant groups settled together in the area surrounding the church, held together by the common hostility of the native settlers. This hostility was so openly expressed that the church held periodic "open house" days at the convent, inviting prominent townsmen to tour the facilities in order to counter rumors and head off hostilities.[20]

A sample of 958 out of an enumeration district of 3,170 from the 1870 census reveals that 56.6% were native born while 43.4% were foreign born (see Tables 5.9, 5.10). This compares favorably with published census data which reveals an overall balance of 44.6% native and 55.4% foreign born for the district. What the published census statistics conceal, though, is the true extent and nature of this "urban village." Whether of native or foreign birth, 94.2% of all residents of this district had a father of foreign birth, while 83.5% had a mother of foreign birth.[21] What the published data conceals is the fact that, for this particular district, "native born" has but one meaning: second generation immigrants. Realizing the hostility of the town, fathers and sons chose to live side by side in a cohesive community, avoiding other areas of town and avoiding company housing where, on paper anyway, biblical instruction and other forms of cultural supervision which would not square well with a new set of workers was still the official policy.

Clearly this was a group of first and second generation immigrants. Compared to an earlier group of factory workers. the immigrant worker would encounter many disadvantages. He participated in property ownership to an even lesser degree than did an earlier generation of "newcomers." His children went to work at an earlier age, and the likelihood that his wife would work in the factory was greatly increased. One real disadvantage encountered, especially in the first generation, was the problem of literacy (see Table 5.11). As many as 40% of the first generation had literacy disabilities.

There was a substantial difference in literacy rates between the first and second generations. For the second generation there was virtually no illiteracy. Children stayed in school until age 10 and acquired basic literary skills. (see Table 5.12). This phenomenon can be accounted for by the unwillingness of the textile mills to employ children under the age of ten, but the attitudes of parents should also be considered. It is quite possible that parents, experiencing the considerable disadvantages of illiteracy, determined that their children would acquire at least minimal skills. Once children did acquire these skills, though, they were taken from school and put into the textile mills to help support their families.

Children remained in school until age 10, after which they began leaving school to work in the factories. As is clear from looking at the employers of child labor, 89% of children officially reported as employed were employed by 3 firms—all textile manufacturers (see Table 5.8, p. 135). In the sample group, no children over age 15 remained in school, whereas in a smaller sample drawn 10 years earlier (see discussion earlier in this chapter) children remained in school after age 12, even if this meant some sacrifices on the part of parents. The parent-child groups from the 1860 sample, although engaged in industrial occupations, were primarily native born and not first or second generation immigrant workers. In 1860, the Amoskeag enforced its policy of not hiring "child" labor (a child for these purposes being under 15 years old), but ten years later, as is evident from the 1870 manuscript census of manufactures, that official policy, like so many others, although still on the books, was not enforced. The increasing numbers of children in school for 3 to 4 years, between the ages of 6 and 9, probably reflect the values and needs of parents as well as corporate employment policies. For parents who either could not read or write themselves or who had peers who had such problems, the disadvantages imposed by a lack of literacy were obvious. Perhaps some parents wanted a family member who could assist in those tasks requiring literacy: checking up on the accounts of a local storekeeper's bill, reading the newspaper, filling out forms or writing letters. Others may have determined that, in spite of the financial difficulties that lack of income from a potential working family member would bring, some minimal literacy was essential to children's survival. Parents may have feared legal repercussions, either directly or through their employers, if they totally neglected the education of their children. For whatever reasons, the children of the second generation achieved a literacy that was denied to their parents on a broad scale.[22]

The "new" residents of 1870 continued the older pattern of residence in detached dwellings designed for single households. Of the general sample, 86.6% lived in such housing, while 10.2% lived in two-family housing. Among textile mill workers, there was a similarly high rate of residence in detached dwellings. 86.4% of mill workers in the 1870 sample lived in single family housing, while 10.5% lived in dwellings designed for 2 families and 3.1% lived in housing designed for three or more households (see Table 5.13). Thus, a pattern of residence that had prevailed since before large scale industry came to town lasted down to 1870. Changes would take place during the '70's, though, and, by 1880, single family housing would account for only 17.6% of the housing in the town's most heavily immigrant industrial area. Housing for four or more families—the tenement house—would house almost 20% of workers by the end of the 1870's.

One can only speculate on the extent to which boarding helped to maintain the detached house as a way of life. While household relationships are not clearly specified, it appears that as much as 30%, or slightly more, of the 1870 sample may have consisted of boarders. If the post-war generation of workers —immigrant workers—did not utilize the added income from boarding to keep the family's children in school for a few additional years, as had been the case in 1860 for a group of native-born workers, then it is conceivable that such income may have been utilized to stave off the move to a "tenement," an experience that was becoming increasingly common with factory workers in Manchester throughout the 1870's.[23]

Although single household residences predominated, it is striking how few of the householders owned their own houses. Of the 226 households selected for analysis, 21, or fewer than 10%, owned real property and only 25, slightly over 10%, reported ownership of personal property. For most men and women, property ownership was not to be attained. This was especially true for the mill worker. Textile workers composed almost 41% of the sample population, but were only 23.8% of the property owning group (see Table 5.14) and only slightly over 1% of textile workers would own real property. Looking at the percentage of textile workers who owned property among the whole sample, it is even smaller, composing about half of 1%. Of those who did own property, though, it can be said that there was a wide variety of different occupations. Five day laborers, 3 general textile operatives, 2 cloth printers, 2 inn keepers, a hat shop operator, an engineer, a stone mason, a bricklayer, and a baker are among the variety of occupations represented by this small "elite." Of the 21 property owners, 17 were first generation foreign born and 16 of those were Irish. If few of Manchester's new residents would own property, then even fewer of the sons would have acquired any stake in property ownership by 1870.

The fact that there was so little distribution of property among mill workers does not mean that they were not working to further themselves economically. A large number of wives and daughters went into the work force, i.e., they went to work in the mills. Fifty-seven percent of Ireland-born women worked in the mills. Undoubtedly some of the 41.8% of such women who stayed out of the work force were housewives who remained out of the work place either by choice or because of the temporary demands that child-rearing placed upon them, but this figure also includes children, the aged, and the disabled. It is striking, then, that so many wives and daughters went into the textile mills. In table form (see Table 5.15), these figures reinforce the differences in employment opportunities between men and women. Irish men could and did find employment outside of the textile mills. Women were not so fortunate, and the alternatives, practically speaking, for women seem to have been to work in the mills or to remain at home. Some few women may have had a wider range of opportunities, but their number was extremely small.

Not only for women, but for the foreign born or in other ways less advantaged residents, factory work rather than a wider range of employment possibilities represented the major career choice (see Table 5.16). The town's least desirable and prestigious employment—textile operatives and unskilled and semi-skilled labor—was reserved for the foreign born, particularly, in 1870, for the Irish and for the newly-arriving French Canadians who would move into the factories in increasing numbers throughout the 1870's. The Irish composed 47.2% of the sample, but over 61% of the textile workers in the sample were Irish. Similarly, the French Canadians composed 3.8% of the population but 5.6% of unskilled textile factory labor. The more "favored" groups—such as the English who went into the machine shops as skilled machine operators or mechanics, or the skilled Scots weavers—composed 4.1% of the population, but only 3.9% of textile workers. The employment situation seems to have been best for those born in New Hampshire (this would also include second generation immigrants); these groups composed 38% of the population, but only 21.2% of the textile labor force. Like the Scots girls, the English present an example of occupational preferment (see Tables 5.17 and 5.18). A disproportionately high number of Englishmen were able to move into the ranks of skilled workers, while the Irish, too, having been in town as a group for some time, moved into the more preferred occupations. Of the 3 groups, the French Canadians reflected their status as the most recently arrived and least favored on the occupational hierarchy. French Canadian men moved into the least skilled and poorest paying jobs—jobs in unskilled labor and in the textile mills. It is significant that the English could afford to keep over half of their women out of the work force, while the Irish, and to a greater extent the French Canadians, could not afford to have non-working wives or daughters. Indeed, for French Canadian women there were only two alternatives: working in the textile mills or staying home to care for house and children, and a greater number went into the work force than stayed home.

Even among French Canadian males, there were few choices in terms of work. None could afford the luxury of being out of work, and between the two categories of textile work and unskilled labor, almost 92% of the French Canadian males in the 1870 sample can be accounted for. In part, the absence of French Canadian males from the ranks of the retired, unemployed, or disabled can be explained by the age structure of this population. In 1870, the French Canadian migration to the textile towns of New England had only recently begun, and those who came were the young and the healthy. The old and the disabled were either left behind or returned to Canada. Work in Manchester was work for those under 30—in many cases for those well under 30 years of age. Until the mid-1870's, it was rare that men and women stayed in the mills or moved into the mills as they grew older (see Table 5.19). The Irish, a group that had been in Manchester longer than the most recently arrived French Canadians or the English-Scots skilled workers, had the largest percentage of older workers, but even for the Irish, factory work was for the younger workers. More than any other occupational area, textile workers were among the youngest of the work force, and work in the mills was reserved for the young, the more recently arrived or less well-off immigrants, and for women (see Table 5.20).

The most "preferred" employment for men and women in their 20's and 30's was skilled and semi-skilled work, either in or out of a factory. Thirty percent of English workers moved into these areas, while 12.7% of the Irish did so, but only 8% of French Canadians were skilled or semi-skilled workers. The earlier work force "imbalance" between men and women in the overall work force had been resolved by 1870. Before 1870, women composed a much larger percentage of the work force, but by 1870 women outnumbered men by only about 8% (see Table 5.21). The changes that took place in the age and structure of the labor force over the 20-year period between 1850 and 1870 reflect the changes that took place in the town as a whole (see Table 5.22). Although women would continue to be a major factor in the labor force, the new workers came with their families and not as "mill girls" and they lived in neighborhoods organized by ethnic background and economic status. The earlier mixture of residents together regardless of economic status was becoming less common by 1870.[24]

In 1850, with predominantly native workers who had some options regarding their employment, the company policy against the employment of children was enforced for the Amoskeag and "encouraged" for other mills. By 1870, with a new set of workers of different cultural background who did not have the freedom of easily returning to their native villages, the policy of excluding children from the mills, although officially affirmed, was unenforced. The French Canadians and the Irish, like the New Hampshire townsmen before them, had to adjust to a new milieu. A rural people come to the factory, they lacked the official protection extended to a previous group of farm-background migrants and, as a result, they experienced, for the first time in Manchester's history, some unique disabilities. Their children left school in large numbers at a relatively early age to go to work in the mills. Their old people remained in the work force, unable to afford the luxury of retirement. More of their wives were required to work outside the home. In all occupational categories for which comparisons can be made, the age of the work force experienced a shift toward the young.[25]

Even given the general trend of an increasingly younger population, the age and sex imbalance (see Tables 5.21 and 5.22) in the textile sector of the town's work force is striking. In no other occupational category was there such a cluster of young workers nor such a large number of women workers as there were in the area of unskilled textile operatives. The mean age of textile workers was 23.1 years, while the median age was 20. Three children under 10 years of age worked in the mills: one 5 years old, one 7 years old, and one 9 years old. By contrast, the number of children in the mills shoots up dramatically when looking at children past the age of 9. Seven 10 year olds, ten 11 year olds, and eighteen 12 year olds worked in the mills. This phenomenon coincides nicely with the ages at which children left school (see Table 5.12). It is probable that two factors influenced this pattern of child labor: parental need for income from all family members able to work; understood, if officially contradictory, company practice: the 10 year old applying for work would not be given overly-close scrutiny. In addition to being younger, textile workers lived in larger households and had slightly more children than was the case for the general population (see Tables 5.23, 5.24).

In the pre-Civil War period, Ann Osgood had saved regularly for her entire career as a mill worker. Even with a "favorable" and seemingly benevolent employer, Miss Osgood had been unable to accumulate any property worth talking about, but she represents the fact that at least some very meager savings were possible for an earlier generation of mill workers. After the Civil War, far fewer textile workers were able to accumulate property. As reflected in the 1870 sample, only five textile workers had been able to acquire real estate and only three reported ownership of other forms of property. Given average wages of $34.42 per month and the fact that 93.9% of all households had one or more children, it is likely that most of the resources of the mill worker and his family were devoted to survival.

Even the income of the elderly was needed for economic survival. Of 34 persons over 60 years of age in the sample, 21 (61.8%) worked, but only one worked in the textile mills alongside the younger work force that prevailed there. Seventeen of this group worked at non-mill unskilled labor and 2 were skilled workers. Idle hands were clearly not a luxury that this new generation of workers could afford, either for its young or for its elderly. Foreign born workers lived in larger households than did the native born, and they had more children to support (2.8 versus 1.9).[26]

No longer did mill workers of this generation find company officials living in their midst. The "better" elements would not choose to live in the new ethnic village neighborhoods. No longer would men of status like Charles Richardson choose to live in the midst of working class housing in the new neighborhoods.

Clarke's 1875 history reinforces the picture of the social divisions that took place during the late 1860's and throughout the 1870's. Clarke included descriptions of "the finest residences" of the city—three mansions owned by a manufacturer, a merchant-politician, and a mill agent. Such men hardly had to worry about the encroachments of their less well-off neighbors, for their grounds ranged in size from 1 to 12 acres. Clearly these men did not choose to live among the working population, a practice that had gone out of fashion after the coming of the new workers.

The 37 "prominent men" whose biographies were sketched by Clarke likewise had little in common with the majority of their fellow townsmen. Only one man, a German, was foreign born, and all were distinguished from their fellow townsmen by their age, ranging from 41 to 86, much older than the town's average worker. These men were set off by profession as well (see Table 5.25).

The two physicians and the one clergyman included were intended to be representative of the honor traditionally due to those professions. But there were too many clergymen and physicians to "waste space" by cataloguing all of them when there were other men who had helped to shape the industry and values of the new town. The real values of the town were reflected in the remaining 34 men Clarke profiled. None were working class, all were businessmen. Clarke perceived that business was the order of the day and he paid tribute to the new order. Not once did he mention farming as a virtuous way of life except to praise the businessmen he profiled who had made the transition from farmers to businessmen. For Clarke these were truly "self made men." There were working farms in Manchester still and, as will be seen in the 1880 data, some did quite well, but they were regarded by the prevailing industrial spirit as representative of a bygone era and had nothing to contribute to the new image of a hardnosed business-oriented community which the many pieces of "boosterist" literature that began to pour from the presses during the 1870's tried to cultivate. To foster the image of a busy, no-nonsense town with a spirit favorable to material success, the "prominent men" who were put forth as "representative" by Clarke were among the most successful in town. In addition to their "primary" business activities as outlined above, these 34 men served together on boards of directors, in town office, in political activities (3:1 Republican), or in "association" with the textile mills (see Table 5.26).

Clarke's history was a celebration of the Manchester economy of the mid-1870's. The impression of a prosperous town with a varied economy where any man who worked hard could get ahead was deliberately fostered. Clarke described the variety of firms, independent of the Amoskeag, located in "mechanics row." There were 15 such firms, all small businesses, independently owned and prospering. Upon looking closer at such firms, though, it can be seen that 11 were involved in manufacturing supplies for use in textile mills: leather loom harnesses, bobbins, carding supplies, or machinery. Even for the 25 non-mechanics row firms discussed by Clarke, 8 or 9 were clearly dependent upon the mills.[27]

The booster literature was correct in its implication that many men did quite well economically in the business-oriented town. Few were foreign born, though, and none of Manchester's "representative men" were mill workers. Clarke and others chose to celebrate the prosperity brought by the mills while avoiding mention of the men, women, and children who worked in the mills. Social divisions were becoming firmer during the 1870's, and although they shared the same town with a huge number of unskilled textile operatives, men like Kidder and Clarke lived in a different world from that of the anti-dancing, anti-drinking, club-swinging Father MacDonald. For the Irish and French Canadian workers, life in Manchester was a matter of survival, of poverty, and of steadily deteriorating economic circumstances. For Kidder and Clarke, life in Manchester in the 1870's was happy and comfortable, involving dinners at the Masonic Lodges, speeches before the Odd Fellows, and the illusion of independence from the mills.

Table 5.1. 1860 Census Sample[28]

Sample Size: 531
Number of Households: 61
Number of Dwelling Units: 51
Range, Household Size: 1-43
Mean Household Size: 8.7

Table 5.2. Foreign Born in New Hampshire, 1860

	New Hampshire	Manchester
	N =	N =
Total Population	326,073	20,107
All Foreign Born	20,938 (6.1)	5,480 (27.3)
By Place of Birth (% of Total Foreign Born)		
Ireland	12,737 (60.8)	3,976 (72.6)
Canada	4,468 (21.3)	800 (14.6)
England	2,291 (10.9)	395 (7.2)
Scotland	741 (3.5)	153 (2.8)
Germany	412 (1.9)	
France	103 (.4)	
Other	186 (.8)	

Source: U.S. Census, City Records

Table 5.3. Work Force of Manchester, 1860[29]

By Industry

Textiles	72.3%
Boots & Shoes	6.5
Engine Works	5.8
Clothing	3.8
Stone Works	1.5
Machine Tools	1.3
Other	8.8

By Industry, By Sex

	Male	Female
Textiles	50.5%	87.4%
Boots & Shoes	7.3	5.9
Engine Works	14.3	
Clothing	1.5	5.4
Stone Works	3.7	
Machine Tools	3.1	
Other	19.6	1.3
N =	3,156	4,551

Table 5.4. Neighborhood Population, 1870

Area	Native*	Foreign-Born*	N =
A	62.1	37.9	4,084
B	76.1	23.9	2,460
C	82.3	17.7	4,296
D	74.3	25.7	4,073
E	44.6	55.4	3,170
F	81.4	18.6	3,253
G	54.5	45.5	1,660
H	82.0	17.9	540

*Expressed as percentage of total neighborhood residents

Source: U.S. Census

Table 5.5. Neighborhood Growth Rates, 1860-1870[30]

Area	% Native	% Growth Rate, 1860-1870
A	62.1	+21.4
B	76.1	- 1.8
C	82.3	+34.6
D	74.3	+18.3
E	44.6	- 0.9
F	81.4	+13.6
G	54.4	+61.0
H	82.0	+ 5.7

Source: U.S. Census

Table 5.6. Work Force of Manchester, 1860-1870, by Industry

	1860	1870
Textiles	72.3	81.6
Boots & Shoes	6.5	1.1
Engine Works	5.8	4.8
Clothing	3.8	2.1
Stone Works	1.5	.9
Machine Tools	1.3	2.0
Other	8.8	7.5
N =	7,707	8,320

Source: Census of Manufactures

Table 5.7. Work Force of Manchester, 1860-1870, by Industry, By Sex[31]

	Male		Female	
	1860	1870	1860	1870
Textiles	50.5	66.2	87.4	94.5
Boots & Shoes	7.3	1.8	5.9	.3
Engine Works	14.3	10.5		
Clothing	1.5	1.1	5.4	3.3
Stone Works	3.7	2.0		
Machine Tools	3.1	4.4		
Other	19.6	14.0	1.3	1.9
N =	3,156	3,800	4,551	4,100

Source: Census of Manufactures

Table 5.8. Employers of Children, 1870[32]

Firm	Number of Children Employed
Manchester Print Works	200
Amoskeag Mfg. Co.	134
Langdon Mfg. Co.	40
John Brugger, hosiery	25
Felton Brothers, shoes	10
A. P. Olzendam, hosiery	7
Gould & Spence, ropemakers	3
Alfred Fairbanks, chair caner	1

Source: Census of Manufactures

Table 5.9. Nativity of Sample District, 1870[33]

New Hampshire	38.0
Other U.S.	5.4
Ireland	47.2
Canada	3.9
England-Scotland	4.0
Other Foreign	1.2
N = 958	

Table 5.10. Parental Nativity, Sample District, 1870[34]

	Father	Mother
Native Born	5.7%	6.4%
Foreign Born	94.2	93.5

N = 958

Table 5.11. Generational Literacy, 1870

	Reading	Writing
Literacy, 1st and 2nd Generations, Combined		
Capable	79.4	76.6
Incapable	20.6	23.3
Literacy, 1st Generation		
Capable	63.7	59.1
Incapable	36.3	40.9
Literacy, 2nd Generation		
Capable	99.8	99.5
Incapable	.2	.5

Table 5.12. Age-Education, 1870[35]

% Persons	Age								
	5	6	7	8	9	10	11	12	13-15
In School	37.5	68.4	83.3	79.3	90.	52.2	41.2	26.7	0.8
Out of School	62.5	31.6	16.7	20.7	10.	47.8	58.8	73.3	98.2
N =	32	19	18	29	20	23	17	30	51

Table 5.13. Housing Patterns, 1860-1880[36]

	1860	1870	1880
Single Household	67.0	86.6	17.6
2 Households	33.0	10.2	47.0
3 Households		2.9	15.6
4 or More Households		.2	19.8

Table 5.14. Real Property Ownership, 1870[37]

	General Population	Textile Workers
Range	$700-7,000	$1,000-2,500
Median	$2,018	$1,900
Mean	$2,790	$1,780
Standard Deviation	$1,784	$ 584
N =	21	5
Sample Size	958	391

Table 5.15. Sex-Occupation Table, Irish Born, 1870[38]

	Semi-Prof.	White Collar	Skilled	Semi-Skill	Unskilled	Textile	Other
Male	7	1	19	5	59	89	9
	3.7	.5	10.1	2.6	31.2	47.1	4.8
Female			1		2	150	110
			.4		.8	57.0	41.8

Table 5.16. Nativity, Workers in Textile Employment, 1870[39]

Birthplace	% Textile Workers	% of Larger Sample
Ireland	61.1	47.2
New Hampshire	21.2	38.0
Canada	5.6	3.8
England-Scotland	3.9	4.1
Other Native	7.1	5.3
Other Foreign	1.1	1.3
N =	391	957

Table 5.17. English-Irish-Canadian Nativity, Occupational
            Comparison[40]

	Ireland	Canada	England
Professional			
Semi-Professional	1.5		2.6
White Collar	.2		2.6
Skilled	4.4		12.8
Semi-Skilled	1.1	1.8	2.6
Unskilled	13.5	13.9	10.3
Textile	52.9	61.1	38.5
Other*	26.3	22.2	30.8
N =	452	39	36

*Retired, housewife, umemployed included

Table 5.18. Foreign-Born Occupational Comparison, By Sex[41]

	Male			Female		
	Ireland	Canada	England	Ireland	Canada	England
Professional						
Semi-Prof.	3.7		5.0			
White Col.	.5		5.0			
Skilled	10.1		25.0	.4		
Semi-Skill	2.6	8.3	5.0			
Unskilled	31.2	41.7	20.0	.8		
Textile	47.1	50.0	30.0	57.0	66.7	47.4
Other	4.8		10.0	41.8	33.3	52.6

Table 5.19.   Foreign-Born Work Force by Age, By Ethnicity, 1870[42]

Age	Canada	Ireland	England
Under 30	69.4	61.6	66.7
30-49	22.3	26.4	33.3
50-59	8.3	6.3	
60 + Over		5.7	
		N = 527	

Table 5.20.   Occupational Categories by Age, 1870[43]

Age	Semi-Prof. & White Collar	Skilled & Semi-Skill	Unskilled	Textile	Not in Labor Force
Under 20	16.7	12.1	9.0	39.6	66.5
20-29	25.	50.	28.2	41.2	13.4
30-39	8.3	13.7	11.5	6.9	5.1
40-49	41.7	6.9	17.9	10.0	6.7
50-59	8.3	12.1	11.6	2.1	5.2
60 + up		5.2	21.8	0.3	3.1

Table 5.21.   Sex Balance, Manchester Work Force, 1850-1870[44]

	Male	Female	% Imbalance
1850	1,877	3,363	79.2
1860	3,156	4,551	44.2
1870	3,800	4,100	7.9

Table 5.22. Occupational Categories by Age, 1850[45]

Age	Prof.	Semi-Pro & Wht Collar	Farm	Skill & Semi-Skl	Unskill	Text.	Not in Labor Force
Under 20				.3	1.6		1.4
20–29	10.0	8.0	11.7	23.6	17.8	35.3	9.8
30–39	36.7	49.6	25.4	41.5	24.2	47.1	17.0
40–49	33.4	27.2	25.5	22.9	29.1	11.8	33.8
50–59	13.4	11.2	22.6	8.8	24.2	5.9	21.1
60 + Up	6.6	4.0	14.7	2.8	3.2		16.9
N =	30	125	102	284	62	17	71

Table 5.23. Household Size, 1870 [46]

	Textile Household	General Population
Mean Size of Household	9.215	6.699
Mean Number of Children	3.414	3.267

Table 5.24. Occupation by Sex for Sample District, 1870

Occupation Level	All	Men	Women
Professional			
Semi-Professional	.9	1.8	
Farm			
White Collar	.3	.7	.2
Skilled	4.5	9.7	1.2
Semi-Skilled	.9	2.0	
Textile	40.8	35.6	45.2
Unskilled	8.1	17.1	.4
Housewife	12.2		22.8
Other	3.3	33.1	30.0
None	28.1		
N =	957	444	513

Occupations After Excluding Housewife/None/Other[47]

Professional	-
Semi-Professional	1.6
Farm	-
White Collar	.6
Skilled	8.1
Semi-Skilled	1.7
Textile	73.4
Unskilled	14.6
N =	533

Table 5.25. Primary Occupations, "Leading Men," 1870[48]

Lawyers & Professionals	12 (32.4)
Mill Officials	6 (16.2)
Manufacturers	6 (16.2)
Bankers	5 (13.5)
Merchants & Commercial	4 (10.8)
Building & Construction	3 (8.1)
Clergymen	1 (2.7)

Table 5.26. Secondary Occupations, "Leading Men," 1870

Bank Directors	24	State Government	13
Business Directors	12	Federal Government	6
Mill "Association"	10	Church Activities	9
Local Politics	19	Subsidiary Manufact.	9

6

Neighborhoods and Accommodation

The late 1870's and early 1880's were years of confusion, division, and turmoil in Manchester. Like other towns, especially textile towns with a large unskilled factory work force, its working population was composed of "men in motion," large numbers of workers (and their families) who moved from town to town in search of work, higher wages, or better opportunities. Low wage jobs and a highly impermanent work force together with the pressures of immigration combined to make Manchester's working neighborhoods (and there were clear and distinct neighborhoods in Manchester by the late 1870's) unstable places to live, with the immigrant church being a great bastion of stability among a mobile work force. In Manchester's industrial district, one neighborhood was chosen as a sample. There were 379 households in the neighborhood in 1880. Of those, only 12 households, or 2.9% could be traced to 1870. While recent studies have led us to expect high rates of turnover among laboring populations, the Manchester data is alarming in that, at rates such as these, the population approaches a kind of total instability. The stable population of the town, then, would appear to be the solid middle class, the group reflected in newspapers, local histories, public office, and social organizations. This apparent division between a relatively stable middle class and a highly unstable working class is deceptive. In Manchester, there was another segment of the population that could legitimately be classified as "working class," and, for this group, population instability was substantially less than it was for the industrial factory worker living in the most highly impacted neighborhoods.[1]

In the 1840's, an active and bitter struggle had taken place between the older agricultural community and the new factory "village"—the intruders. As has been seen earlier, the industrial village prevailed in terms of political influence in the community. It would be a mistake, though, to assume that political defeat meant the death or disappearance of Manchester's farming community. To be sure, the old farms located in the path of the factories and the industrial settlement disappeared. The farmers, though, as opposed to the farms in the industrial settlement, are another question. They did not disappear; they moved to other parts of the city, and they stayed on over the years to a surprising degree. Even as late as 1880, it would be a mistake to think of Manchester as exclusively urban. To be sure, Manchester's factories were well on their way to becoming the world's largest cotton textile producers. Unlike some other textile towns, such as Lawrence, Manchester had enough land to accommodate both farmers and factory workers. Because of the Amoskeag's policy of encouraging compact industrial settlement and because of the necessity, given long hours, of living near the work place, there would remain enough "rural space" within the boundaries of Manchester, adjacent to the factory villages, to allow significant farming activity. The very existence of such an area also provided farmers with greater opportunities to move into the town's more desirable industrial jobs as well as providing the more favored of the work force of the factories with an important alternative to life in a constantly changing, often tumultuous, industrial neighborhood.[2]

Of the 226 households in Manchester's largest "rural" district, 64, or 28.3%, could be traced back to 1870. Moreover, 54, or 23.8%, could be traced back even further to 1860. This is a sharp and remarkable contrast with the industrial neighborhoods. There such continuity was virtually unknown. Manchester's "rural" district did not consist solely of farmers and their families. Many native born "Yankees" chose the rural district as a means of escaping from the turmoil and cultural alienation of the industrial neighborhoods. Usually such workers were the more skilled of the industrial population. As they had done in the 1840's and 1850's, Manchester's farmers put the idle hands in their families to work in the town's factories, and they supplemented their income by taking in industrial boarders. Shoemakers, mechanics in the mills, apprentices, teamsters, masons, unskilled factory "operatives" and day laborers—men and women of all these occupational categories could be found boarding with the town's farmers. Some former farmers had moved over into industrial occupations. For them, continued operation of a farm, on a limited scale, must have provided an emotional tie to their heritage as well as a sometimes lucrative sideline. All benefited by the relative stability of the rural district. For those who enjoyed this stability, there was a real economic advantage. They were able to wait on the sidelines, as it were, for the best job opportunities that the industrial structure of Manchester had to offer. Frequently their neighbors, Yankees like themselves, who were overseers or officials of the mills would provide them with "tips" on choice jobs in town.[3]

One man much cultivated by his neighbors was Frederick Lougee. A man with a reputation for being "on the rise" with the Amoskeag, Lougee lived, with his wife Mary, in the midst of rural neighbors and made the trek into the industrial area daily to perform his duties as one of the mills' chief overseers. Lougee chose to live in the rural part of town because of its very isolation—

both physical as well as cultural and esthetic—from the industrial neighbor-hoods. At 56 years of age in 1880, Lougee had been born in a rural area of New Hampshire of Yankee parents. As one of the Amoskeag's officials, he un-doubtedly could have lived anywhere in town. He chose to live among the na-tive born in a rural setting, and his neighbors would almost surely have bene-fited from his information with regard to job opportunities and from the built-in "introduction" that such a neighbor provided.

Lougee had begun work for the Amoskeag as a mechanic, a skilled worker. By 1860, he had risen to master mechanic and had managed to accum-ulate an estate worth over $2,000. By 1870, Lougee had become an overseer and stashed away another $1,700. In wealth, in prestige and position, and, increasingly, in cultural background, Lougee was set apart from the men and women whom he suprevised on a daily basis. Increasingly his work force was made up of immigrants, but he chose not to live with or near them. In this sense, he typified the standoffishness of the overseer. As the years passed when natives dominated the work force, overseers like Frederick Lougee would come to have less and less in common with the men and women with whom they worked.

Lougee did more than retain "emotional" ties to his farming past. While going off, day by day, to supervise the factory operations, he relied upon hired help as well as his own "spare time" labor to operate an active working farm. His farm of 36 acres was valued at $3,500, and he cultivated 8 acres on a regular basis. During the busiest times of the year, Lougee hired a farmhand to help out. He did not hire one of his rural neighbors, though, but employed a hired hand who made the reverse of Lougee's own daily trip: the hired man traveled to Lougee's farm daily for 20 weeks from the industrial neighborhoods and was paid $100 for the year for his labor. It is doubtful that many of his neighbors would have worked for that.

Frederick Lougee's farm did not make him rich. It was, in fact, an economic drain on his assets that didn't even pay its own way. Totaling the value of all of the farm's "produce," one sees a total yearly "income" of $193, of which, remember, $100 was paid out in labor. Most of this "produce" was probably consumed by the household. Certainly this was true of the 2 cords of wood produced. Likewise, the 50 bushels of apples and 4 bushels of peaches from the farm must have kept Mary busy washing, baking, and preserving. Other than this, the Lougee's farm produced 130 eggs, 25 bushels each of rye and oats and 6 tons of hay. In terms of a rational business investment, Fred-erick Lougee's farm was a poor choice for a man who was reputed to be business-wise: it didn't even return 50% of the more than $460 annual operating cost (exclusive of labor). Moreover, it required a lengthy trip to work each day and what must have been truly exhausting after-hours labor for a 56 year old man with a reputation for working tirelessly during the day in the mill. Clearly, the rural life was a labor of love. It represented an emotional and a cultural choice for a factory supervisor financially able to afford such a choice. His decision represents more than just personal whim, though. It symbolizes the social divisions that had come to prevail in Manchester between the immigrant and the native, the long term and the transitory worker, and the skilled (or favored) and the large numbers of unskilled in the factory's work force. Unlike the earier undifferentiated residential structure, by 1880, Manchester's neighborhoods each had their own unique character.[4]

Being substantially more "settled" than the industrial neighborhood sample, the rural neighborhood provided an important non-middle class element of continuity from year to year, especially given the day-to-day contact between rural residents and industrial workers. In the 231 households sampled, there were 41 non-farm boarders. The occupational breakdown of these 41 is telling (see Table 6.1, 6.2). In a work structure dominated by unskilled factory operatives, not a single one boarded with rural families. The simplest explanation for this involves time and distance. Given work days that approached 12 hours, factory workers would have necessarily preferred to live close to the mills. Rural peacefulness may not have been regarded as worth the long trek to the rural area.

The contrast between the rural district sample and the sample drawn from the district dominated by company owned housing is telling. Given long hours, Manchester's unskilled textile operatives lived as close to the mills as they could. Over half of the residents in this district were boarders, and almost 62% of these were unskilled textile operatives. At least as plausible as the explanation involving distance from the mills is the factor of nativity and ethnicity. A full 86.3% of the residents of the rural district were native born, and 75% were native born of native parents. In short, the Yankees had set themselves aside from the new immigrant working class neighborhoods. That is not to say that the native born did not work in the town's industries, but they did stay out of the lowest paying jobs!

The extent to which their longevity in the community gave the native born an edge is seen when comparing household status to occupation. Among heads of household, farming was the most prevalent occupation, with 41.1% of heads of households engaging in farming as their principle occupation (see Table 6.3). Fewer than a quarter of farmers' sons, though, followed in their fathers' footsteps once they were old enough to begin working (see Table 6.4). Farmers' sons went off to work in the industrial structure of the town, but, it is important to note, they did not take up unskilled textile factory work except for a brief period when they first entered the work place. They preferred skilled work and even unskilled, but remunerative, labor to the lowest level textile factory jobs. Like the sons, farmers' daughters and wives avoided the textile mills. In fact, farm and rural wives and daughters generally remained out of the labor market altogether. Over 95% of farm wives and 77% of daughters over 15 years of age remained at home. While income from these "extra" hands might have helped out, natives apparently felt aversion to the mills and were financially secure enough that they could keep their wives and daughters home.

The job patterns and choices of the rural district residents are worth further examination because of their importance as a stable population group in a sea of instability and also because of their closeness to the working population of the town. With intimate daily contact between Manchester's farming families and their relatives, neighbors, and boarders who went off to the industrial district to work daily, it is significant that only slightly more than 10% of farm sons entered the unskilled work of the textile mills. Being familiar with the opportunity structure that a mill town had to offer, seeing those opportunities since youth, farming sons of job age realized that the town had better jobs to offer than the unskilled work of the textile factories: these were seen as dead-end jobs, holding inadequate present rewards and little future. They preferred unskilled general labor in the construction trades (something for which the farm would have prepared them) to tending the textile machines. If they entered the factory at all, they did so at the higher skilled levels, perhaps taking advantage of their friendship with neighbors like Frederick Lougee to obtain an introduction, an apprenticeship, or an advantageous position.

Even farm daughters rejected the factory and were permitted to do so by their fathers. This stands in sharp contrast to the earliest days of the factory town when farmers from all of Manchester's neighboring towns wrote and "applied" in person to the factory agent, literally begging that their daughters, regarded as unproductive and a burden at home, be "given an opportunity" to work in the mills. By 1880, only 11.5% of farm daughters of working age (15 and up) would work in the factories, while an amazing 77% of farm daughters of working age chose to stay at home. Either unskilled textile factory work offered lesser rewards than did working at home on the farm (and, given the manuscript census data on the income for these very farms it is obvious that such was not the case) or, no matter what the financial incentive, factory work had either become degrading or was so conceived of by the natives. It is clear that, by 1880, farm daughters in the vicinity of Manchester could not be induced to work in the textile mills while sons used the farm as a springboard to the more preferred areas of employment in the textile town.[5]

Linking data from the manuscript census of agriculture with the manuscript census of population and with wage data helps to explain the choices of sons in the rural district. Of 114 active farms in the Manchester sample, the average or mean value per farm was $3,763. To be sure, this was far more than most men managed to accumulate in terms of an estate. In terms of a farm that produced enough income to live, though, small farms of this sort were simply inadequate. While the urban farmer may have been a relatively wealthy man on paper, when his earnings from the farm are compared to the annual earnings of other men in Manchester, it can be seen that the urban farmer did not fare so well (see Table 6.5). A very few farmers, to be sure, did do very well for themselves, but many others fared much less well both in absolute terms and vis-a-vis other occupational categories. Seventy-one percent of all farmers earned less than $450 per year from farming operations. For these men, the vast majority of Manchester's urban farmers, the temptation to send their daughters off to the mills to help supplement the family income must have been at least as real as it was for the farmers of the 1840's who begged for "opportunities" in the mill for their daughters. The temptation, though, as has been shown, was well resisted. Given farm income, it is easy to see why sons chose to go into non-farm occupations. Especially for skilled workers, yearly income and living standards would be substantially better than what could be expected from the farms. Thus the decision of farm sons to move off the farm in search of higher earnings makes sense. Moreover, the way in which farm sons went about making their move from the farm and into the industrial milieu gave them a real advantage. They were better prepared to take their place in the industrial job structure than were the sons of industrial district residents, odd though this may seem. Unlike the son of the industrial worker, the farmer's son felt no real pressure of time. He could afford to sit back and, with the advice of parents, family and neighborhood friends, wait for the best opportunities. Once those opportunities came his way, he would be there—on the spot and keenly aware of local conditions, markets, and personally familiar with important decision makers in the mill hierarchy. Given the transitory nature of the vast majority of the industrial population, this was a tremendous advantage.

The way in which the rural district sons could, and did, bide their time while their industrial counterparts were thrust into the job market can be seen in the differentials between ages of school attendance in the three areas (see Table 6.6). In the rural area, 62% of children ages 15-16 remained in school, whereas only 24.3% of the industrial district's children of this age group remained in school. Farm earnings, supplemented by income from boarders and from family members working in the factories enabled rural children to remain aloof from the work world of the factories for longer periods than was the case for the children of the residents of the industrial district. Relief from pressure to get out of school and into the job market meant that farm children would not be so pressed to take any available job in order to help out family finances.

For most farmers, continued life on the urban farm meant holding onto a way of life with which they were familiar and giving their children greater opportunities than could be the case should they abandon farming and move to the industrial settlement. There were larger, commercial farmers in Manchester in 1880, though. Some, like Frederick Allen with his $25,000 farm of 105 acres or Isaac Huse, with his $21,000 farm and his continued political presence, ran their farms as strictly a business, rather than an emotional and cultural, affair. For these elite few, farming was a very rewarding business, and they took their place beside the commercial and industrial elite of the town. For most, life in the rural district of the industrial city that Manchester had become by 1880 represented a kind of cultural continuity, involving isolation from the troubles of the industrial village, and, perhaps most importantly, ethnic solidarity among Yankees.[6]

The very existence of a "rural" and Yankee district in 1880 hints at the divisions that were glossed over in the boosterist literature of the town's commercial advocates. In the town's earliest years, there was hard fought conflict between rural and industrial values. The native born Manchesterites had struggled against a set of newcomers, also native born and usually New Hampshire born, whose presence seemed to threaten their way of life. While this initial conflict may have resulted in a transfer of political control and in the disappearance of some of the old farms, it did not result in any sharp residential differentiation; that is, distinct neighborhoods did not take shape much before the Civil War. Mill worker lived alongside mechanic and nearby farm laborers. With the coming of the Irish, things began to change. A process of neighborhood differentiation set in. Initially, this consisted of Irish textile workers who chose not to live in company housing, forming their own neighborhood centered around the first Catholic church in town. By 1880, that process of neighborhood differentiation was well under way. Distinct "urban villages" had taken shape and were continuing to be formed. The farming-rural district that has been examined so far in this chapter was simply one of those sharply distinct neighborhoods.

The city censuses of 1882 and 1884 recognized a kind of Balkanization of the city's neighborhoods. The city marshall divided the residents of *each street* in the city according to ethnic composition. In Ward 5, the city marshall made the following classifications:[7]

American	42.6%	Nova Scotia	.1%	Sweden	.2%
Canadian	25.4	New Brunswick	.1	France	.01
Irish	28.3	Prince Edward Island	.02	China	.07
German	.4	Newfoundland	.03		
English	2.0	Poland	.02	N = 8,022	
Scots	.8	Prussia	.01		

In a working neighborhood, these classifications reveal the ethnic background of the work force. Had this same census been taken four years earlier, the French Canadian population would have been significantly less. By the mid-1880's, the French Canadians were becoming a major element in the transformation of Manchester's textile work force, and in the formation and hardening of neighborhood lines. When the city's voting wards are utilized as a basis of classification, the ethnic nature of the neighborhoods becomes more clear (see Table 6.7).

Even the ward figures conceal the extent to which ethnic neighborhoods had taken shape in Manchester by 1880. The figures become more meaningful when broken down by street. From the ward figures above, it would seem that Ward 5 was a holding action for natives. In reality, though, many of the "natives" in this heavily immigrant working district were the sons and daughters of the foreign born, quite unlike Ward 8, for example, where the native born held off the influx of foreign born quite successfully.[8] Within Ward 5, the natives, Irish, French Canadians and English-Scots held their own on individual blocks and streets. Along that section of Elm Street, the town's main thoroughfare, for example, where it ran through Ward 5, French Canadians predominated with 60% of the residents. The Irish, who had formerly held sway along this portion of Elm Street, by 1884, composed only 10.3% (N = 1,044). Along Park Street, the situation was reversed, with natives composing 47% (and many, remember, were the children of the Irish), the Irish composing 35.9% of Park Street's population, and the French Canadians, having only begun to move onto Park Street, 13.5% (N = 1,042).[9] These figures reveal part of the process of transformation that was underway. The natives who remained in the most heavily industrialized districts were fighting a losing holding action, while the various ethnic groups, mostly Irish and French Canadians, staked out their own places in the city. This retreat from the new ethnics was what the existence of a separate rural district represented in 1880 (see Table 6.8). Altogether, 75.9% of the rural sample district was native born, with 55.5% New Hampshire born of native parents. Yankees, on the retreat from an industrial district overwhelmingly foreign born, set up their own neighborhoods just as did the Irish and the French.

Perhaps it was what they perceived as the disorganization of the new ethnic neighborhoods as much as the changing ethnic character of the older town that caused the natives to flee to the outskirts by 1880. Manchester had changed in many ways. Houses of prostitution, for example, operated more or less openly despite occasional well-publicized raids. Newspapers frequently named the women arrested in such raids, describing them in pejorative terms and often identifying them by ethnicity. The same was true for their customers who were usually charged with "disturbing the peace." The frequent occurrence of Irish and French ethnicity, either openly or implicitly, in such accounts detracted from the desirability of the ethnic neighborhoods.[10]

The French Canadians, only recently begun to arrive in Manchester in numbers, were frequently urged to "Naturalize!" in newspaper stories and editorials. The impression that French Canadians were undesirable or hopelessly incompetent was fostered by newspaper accounts throughout the late 1870's and early 1880's. One such account told of Mrs. D., the wife of a woodchopper who was employed by one of the town's textile mills. She was portrayed as a pathetically ignorant woman whose ignorance, negligence, and inability to speak English caused her, through careless blundering, to smother her child in bed. Newspaper accounts indicate the shock of the older community at a people woefully ignorant of child rearing practices and convey the disgust of the medical examiner who questioned Mrs. D. In order to question her, it should be noted, the medical examiner and the police had to communicate via an interpreter and their initial efforts were frustrated until they could find a "reliable" interpreter. Even more than had the Irish, the French Canadians, by their increasing presence, symbolized the social divisions that were coming to prevail in Manchester.[11]

The most striking thing, to the native mind, about the French Canadians was their inability to speak English. This language problem did not merely divide neighborhoods, it carried over into the work place as well. Mary L., "a French girl," went to work in the Amoskeag as an unskilled textile operative, perhaps as a bobbin girl, and was unable to speak a word of English or communicate with her Yankee overseer. Having obtained work, in 1878, when work was hard to get, especially for a non-English speaker, Mary was afraid to let on that she didn't understand the nature of the job or its dangers, and so she kept quiet when the Yankee overseer and second hand came by. The company was instituting a series of wage cuts (which would eventually result in a major labor disturbance by the mid-'80's), and Mary was careful not to give any excuse to a factory management eager to cut back. Not realizing what she was doing, Mary caught her long dress in the machinery and eventually required amputation of a leg. Girls like Mary were common in Manchester, and eventually the Amoskeag, like the medical examiner who examined Mrs. D's child, would have to face up to the language and cultural problems posed by immigrant workers.[12]

Without keeping in mind the continually widening influx of French Canadians, it would be impossible to understand the popularity of Kearneyism in Manchester during the late '70's and early '80's. Kearneyist speakers began to attract larger and larger crowds of workers as the mills instituted their wage cuts toward the end of the 1870's. Such speakers offered, via the ploy of blaming immigration, a quick and easy explanation of the mill workers' plight, and both skilled workers, who feared loss of their job status, and the unskilled, who saw the potential for tremendous wage cuts in their already low salaries lying ahead of them, were attracted to the Kearneyites. Dennis Kearney's accusing finger, pointed most blatantly at the Chinese (and, by implication, at other "foreigners" as well), won great popularity among Manchester's textile workers. The promise of a Kearneyite speaker was a sure fire way to draw a crowd in the late '70's. The Knights of Labor, active in Manchester in the late 1870's, used the popularity of immigrant exclusion to pack their rallies. At one point in 1878, they plastered the town with placards and posters announcing the visit to Manchester of Kearney himself, who promised to give a full and complete explanation to the textile workers of Manchester of their plight. While the "Kearney" meeting was packed, Kearney did not show up, nor, apparently, had there even been any plans that he would. Instead of the original, though, Manchester's workers heard one of the many Kearney imitators: the importance of controlling the foreign influx was linked with the evils of women and children competing with men for jobs.[13]

Manchester was a strange and ambivalent place in the late '70's and early '80's. It would appear that the town, in spite of the continued native political and commercial dominance, had made its peace with the Irish. An Irish mayor had been elected; the once embattled Father MacDonald was not only joined by a number of other priests, but achieved prominence and respect in the town at large. The Amoskeag had a number of Irish overseers and Amoskeag officials were to be counted in the ranks of the Irish. Regular newspaper accounts of Irish fund raising efforts, building committees, and fraternal events appeared as often as the "special" events of the older groups. News of preachers, revivals, and missionaries was about equally distributed between Protestant and Catholic denominations. The only sour note in the rapprochement that had taken place between the two groups after the Civil War was the issue of the undesirable French Canadians. Perhaps this helps to explain the appearance in Manchester newspapers during the late 1870's of such newspaper series as "The Escaped Nun," wherein an alleged former nun "exposed" the "unnaturalness" of her former faith. Appearing at a time when Yankee-Irish hostilities had visibly cooled and differences were being increasingly smoothed over, it would seem that the new wave of French Canadian immigrants and depressed employment conditions combined to stir old, seemingly forgotten prejudices.[14]

The coming of the French Canadians caused other problems anew, too, problems that the town had not seen since the years of heaviest settlement in the 1840's. An evergrowing municipal budget not only alarmed the town, but drove it nearly to bankruptcy in the late 1870's as fiscal responsibility became a major issue. The two major items of town expenditure that would become involved in the dispute were the two that related most directly to the problem of the new immigrants: schools and police. The one other major municipal department escaped budgetary scrutiny altogether. No one seemed to consider the fire department, long a corporation "pet," as a likely candidate for reduced expenditures at a time when such reductions everywhere seemed critical. First rate fire protection was essential to the textile mills, and the Amoskeag still controlled the town. The need to provide first rate fire protection was so essential to the Amoskeag, in fact, that the company laid out, designed, and built the city's reservoir and water distribution system. Similarly, whatever updating of the system was required in order to obtain first rate fire protection and advantageous insurance rates was done by the company. With this kind of official concern, coupled with the concern of the city's "boosters," there would be no tampering with fire department budgets![15]

Education, though, was something else. The beneficiaries of the city's school system was not the corporation, but the increasing number of immigrant children. The city's primary school teachers earned $35 per month, and there was concern about the increased number of teachers that would be required to deal with what was perceived as a prolific foreign element. In part, this problem was solved through the evening schools. These were schools intended mainly for "boys and girls" of school age who worked in the textile mills during the day, although adults who required education in literacy in order to pass the citizenship tests could, and did, attend as well. By 1877, the evening schools were thoroughly entrenched and offered a cheap way out of the problem of a rising population of school age children. In 1877, the evening schools held regular 21-week terms and enrolled 368 pupils, most of whom worked by day in the mills. School was held, of course, in the most heavily industrialized part of town, while in the native section day school went on as usual. In this way, children could leave school at about age 13 (see Table 6.6, for industrial district sample data), go to work in the mills at the lowest paid jobs, and still comply with state law. Here, again, as in the case of the town's kid glove treatment of the fire department, the town served the best interests of its bread and butter industry. This also helps to explain the popularity of the Kearneyist orators' complaints about women and children depressing the wage structure.[16]

The other area of budgetary controversy involved the police department, where expenditures had risen over 100% between 1867 and 1880. Since this department was not vital to the corporation and since cuts here would most adversely affect the transient population, the solution seemed simple enough. Salaries were reduced and police officers dismissed. The day had long since passed when the mills' chief financial officers had lived in the industrial district alongside mechanics, artisans, and mill operatives. In earlier years, when there had been no sharp "urban village" distinction between ethnic and occupational groups, a budget cut of major dimensions would have adversely affected the entire community and would have been unthinkable. By 1880, though, an increasing differentiation between districts, neighborhoods, and streets meant that measures that hurt one group might have little effect upon another group. The prostitution and crime associated with the working class neighborhoods and the rise of the foreign born barely touched the everyday lives of the elite, isolated natives. The natives were the group with the greatest year to year population stability and, as such, were a politically sensitive group. Not in town, or likely to be in town, long enough to have any say in local affairs, the industrial workers at the lowest levels could be safely ignored in terms of municipal services.[17]

The neighborhoods reserved for the comfortable and well-off and for the Yankees did not feel the sting of school budgetary policies or of police budget cutbacks. By 1880, some neighborhoods could be pointed out as reserved for immigrants or second generation natives by demographic characteristics alone. Manchester's factory work did not appeal to the delicate. It remained work for the young and the strong and it remained demanding and exhausting. As old age approached, workers got out of the most demanding, lowest paid textile work if they were able to do so (see Tables 6.9, 6.10). Here, again, the natives stood at an advantage; being on the spot, they seized jobs as mechanics, loom fixers, second hands, and other "preferred" jobs whenever they presented themselves. In Manchester's industrial sample district, 69.1% of the population was under 30 years of age in 1880, versus an under 30 population of 51% for the rural sample district. By comparison with their fellow townsmen who lived in a more relaxed atmosphere, Manchester's factory population showed a youthful imbalance. Not only were factory workers younger, but they had more children (hence felt the sting of "evening schools" versus the regular school system) than their non-textile or more skilled urban neighbors (see Table 6.11). They were also far more likely to live in multiple family dwellings versus the one or two family dwellings that prevailed in the less industrialized neighborhoods.

For those who were fortunate enough to live in the rural area, little had changed from 1860 to 1870 in terms of the physical pattern of life: the single family dwelling was overwhelmingly predominant in 1880, just as it had been in 1870 and 1860. In 1880, 89.3% of all rural district residents lived in detached, single family dwelling units. The remaining 10.7% (N = 920) lived in two family units. Such was decidedly not the case, though, for their townsmen who lived in the industrial sample district (see Table 6.12). There the picture was one of tenement houses creeping into a formerly less impacted setting. Only 17.6% lived in single family residences, while 5% lived in large tenement houses accommodating nine families. Not only do these district differentials point to a marked contrast between the way of life for the elites versus the way of life for the lower level factory workers, but, in terms of the factory operatives themselves, this represents a sharp change in living conditions from 10 years earlier. In a sample from a similar district (the boundaries of which were partly congruous with the 1880 industrial sample district) from 1870, it becomes apparent that it would have been almost unheard of for a tenement house, even for low income textile operatives, to contain more than three families (see Table 6.13). By 1880, almost 20% of the working district population lived in tenement houses containing four or more dwelling units—a situation that was unheard of 10 years previously, and that remained unknown in the "better" parts of town.

The decade of the 1870's saw a continuation of the post-Civil War trend of polarizing the population between the relatively affluent and the growing unskilled work force of immigrants needed to fuel the Amoskeag's phenomenal post-War growth. Now it would be out of the question for an Amoskeag executive to live, in an undifferentiated way, alongside common workers. Administrators, overseers, and the most highly skilled craftsmen together with the middle class separated themselves from the increasingly immigrant work force. They lived as they had in the past, in single or small multiple family dwellings, while the standard for non-corporation owned workers' housing became the multiple family dwelling (see Table 6.14). Those who lived in such housing were those who held the least skilled, least desirable jobs that the town had to offer. Moreover, they were the foreign born. Of the native born, those with foreign born parents were most likely to live in multiple family housing (see Table 6.15).

Not only in terms of crowdedness and new housing styles, but also in terms of annual income, the newly developed immigrant neighborhoods stood apart (see Table 6.16). In the rural sample district, 54% of the heads of household for whom annual income could be calculated earned less than $450 per year. In the industrial district, by comparison, 81.3% of heads of household earned below $450. This does not mean, of course, that there was not supplemental income from boarders, working wives, sons, daughters, or some other source. In fact, it is understandable, given the low income level, that there would be a powerful economic incentive, in the industrial neighborhood, to put every available family member, every idle hand, to his or her optimum economic utilization.

What the economic pressures of the factory district meant for wives was that 18% of them would go to work outside of the home and, in Manchester, for women, this meant work in the textile mills (see Table 6.17). Only 5% of farm wives worked in the mills. Likewise, sons and daughters found themselves put out of the nest and into the work place in order to help contribute to the support of their larger families. When daughters, especially, left the home to enter the work place, they went into the mills at the lowest skilled jobs: 98% of working daughters in the industrial district went into such jobs, while 68% of their brothers did so. Again, the contrast with their Yankee neighbors is striking. Only 9.5% of rural sons and 11.5% of rural daughters went into the factory. It should be pointed out, too, that those who worked at unskilled textile jobs were the immigrants: 57% of Irish workers worked in the mills, while the French Canadians, the most recently arriving group, found themselves in a position similar to that which the Irish had found themselves in 30-35 years earlier, with 71% of working French Canadians in the lowest paid textile mill jobs (see Table 6.18).

In spite of the industrial flavor of its residents' occupations, the company housing district was more similar to the rural district than to the immigrant neighborhoods in the dominance of the native born. Altogether, 79.6% of residents in this district were native born, and 68% were of a native born father (see Table 6.19).

The homes of the immigrant working population, in addition to being more "compacted" into tenements, were physically more crowded than the homes of their more fortunate Yankee neighbors. Manchester's transient working population had more household members and more children than did the settled population of the town. Both populations could legitimately be termed working populations, but the difference between the way of life led by each group was considerable. The Irish were emulating the pattern of the natives and trying to use networks of countrymen, neighbors, and kin to obtain "inside" information about the better jobs, the employment prospects, and looking always for a path to the more preferred jobs. The French Canadians, not having yet established ties to the knowledgeable sources that a more stable population group would present, and being the newest group of migrants to Manchester, were at a distinct disadvantage (see Table 6.20).

Numbers alone do not adequately convey the differences between the two neighborhoods and between groups in the town. What has been referred to as the "rural" neighborhood of 1880 was a fairly well spread out district. It was a district of scattered houses dispersed along "roads" that were never listed in official censuses by name simply because no one had, officially, gotten around to assigning them a name. In the compact industrial setting, though, multi-family housing was packed together fairly tightly. The "rural" district housed less than 1,000 people in an area much larger than its industrial counterpart where over 2,000 people lived.

In Manchester's earlier years, women would have far outnumbered men in the general population, but, by 1880, the sexes were fairly well balanced: 45% men, 55% women. This overall population balance, though, did not carry over into the work place. 97.6% of all women who worked were employed as unskilled textile operatives—tenders of the machines. By contrast, only 44% of working men were held to the lowest paid jobs in the mills. It would seem, then, that men had more, and better, employment opportunities than did women. The popularity of Kearneyist rhetoric was not without justification. Manchester's working population perceived that not only a large supply of immigrant labor, but also a large number of young women in the mills depressed wages below what they might otherwise have been. In terms of absolute numbers, women outnumbered men in the lowest skilled textile jobs. When looking at this occupational category by age, though, it becomes apparent that women did not stay in these positions as men did (see Table 6.21). The women who held the lowest skilled mill jobs were *young* women. By the end of their 20's, women left the mills in large numbers. By the childbearing and rearing 30's, the percentage of women in the mills fell off sharply.

By contrast, although men never achieved an 87% rate of employment in the mills, a significant percentage of men remained employed in low paying textile work until "retirement," a phenomenon that was delayed far longer for men than it was for women. Looking at the entire population over 65 years of age, it is apparent that virtually all women had left the working world, while over half the men continued to work—presumably until they died. At a time of continual wage cutbacks, the explanations offered by Manchester's labor organizers that an influx of foreign workers together with a work pool of "women and children" were the cause of the workers' plight must have seemed plausible and, to a certain extent, reflected local prejudices and conditions.

The Amoskeag had viewed Manchester, in an earlier period, as "a kind of industrial Garden of Eden where nothing happened without the advice and consent of the company's agent," but by 1880, this industrial paradise had undergone considerable departure from an ideal which never accurately reflected reality. For one thing, a kind of sorting-out process had taken place whereby the more highly skilled, cleaner, more desirable jobs in the mill were reserved for the native born and their progeny, while the highly mobile Irish and the newly arriving French Canadians went into the lowest paying mill work. This is clearly revealed in the parental nativity of the factory district workers (see Table 6.22).

As the composition of the work force changed, so did company policy toward the workers and the town. The earliest years, before the Civil War, had been characterized by an acute awareness of common interests and company developed sense of community between company, workers, and town. In 1855, when workers struck, the company presented a rigid facade of unrelenting sternness, but in practice engaged in a kind of behind-the-scenes jawboning whereby Agent Ezekiel Straw and other company officials sought an accommodation that would both alleviate grievances for workers and "save face" for the company. Such a course of action was possible because, in spite of antagonistic rhetoric, workers and company officials lived side by side in a more or less homogeneous community. After the Civil War, this homogeneity broke down rapidly and the company began to formulate new policies to deal with a different kind of work force (see Table 6.23).

The company's policy toward the "Scots girls" represented the transitional phase of the company's labor policy. On the one hand, the strictest moral supervision was exercised. Agents in Europe investigated the "girls' " backgrounds, letters of reference were demanded, dwellings in Manchester were provided—in short, the older paternalism in some ways continued and prevailed. Yet there was also a newer aspect here: the rationalized business approach. The Scots girls were an investment which the company insisted be "paid back." Paternalism did not go so far as to extend free passage, no matter how important such a group of workers may have been regarded. Not only was the Scots' experience significant in terms of the businesslike approach of the company, but it also signified the split in the Amoskeag's work force between the "elite" skilled workers, and others who would be deemed essential to postwar production needs, and the huge numbers of unskilled "operatives" needed to man the factories.

The Scots girls signified both a clinging to and a turning away from paternalist policies. Most post-war workers did not receive the favorable treatment accorded the Scots girls. Not until after 1900 did the company again firmly embrace a paternalist philosophy such as it had symbolized in its earliest years. Tamara Hareven has described the gamut of company sponsored activities, clubs, and programs designed to formulate a new labor policy after 1900. In the 1880's, though, the company was in the position of having moved away from its older, community-oriented paternalism, finding a strictly rationalistic business approach increasingly inadequate (at least in terms of forestalling labor disturbances), and not yet having adopted its revamped, twentieth century brand of paternalism.[18]

On the surface there seemed many elements of continuity between the earlier pre-war years and the maturing years of the Amoskeag. Just in terms of local leadership, the Straw family seemed a bastion of continuity. In 1886, Herman Straw, E. A. Straw's son, headed the company as its agent. Father and son were different men, though, and, more importantly, they functioned in different times and under highly disparate circumstances.

Herman Straw, on the job for only one year, could not approach the strike of 1886 as his father had handled the disturbances of 1855. The older cultural homogeneity that had enabled the elder Straw to "jawbone," to appeal to a pool of shared interest and culture, was long gone by 1886. The company found itself faced with different workers and a vastly more hostile, self-aware, and unrelenting situation wherein there was no room for accommodation on either side. By the 1880's, workers and managers no longer shared a common cultural background. They no longer lived side by side in the town. They were more skeptical about the argument that the company would advance the best interests of both, and that what was good for one set of interests would benefit the other as well. In the case of the newly arriving French Canadians, company and workers no longer even shared language, thus further impairing communication at a time when it was vitally needed. After 1886, the importance of bringing ethnic representatives into supervisory level positions became obvious. Bilingual supervisors who could function as middle men, as earlier native overseers had done, were increasingly in demand following the labor disturbance of 1886.[19]

If the company and its representatives did not share the language, culture, or neighborhoods of the mill workers, though, there was another group of men who did share these new workers' backgrounds. It would be to these men, rather than to a paternalistic management, that Manchester's workers would turn in the mid-1880's. The Knights of Labor had become active in organizing Manchester's work force, and the leadership of the Knights, like the working population of the mills, was drawn from the ranks of Irish and French Canadian immigrants.

Wages in Manchester had been falling since the 1870's. In addition to this substantive deterioration in the condition of Manchester's work force, there was also an absence even of the illusion of a concerned, activist employer as the Amoskeag allowed its overt paternalist policies to fall by the wayside. In the years between Ezekiel Straw's leadership and the appointment of his son, Herman, the single most visible symbol of continuity and paternalist rule— the Straw family's presence at the top of the mill's administrative structure— was gone, replaced by a more strictly rationalistic business leadership controlled from Boston.[20]

Each time the company cut wages, it promised workers that "in the good times coming," when business recovered, cuts in wages would be made up for by (it implied) more than commensurate wage increases. As the 1880's progressed, the promises of the Amoskeag seemed to grow increasingly empty. The working population of the 1880's no longer had the same faith in the mill managers as had the workers of the 1850's or the "elite" workers of the rural district. The late '70's and early '80's witnessed a new militancy among the foreign born mill workers. Labor organizers, sharing a cultural heritage with Amoskeag workers that was unknown to many supervisors, were able to appeal to an increasing unwillingness to accept the company version. Throughout the wage cuts of the early '80's, increasing attention and credence was given to labor leaders and less reliance was put upon the good intentions of the company leadership. Given this aroused degree of sensitivity, then, it is not surprising that, in February 1886, when the company announced an end to wage cuts and granted a raise of 7%, there was trouble. Workers reacted with suspicion and discontent rather than with gratitude and praise that a loving "father" might reasonably expect from his loyal child. By the 1880's, the Amoskeag's work force of unskilled foreign workers could no longer look upon their employer in the same manner as had at least some of an earlier generation. The image of factory managers as kindly fathers was dead.[21]

For the more highly skilled of the Amoskeag's workers, such as the gingham weavers, the company's announcement of a 7% wage increase, ironically, seemed only to confirm their worst fears and suspicions. They had endured years of cutbacks, with only vague promises of the company's good will and good intentions to sustain them. They were beginning to feel the pressures of the lesser skilled and of a multi-ethnic work force moving into the weave rooms. Being less specialized than the mechanics, they felt themselves being squeezed out of the middle-level skilled jobs while excluded from the most highly skilled work. Agent Herman Straw had been on the job less than one year in 1886. Although he would eventually modify the company's labor policies to reflect a certain similarity to the paternalism of his father's day, Straw was not perceived, in the mid '80's, as his father had been in the mid '50's. Workers did not turn to him as friend, ally, and counselor as some had done to his father. Neither did workers turn to their foremen. Instead workers discussed their grievances amongst themselves after work, at homes and in saloons, and at lunch hour well outside of the overseer's hearing. Both of the rooms where trouble first broke out were supervised by Yankee overseers of the old school—worshipful of the company, living apart from the workmen, and detached from the newer ethnic groups. The overseers were Odd Fellows, Masons, and men who "labored untiringly in the interests of the corporation."[22]

It is little wonder, then, that the labor disturbance of 1886 caught the company completely by surprise. It is entirely understandable that "only the vaguest rumors of discontent" reached the company's officials. Channels of communication were no longer open between mill workers and company officials. The working neighborhoods of the town were abuzz for months with discontent and for days with the rumor that the discontent of the Amoskeag weavers was virulent. Almost any of the working families in Manchester's industrial district could have given the company insight into the seriousness of the situation: the weavers were about to confront the Amoskeag, not with a humble petition from a loving "child," but with a demand: wages must be raised at once a minimum of 10%.

Workers in two rooms were content to present surprised company officials with their "notice" on a Saturday morning. They had expected to find Agent Straw in his office. Since he was in Boston, though, they would be content to wait for his return to discuss the situation with him personally. One room was not to be put off. They demanded "that the matter be adjusted at once." Unsatisfied with the plea of helplessness on the part of Straw's aides, over 150 workers walked out at once, to be followed by over 5,000 on the following Monday.[23]

The importance of the 1886 strike lies in its coming at a juncture where company policy was about to be readjusted to meet changing circumstances. After the Civil War, the company had moved away from its older stress on paternal concern for its workers. By the mid-1880's, the company was beginning, again, to see the virtues of a paternalist facade. To be sure, the older paternalism with its rigid control over every aspect of workers' lives and every detail of town governance was inappropriate to the '80's, but, so, too, was the rationalistic business ethic that had begun to take its place. By the mid-'80's, the company would begin working to formulate a new kind of paternalism, the purpose of which was to help to avoid exactly the kind of confrontation with which mill workers and executives suddenly found themselves faced in February-March 1886.

The company had begun to realize that a town with a relatively stable and loyal middle class but with a large, mobile, and unreliable (in terms of loyalty) working element would not serve its needs. What the company hoped to foster, after 1886, was a working population that would feel, as at least some of its earlier counterpart had felt, that what was for the good of the company was for the good of the workers. How little this was so in 1880 can be seen by looking at the relatively "stable" core of the industrial neighborhood. It should be remembered that this constitutes only 12 out of 379 households. Nevertheless, this group, remaining in town as it had since 1870, is revealing of the sorts of ties that served to keep workers in town: they had a stake in the community. They also represent the kind of working population that future company policy would attempt to cultivate, a stable work force with ties to town and factory.[24]

Only three of the "stable" households were affluent enough to afford a single family home in 1880. They reached this affluence in differing ways. Richard Horan, 44, and his wife, Julia, 42, lived alone in a single family home in 1880, a highly unusual situation for a workman and, undoubtedly, an enviable one. They had not achieved this situation on their own, though. Ten years earlier, Horan's mother-in-law and sister-in-law (his wife's sister) had lived with him and his wife, and they had worked in the mills in order to meet expenses. As a day laborer, Horan worked hard, but he earned more than an unskilled operative, and both he and his wife utilized their free time, undoubtedly helped by the housekeeping aid that his in-laws must have provided, to rid themselves of the stigma of illiteracy. Perhaps they attended the increasingly popular evening schools. At any rate, Horan probably utilized his ties with his resident in-laws to build a nest egg, acquire the crucial ability to read and write, buy a home, and, eventually, enable Julia to retire to keeping house.

Catherine Hayes, a widow of 60 years of age, maintained a home for herself and her two adult children, John, 29, and Mary, 22. She helped to meet the expenses of a single family dwelling by taking in a boarder, Patrick Congdon, who, at age 70, still went to work as best he was able as a day laborer. The two adult children, of course, did their part as well—there was no room for the idle. John worked as a clerk in a retail store, where he undoubtedly heard the same sort of daily "lessons" that Joseph Kidder preached to the clerks in his store: the virtues of hard work and the guarantee of advancement. His sister, Mary, held a job with a promise of a less bright future: she worked as an unskilled operative in the Amoskeag. Things had improved for Catherine Hayes since 1870. Then she had another child at home, Mary was in school, and she had to take in two boarders, the Adams brothers, both farm laborers, in order to make ends meet. Still, she had been relatively well-off. Her eldest son, William, 22, was still at home in 1870, and undoubtedly earned good money as a skilled iron moulder. The Hayes family was prosperous enough, in 1870, to have accumulated an estate of $5,800. By 1880, Mrs. Hayes, having worked, saved, made a settled home for her family and raised her children, could settle back in relative (and, for her neighbors, most unusual) comfort.

Compared to their neighbors, the O'Neill family, the Hayes' were well-off indeed. Timothy O'Neill, 49, also maintained a single family home, but with much more difficulty than Catherine Hayes. With six children of his own and his brother's son to raise, Timothy O'Neill found that he could not get by on his wages as a day laborer. The family income was supplemented by that of O'Neill's three eldest children. Both Kate, 22, and John, 15, worked for the Amoskeag as unskilled tenders of the factory's machinery. The hope of the O'Neill's was Jeremiah, 19, the eldest son whose "inheritance" was the appointment as an apprentice machinist which his father's "connections" had undoubtedly helped to acquire. Perhaps, if things worked out well, John could move into a similar position in a few years and work his way out of the least skilled mill job which family finances mandated that he hold temporarily. O'Neill may even have dreamed of the day when his youngest, Daniel, 8, could become a skilled worker. In the meantime, three of the O'Neill children worked so that four could remain in school and the family could hold onto its home. In addition, the O'Neills had the Healy sisters: two sisters, in their 20's, who worked in the mills and boarded with Timothy and Margaret O'Neill and their family.

If a single family home was an elusive goal for most of the town's working population, then the "next best" solution was the two-family home. For one worker, James Dollard, the two-family home was really a single family home in expanded form. Dollard had worked as an unskilled textile worker, earning low wages, for 10 years. He must have saved painfully, for his labor and that of his children enabled him to acquire a hoard of about $800. Dollard did two things with his hard-earned money: he purchased a two family home; he brought his brother, Martin, 36, and his family over from Ireland to live in the house's second apartment. Dollard put his children to work as soon as possible to make ends meet. Both Katie, 15, and Matie, 13, worked with their father in the mill. It had undoubtedly taken some talking of a very persuasive nature to induce the overseer to put Matie on: the company was still sensitive to employing children so young (see Table 5.8). Perhaps Dollard was able to use his influence as one of the few long-term workers together with the sympathy that would have resulted from the recent death of his eldest son, Martin, on February 12. The overseer may have realized that his allowing Matie to work, despite her age, would be the only way that one of his most reliable workers could survive financially. James' brother, Martin, had only one child. Since the child was old enough to take care of herself, and since James' wife would be at home during the day, both Martin and his wife took jobs, again as unskilled operatives working together with James Dollard, their sponsor, in the Amoskeag. In all probability, Martin's 12 year old daughter would not go to school much longer: the two families needed all the cash they could get, and taking in a boarder undoubtedly helped Martin and his wife to pay for their share of the house's cost, together, perhaps, with helping to pay back James for bringing them to Manchester.[25]

Manchester's other "stable" families were not all that different from the Dollards. They met their expenses by working: children went to work, and they went to work young, while the family took in boarders to make ends meet. They provided the boarders with room, board, an alternative to life in the housing owned by a company which was regarded as not to be trusted, and often, because of their longevity in the community, an entree to overseers, work rooms, and methods of adjustment to the factory which could not be gained through the "official" channels. In some cases, one or two favored sons would be afforded privileged treatment: the family's "influence" or "connections" which resulted from their unusual persistence amidst a sea of constantly changing faces, would be utilized to obtain much envied apprenticeships. To make a brother a machinist, moulder, or mechanic took the work (and income) of siblings and the influence of parents. For the most part, Manchester's "stable" households were not headed by unskilled textile workers. There were exceptions, such as James and Martin Dollard, but it is important to note that of three "stable" houses headed by textile workers, the Dollard household was the only one wherein the head of the household was an unskilled operative. Edward Brickley was a textile worker, but he was a skilled dye house man who held a critical job in the manufacturing process. Because of this, he was able to afford the unusual luxury of keeping all five of his children in school. Similarly, William McLaughlin had worked his way up, had accumulated a nest egg, and, by 1880, no longer had to take in boarders to make expenses.[26]

It should be remembered that these were the "exceptional" households among Manchester's working population. They "stayed put" by virtue of their skills, the willingness of all in the family to work, their hope of advancement for their sons because of their very persistence, and their ability to take in boarders to supplement family income. Being immigrants, they held little hope of great upward personal mobility, but they did see such possibilities for their sons. When a son could not be guaranteed some hope of a future that held more than an unskilled textile job, like the case of Daniel Lyons, 28, he often left town in search of greener pastures elsewhere. Lyons left his mother, sisters, and a younger brother at home to join the Navy. In all probability, he would also advise his younger brother, James, 19, to follow in his footsteps and not to be trapped in the dead-end mill job which he held in 1880.

Manchester's "stable" workers were still relatively loyal to the Amoskeag because their fate was tied to that of the company. For the majority of the less settled, more mobile work force, though, the company did not loom so large in their lives. This was the situation that Herman Straw had to reverse in 1886. But the younger Straw would find himself far more closely circumscribed than his father had been. Manchester and the Amoskeag had undergone considerable growth since the days of the elder Straw, and the company treasurer at Boston exerted far more control than he had done in the earlier years. Straw's appointment was both a recognition of the value of a paternalist approach and a hope that his very appointment might stave off the troubles of the 1880's.[27]

The situation was much changed from the 1850's. By 1885-86, the Amoskeag's workers, especially the more skilled workers, were organized, had a set of grievances, a set group of leaders, were no longer culturally monolithic, and, as evidenced during the strike, had the overwhelming sympathy of the vast majority of unskilled workers who joined them for three weeks. The unskilled continued to support the strike even though they were rigorously excluded from the meetings of the skilled workers where strike issues were discussed.

The Amoskeag weavers lost the strike of 1886. The official company version of the strike held that "the corporation . . . stood firm as a rock throughout the trouble, and, while absolutely nothing had been gained by the employees, much had been lost." There is some reason to suspect the opposite, though. Amoskeag workers may have won some important gains from their "lost" strike. The strike forced company officials to recognize the wisdom of adopting a new-paternalist employment policy. It also forced the company to recognize the reality of an ethnically pluralistic work force. While the Irish had already been accommodated to some degree, the company would now make further modifications in its labor policy aimed at further conciliating the Irish, winning the loyalty of the French Canadians who had begun to pour into town, and creating a work force with ties to both company and town.[28]

The situation that the Amoskeag set about to reverse after 1886 was a difficult one. Low skilled and low paid textile workers were segregated into certain neighborhoods that bore striking differences from the more exclusive areas of town. Within these neighborhoods, as 1886 indicated, a sense of difference and feelings of anger arose. Such workers had little stake in either company or community. Indeed, for the roughly 7% who lived within the households of others, as boarders, there was little reason for any feelings other than hostility toward their employer (see Table 6.24). They were trapped in dead-end jobs and living in a town where they were not likely to remain for long. In the industrial neighborhoods, sons regularly followed fathers into the mills at the lowest entry levels—as unskilled operatives, tenders of the machines. The only exception of any importance occurred to those few families that had achieved some degree of persistence and thus were able to utilize influence, friendship, or superior knowledge of local conditions to obtain the best job opportunities for their sons. (Daughters would go into unskilled mill work if they went to work at all.) Such was also the case, as has been seen, for "rural" sons—a small elite group within the working community was able to use its position to wait for and seize what better job opportunities the town had to offer, but, for the immigrants and for the vast majority of the mill's unskilled labor force, the reality of life was temporary residence in a transient situation (see Table 6.25).

The occupational routings of the daughters of Manchester's industrial workers is in some ways more telling than that of sons. Since the infancy of textile manufacturing, the factory was touted as a way to put "burdensome" daughters to some economically productive employment. In the earliest years, these views won widespread acceptance among Yankee farmers, and it was not unusual to witness farmers "applying" for work opportunities for their daughters. By 1880, this situation no longer prevailed. Farmers had come to regard mill work as so undesirable that they chose (and could afford) to keep their daughters at home and economically unproductive rather than allowing them to go into the mills. Immigrant workers, on the other hand, saw, in their daughters, a crucial economic asset, and it was a rare thing, indeed, when an Irishman or a French Canadian, pressed by larger families and lower wages, did not put his daughters into the job market as soon as he possibly could. In

Manchester, the job market for daughters meant the lowest paying unskilled jobs in the Amoskeag or in one of her associates.

Shocked at the degree of labor militancy manifested in 1886, Amoskeag officials saw all of their troubles coming from the transient immigrant districts. In the native born they saw a group of quiet, tractable workers, many of whom saw their fate and the fate of the Amoskeag as one and the same. It was this pattern that the company would hope to replicate in the immigrant neighborhoods. Mill officials had already begun to publicize the virtues of considering a career with the textile factory. To do this, they publicized the careers of the early "mill girls" such as Hannah Pope, who remained in Manchester as old age approached.[29]

Hannah Pope was born in rural New Hampshire in 1816, and had been one of the first "mill girls given an opportunity" with the Amoskeag when it began operations in 1839. She remained alive and living in Manchester well into the 1880's, and it was hoped that immigrant workers would see, in her career and those of other "mill girls," a model for themselves to follow. Hannah Pope kept her eyes open for opportunities in Manchester—both within the factory and in the increasingly industrial setting surrounding the factory. She considered possibilities not only for herself, but also for her family back home on the farm. When a desirable semi-skilled job became available, she wrote her younger sister to come to Manchester at once and used her influence with the overseers to persuade one of them to take her sister on. Likewise, she and her sister both kept watch for likely opportunities for her brothers. Coming on their own, with no knowledge of the factory process, straight off the farm, and with no one known to be "reliable" to make introductions for them, they would have stepped into the lowest skilled, lowest paid jobs that the mills had to offer, as did so many immigrants. But their sister had local "contacts," and she kept watch, let them know the most opportune time to come, and made the necessary introductions and recommendations. Eventually Hannah Pope would bring her entire family—including her father—to the city. From the Amoskeag's viewpoint, the Popes proved to be reliable, loyal, and ambitious. Having "taken care" of her family, moreover, Hannah Pope looked out for herself as well. She set her sights on Stephen Austin, a skilled carpenter and woodworker with a secure job with the Amoskeag. After bringing her family to the city and seeing that they were able to look after themselves, Hannah Pope married Stephen Austin and retired from the textile mill.

Hannah Pope Austin, as well as some of the relatives whose migration she advised and assisted, still remained in Manchester in the 1880's. They lived a fairly genteel life among their fellow Yankee neighbors. Removed from the turmoil of the industrial neighborhoods, they could look back on the earliest years of the city as a time when, as Hannah Pope Austin would put it,

Manchester was "a pretty tough place." Had she lived in another part of town, perhaps she would have been far less assured of the placidity of the mature town.[30]

The Amoskeag faced a town divided between two major population groups in the 1880's. No doubt the mills would have preferred to continue to employ workers like Hannah Pope—they were placid, loyal, and relatively permanent. The company faced the reality of dealing with a turbulent foreign born work force, though, and the great challenge for the future would be whether or not immigrant workers could be transformed into the kind of workers that the company desired: since cultural influences could no longer avoid labor turmoil, it was hoped that a renewed, yet altered, paternalism would serve the company's needs.

Herman Straw's appointment symbolized the shift in company policy and its coming to grips with the problems posed by a huge immigrant work force. Manchester-born of the old Yankee elite, with a crucially important family, it was hoped that Straw could win the loyalty of all groups. The settled native population would see in him one of their own. The Irish, having already been assimilated to some degree, would benefit, along with the ever-growing French Canadian work force, from the policies that Straw would implement: children's playgrounds, kindergartens, health clinics, home economics workshops, and a host of other measures (Tamara Haieven has dealt with these measures in detail). As of the mid-'80's, the success of changing policy would be uncertain and would have to await the test of time. The purpose of implementing changes, though, was clear: the social divisions that had come to plague Manchester in the post Civil War years could not be allowed to disrupt the factories again as they had in 1886. The solution that company executives found was a tradition present from the earliest days of the industrial town.[31]

Table 6.1. Boarders' Occupations, Rural District[32]

Semi-Professional	2.4%
Skilled	17.1
Semi-Skilled	4.9
Unskilled	14.6
Textile Operatives	0
Retired, etc.	61.0

N = 41

Table 6.2. Boarders' Occupations, Company Housing District[33]

Semi-Professional	1.2%
White Collar	5.2
Skilled	21.1
Semi-Skilled	1.2
Unskilled	3.8
Textile Operatives	61.9
Other	2.6

N - 344

Table 6.3. Household Status by Occupation, Rural District[34]

	Profes-sional	Semi-Prof.	Farm	White Cclr.	Skilled	Semi-Skill	Unskill	Textile	Retired, At Home, etc.
Head	3	23	95	3	54	11	10	15	17
Spouse				2	1			5	179
Son		7	14	1	13	4	19	7	94
Daughter	1	2		1	1	1		7	150
Parent			5		1	5			25
Sibling		1	1	1	3	2	3	6	8
Other Relative		1	1	1		2	4		17
Boarder & Svt.		2			7	3	7	1	25

Table 6.4. Occupation of Sons (15 Years Old and Up), Rural
            District [35]

Semi-Professional	10.6%
Farm	21.2
White Collar	1.5
Skilled	19.7
Semi-Skilled	6.1
Unskilled	28.8
Textile	10.6
Other	1.5

Table 6.5. Yearly Income Levels, Heads of Households, Rural
            District [36]

	Under $450	$450–600	$601–750	$751–1,200	Over $1,200
Farm	75	8	5	13	4
Skilled		16	22	2	
Semi-Skilled	5			1	
Unskilled	1				
Textile	8	1		3	

N = 164

Table 6.6. Children Attending School, by Age, 1880 [37]

	6-9	10-12	13-14	15-16	17-18	19-20		
Rural	90.4	100.	92.8	62.	25.	6.8	N =	318
Industrial	86.0	100.	64.5	24.3	9.3	1.5	N =	1296
Company Housing	54.5	86.6	75.0	17.6	–	–	N =	144

Expressed as % of each age category attending school.

Table 6.7. Nativity by Ward, 1884[38]

	1	2	3	4	5	6	7	8
Native	65.8		54.9	16.9	42.6	81.6	72.1	
French	20.5		41.9	80.0	25.3	6.7	9.3	
Irish	7.9		.7	2.7	28.3	6.3	10.4	
German	3.5	data not available	.7		.4	.8	4.7	no data
Swede	2.1		.2		.1			
Scots			.2		.8	.8		
Chinese			.7		.1	2.6		
English			1.0		1.9	1.1		
Misc.	.2				.3		3.1	
N =	3,364		581*	112*	8,022	3,415	2,240	

*By family, not individual

Table 6.8. Nativity by District, 1880[39]

	Rural	Industrial	Company Housing
Native U.S.	75.9%	48.2%	79.7%
Engl-Scotl-Wales	5.2	5.6	2.9
Ireland	7.7	40.0	3.0
Canada	5.5	5.7	10.8
Other Foreign	1.8	.4	3.3
No Data	3.8		.5
N =	920	2,037	666

Table 6.9. Age by Residential District[40]

	Industrial	Rural	Company Housing
Mean	24.3	32.4	29.7
Median	21.1	29.8	26.8
Range	newborn-90	newborn-89	newborn-79
Std. Dev.	17.9	20.9	14.0

Table 6.10. Age by Ten-Year Intervals, by District[41]

	Industrial	Rural	Company Housing
Newborn-10	26.3%	17.9%	5.3%
11-20	22.4	16.8	18.8
21-30	20.4	16.3	41.7
31-40	14.6	16.2	13.5
41-50	7.5	11.5	10.7
51-60	5.3	10.0	7.0
60 + up	3.5	11.3	3.0

Table 6.11. Children Per Household, by District[42]

	Industrial	Rural	Company Housing
Mean	3.39	1.90	3.57
Median	3.29	1.75	2.32
Range	0-9	0-7	0-9
Std. Dev.	2.15	1.62	3.24

Table 6.12. Industrial District, Size of Dwellings, 1880[43]

	% This Size		% This Size
1 Family	17.6	6 Family	2.3
2 Family	47.0	7 Family	1.6
3 Family	15.6	8 Family	3.6
4 Family	3.2	9 Family	5.0
5 Family	3.7	No Data	.4

N = 2,037

Table 6.13. Dwelling Size, Industrial District, 10-Year
Interval [44]

	1870	1880
1 Family	86.7%	17.6%
2 Family	10.2	47.0
3 Family	2.9	15.6
4 or More Families	0	19.4
No Data	.1	.4
N =	958	2,037

Table 6.14. Occupation by Dwelling Size, Industrial District [45]

	Profes-sional	Semi-Prof.	Farm	White Collar	Skilled	Semi-Skilled	Unskilled	Textile
1 Family		5		5	25	5	31	242
2 Family	3	8	2	8	57	10	59	664
3 Family	1	3	1	2	16	2	21	211
4 + Up		1			8	1	43	280
% this category in 4 + family units	–	5.8	–	–	7.5	5.5	27.9	20.0

N = 1,714

Table 6.15. Dwelling Size by Nativity[46]

	Native	England, Scotland, Wales	Ireland	Canada	Other Foreign
1 Family	175	21	146	17	
2 Family	465	50	374	63	7
3 Family	152	20	111	34	
4 + Up	291	24	185	2	1
% This Group in 4 + Cat.	29.6	20.8	22.6	1.7	

Dwelling Size by Father's Nativity

1 Family	21	15	311	12	
2 Family	68	31	779	69	
3 Family	12	5	269	31	
4 + Up	7	5	377	1	6
% This Group in 4 + Cat.	6.1	8.9	21.7	.9	

Table 6.16. Annual Income Level, by Occupation, by District[47]

	Industrial 273*					Rural 164*				
N =	Under $450	$451–600	$601–750	$751–1,200	Over $1,200	Under $450	$451–600	$601–750	$751–1,200	Over $1,200
Semi-Prof.			.4							
Farm						45.7	4.9	3.0	7.9	2.4
Skilled	1.8	3.3	9.5	5.5			9.7	13.4	1.2	
Semi-Skill	1.8					3.1			.6	
Unskilled	40.3					.6				
Textile	37.4					4.9	.6		1.8	
% Totals	81.3	3.3	9.9	5.5		54.3	15.2	16.4	11.5	2.4

*Sufficient data for comparisons of 52 industrial occupations, 273 and 164 households respectively in each district

Table 6.17. Relationship by Occupation, Industrial District[48]

	Profes-sional	Semi-Prof.	Farm Wkr.	White Colr.	Skilled	Semi-Skill	Unskilled	Textile	Other
Head		9	3	4	64	10	116	102	77
Spouse	2				3	1		56	247
Son		4		6	27	5	11	117	324
Daughter		1		3	1			221	339
Parent								1	25
Sibling		2						29	9
Other Rel.	1			2			4	23	24
Servant									7
Boarder	1	1			11	1	15	89	26

Company Housing District

	Profes-sional	Semi-Prof.	Farm Wkr.	White Colr.	Skilled	Semi-Skill	Unskilled	Textile	Other
Head		2		5	13	3	8	48	12
Spouse		3		5	6		1	7	69
Son		1			4			9	14
Daughter								12	20
Parent								1	2
Sibling		1			2		1	5	1
Other Rel.									2
Servant							24		
Boarder		4		18	73	4	13	213	9

Table 6.18. Birthplace by Occupation, Industrial District [49]

	Profes-sional	Semi-Prof.	Farm	White Colr.	Skilled	Semi-Skill	Unskilled	Textile	Other
N.H.	2	4	1	3	32	5	6	180	584
Other N.E.		1	1		10	1	2	46	50
Other U.S.			1	1			1	17	26
Ireland	2	9		6	45	11	134	280	327
Canada		1		4	8	1	8	54	40
Eng-Sc-Wls		1		1	9		3	63	38
Other Fn.		1			2			2	3
Company Housing District									
N.H.		8		21	51	2	22	126	71
Other N.E.		3		5	25	3	11	65	30
Other U.S.				2	9	1		23	7
England								17	1
Ireland							6	13	1
Canada		1		1	9	1	7	37	14
Other Fn.					2		1	14	4
Unknown					2				1

Table 6.19.   Birth by Housing Ownership, Company Housing
              District

	Birthplace		Father's Birthplace	
	Private Housing	Company Housing	Private Housing	Company Housing
New Hampshire	17.1	33.6	11.6	29.4
Other N.E.	8.9	13.2	6.8	12.6
Other U.S.	2.3	4.5	3.8	3.8
England	1.7	1.2	2.3	2.3
Ireland	1.5	1.5	3.2	1.7
Canada	6.6	4.2	7.8	4.1
Other Foreign	.6	2.7	2.3	7.2
Not Known	.5	-	1.5	-
N = 666			N = 666	

Source: U.S. manuscript census

Table 6.20.   Household Size, by District[50]

	Industrial	Rural	Company Housing
Range	1-22	1-24	2-27
Mean	6.5	5.3	10.8
Median	6.2	4.8	7.9
Std. Dev.	2.9	3.6	8.1

Table 6.21. Textile Employment, By Sex, By Age, Industrial District [51]

	Under 15	16-19	20-24	25-29	30-34	35-39	40-44	45-59	50-54	55-59	60-64	65 +
MEN												
Textile	4.9	65.4	57.6	32.5	33.9	40.0	32.7	32.1	12.9	26.7	4.2	0
Other*	93.6	16.3	0	1.3	1.7	4.0	6.1	0	3.2	13.3	16.7	43.5
WOMEN												
Textile	5.8	82.6	87.1	50.0	41.4	24.3	22.6	21.1	8.1	8.7	3.8	0
Other*	94.2	16.0	11.6	48.0	57.5	72.9	77.4	78.9	89.2	91.3	96.2	100

Percentages indicate percent of sex involved in this occupational category   Men, N = 917;
Women, N = 1120

*Category includes retired, disabled, otherwise removed from employment market

Table 6.22. Occupation by Parental Nativity, Industrial District[52]

	Native	Ireland	Canada
Professional	2.9	.4	–
Semi-Professional	14.7	.9	3.4
Farm	5.9	.1	–
White Collar		1.2	8.6
Skilled	38.2	9.6	10.3
Semi-Skilled	5.9	1.8	1.7
Unskilled		17.8	6.9
Textile	32.3	68.2	68.9

Table 6.23. Birthplace by Occupation, Industrial District, 1880[53]

	Professional	Semi-Prof.	Farm	White Collar	Skilled	Semi-Skill	Unskill	Textile
Native	50	29.4	66.9	26.7	39.6	33.4	5.8	37.8
Ireland	50	52.9	33.3	40.0	61.1	61.1	87.0	43.6
Canada		5.9		26.7	7.5	5.6	5.2	8.4
Other Fn.		11.8		6.7			1.9	10.1
N =	4	17	3	15	106	18	154	642

Table 6.24. Boarders' Occupations, by District[54]

	Industrial	Rural	Company Housing
Professional	.7		
Semi-Professional	.7	2.4	1.2
Skilled	7.6	17.1	5.2
Semi-Skilled	.7	4.9	21.2
Unskilled	10.4	14.6	1.2
Textile	61.8		61.9
Retired, etc.	18.1	61.0	2.6

Table 6.25. Children's (15 and Older) Occupations, by District[55]

	Industrial	Rural	Company Housing
Sons' (15 & Older) Occupations, by District			
Professional	1.2		
Semi-Professional	2.3	10.6	12.5
Farm		21.2	
White Collar	3.5	1.5	20.8
Skilled	15.7	19.7	25.0
Semi-Skilled	2.9	6.1	
Unskilled	6.4	28.8	4.2
Textile	68.0	10.6	37.5
Daughters' (15 & Older) Occupations, by District			
Professional		1.7	
Semi-Professional	.4	3.3	5.8
White Collar	1.3	3.3	
Skilled	.4	1.7	23.5
Textile	90.5	11.7	70.6
At Home	7.3	76.7	
N =	244	60	

Conclusion

From its foundation as a major textile manufacturing center in the early 1840's until the mid-1880's, Manchester was free of major labor disturbances. From the perspective of the factory owners and managers, Manchester truly was the "industrial Garden of Eden" which they frequently pictured it as in their public statements. That perspective, of course, was very different from the viewpoint of the men and women who worked in Manchester's mills, especially those who worked at the lowest levels, the unskilled textile operatives. These men and women had ample reason for grievances against their employer-guardians, yet, in a 45 year period, they staged only one minor action to protest their plight. This quiescence can be explained given the context within which Manchester's working population lived their lives. The Amoskeag dominated local affairs and set policies which would, in practice, divide both townspeople and textile workers. Extreme in and out mobility would serve further to divide Manchester's working population. Much effort was expended in learning the ropes, in adapting to a new setting, and in survival. Many of the least skilled would barely have time to adapt to their circumstances when they would move on. With the coming of the Irish and the French Canadians, barriers of culture, religion, and language would divide the working population of Manchester physically into neighborhoods as well as dividing them in terms of interests and awareness. Given all of these divisive factors, it is hardly surprising that labor disturbances did not become serious. What is surprising is the variety and extent of resources that the textile workers utilized in the process of adaptation and adjustment.

There were few who did not realize that, in Mancheser, it was possible to be born in a company tenement, to be educated in a company dominated (and sponsored) school, to worship and be wed in a company-built church, to work out one's life in the company's factories, picnic in the company-built parks and, ultimately, be buried in the company-built cemetery. This scenario is, of course, an overstatement. Because of the high degree of in and out mobility, it is highly unlikely that many men or women at all would ever experience such an extreme of a company dominated life. Nevertheless, it was possible, and the very possibility served to remind the men and women of Manchester of the shadow of the Amoskeag over their lives.

From its very beginnings, the Amoskeag overwhelmed. The building of its first industrial "village" caught by surprise and politically overwhelmed the older farming community. The society that the Amoskeag created would be ideally suited to neither the needs of the older farming residents nor to the needs of the industrial workers, but would be designed to fit the needs of the company that mapped the streets, built the schools and churches, laid out the parks and public squares. The "newcomers" who came from the small towns of New Hampshire and Massachusetts in the early years would have tremendous adjustments to make. They would find a new and strange work environment, living environment, and community setting. Culturally similar to the residents of rural Mancheser, the division and mutual hostility between the early "newcomers" and the older town residents served to distract both from focusing attention on the problem of how to address the changes in their lives that the Amoskeag had brought about. The process of adjustment took time, and, for most mill workers, no sooner would they have adjusted to a new work setting and discipline, new housing arrangements, and a new communal setting than they would move on, either to return home or to move to another textile town in search of the higher wages or more desirable jobs that only "experienced" hands could expect. The textile workers at the lowest skill and wage levels, those most likely to be or become discontent, would be those most likely to move on. The divisions between the unskilled and the more skilled was an important one. The skilled workers would enjoy not only better wages, but would also participate to a far greater degree in the opportunities that rapid community growth could provide. Skilled workers, far more than the unskilled, were able to buy proeprty and profit from real estate speculation. They could look forward to passing on "opportunities" for the better jobs to their children. This was in the Amoskeag's best interest and, undoubtedly, a factor in forestalling labor unrest.

Given the divisions between the unskilled and the more fortunate semi-skilled workers, and given the transiency of the least skilled and the kind of adaptations they would have to make, it is surprising that Manchester's working people were able to voice protest to the extent that they did. A basically temporary population, they were able to utilize the prolific local press to a surprising degree. They utilized it to pass on job information, to warn their fellows off from the least favorable overseers, to protest company work rules and housing arrangements, and to voice a general and widely shared distrust of the "corporations" of Manchester.

As the Irish moved into the lowest level mill jobs, the cultural hostility dividing Manchester's working population renewed and intensified. As the

Irish formed their own neighborhoods, encouraged to do so by company policy, they became set apart physically as well as culturally from the native born, and the Amoskeag was the chief beneficiary. The very presence of the new immigrants and their neighborhoods caused native born workers to view the Amoskeag's resident native-dominated management more as an ally than as an adversary. Until at least 1860, the presence of the Irish immigrant neighborhoods would serve further to divide the working population of Manchester and reinforce the successfulness of the Amoskeag's paternalist policies.

For the Amoskeag's management, the Civil War may have been a blessing in disguise. Many of the most transient and least skilled, the most dissatisfied, would leave town for the duration of the war, while the skilled machinists and metal workers, a more stable group, remained to work on the production of weapons. Those who stayed were those who had benefited most from the Amoskeag's policies: skilled workers, builders, entrepreneurs, merchants, and farmers. They had little in common with the unskilled mill workers and saw little reason to protest their plight. Many of this group would benefit from the post War influx of immigrant workers. As Manchester's growth continued unabated throughout the 1870's and early 1880's, the majority of the new immigrant workers would move into private housing: landlords, builders, merchants, and those more skilled workers with money invested in property would benefit from the Amoskeag's growth and from her policies. The least skilled textile operatives would be divided from those on a higher occupational level by neighborhood, skill, and property, and divided from one another by language as well as by culture and religious belief. No matter what language he spoke, though, the unskilled textile operative would find himself part of a population that bordered on a disastrous level of population instability, with tremendous levels of in and out migration. Being constantly "new" in town, the textile operative tended to look toward a few local opinion leaders—clergymen, merchants, more highly skilled workers—for help and advice in adaptation and adjustment. If the Amoskeag's policies pleased the more stable population, then the grievances of the least skilled textile operatives could be overlooked safely. As long as the more skilled population judged itself in comparison to the least skilled, there would be little trouble in maintaining social control. As skilled workers looked about and saw the rise of multiple family tenements, the deterioration of immigrant neighborhoods, the increasing prevalence of evening schools, and the presence of a group trapped in low skilled and low paying jobs, they would tend to judge their own situation, by comparison, as relatively well-off. They could keep their children in school for longer periods of time, they could keep their wives and daughters out of mill work, and they could wait for the more opportune jobs for their sons.

The rising numbers and influence of the foreign born, though, would mean that the Amoskeag's relative indifference to the plight of the operatives would have to come to an end. The company could not afford to allow labor turmoil to become prevalent or frequent. The 1855 strike had demonstrated that. In dealing with the 1886 strike, the Amoskeag would face new and formidable problems. Manchester was not culturally homogeneous. Immigrant neighborhoods had grown in number and in the numbers of problems that they presented. The residents held little, if any, property. They generally held the least desirable jobs. They did not identify with the interests of the Amoskeag. From the Amoskeag's point of view, it could not afford to have a large segment of the work force regard the company as an adversary for a long period of time. After 1886, policies would be designed to avoid growing antagonism.

Throughout this period of Manchester's history, the textile operatives, the very core of Manchester's industrial population, were at a disadvantage in terms of income, property acquisition, and job advancement. In view of this, what is remarkable is the extent to which textile operatives were able to adapt to the setting in which they found themselves. An ever-present group of "newcomers," textile workers turned to a variety of sources for support and assistance in adapting to their new community. They came to rely on networks of acquaintances from their hometowns, their homelands, or their families to introduce them to new ways of life and to guide them through the turmoil of arrival, settlement, and adjustment. Such informal networks provided alternatives to local opinion leaders and served well to introduce immigrant workers to their jobs, their landlords, their churches; they warned workers of overseers to be avoided, introduced them to new friends, interceded with the bosses, and, in almost countless other ways, showed them the way to survive. In their turn, the immigrants who had once been "green" would help other newly arrived countrymen, townsmen, friends, and family. Much energy and effort was expended on survival and adaptation. After 1886, it would be the task of the Amoskeag to win over the loyalty of the community of immigrant workers.

In summary, this study has focused on the work, family, and community patterns of newly arrived workers making the historic transition from rural to industrial life. Its specific context has been the initial period of industrial growth and development of Manchester, New Hampshire and the patterns of adjustment and adaptation experienced by Manchester's working population from 1840 to 1886.

This study has employed quantitative data drawn from the early industrial town's tax records of over 1,700 taxpayers ranging from the town's wealthiest to the town's poorest adult males. Manuscript schedules of the census of population were utilized from the 1850 through 1880 censuses. Over 5,200 cases were analyzed using SPSS and linkages were made, wherever possible, to the census of agriculture manuscript materials as well as to directory data. Company savings bank records of over 1,100 accounts were utilized.

This study has concluded that the arrival, settlement, adaptation, and adjustment to urban living, industrial work, and a paternalistic community setting was a complex process in which workers experienced both victories and defeats.

In terms of economic achievement, the data demonstrated much of what would be expected: few economic victories, in any sense of that term, were won by unskilled textile operatives. Wages were consistently lower than for other unskilled labor. Levels of savings were consistently low. Indeed, to call such accounts "savings" is almost a misnomer. For textile operatives, savings accounts were little more than arrangements for temporary safekeeping of meager funds. Likewise, in terms of property ownership, textile workers achieved little. They constituted the overwhelming bulk of the working class in Manchester during a period of unprecedented growth, yet, if any working class members benefited from such growth, it was the skilled building tradesmen rather than the numerically far greater textile segment.

This study has suggested that there were areas where workers did achieve some success, though. If we are to look for successes among the working class, perhaps the place to look lies in the long and complex process of the building of a sense of community. Manchester's working class community was not one community at all, but, rather, it was a series of communities characterized by ethnicity, level of skill, religious background, and ties to kin and countrymen. The process of neighborhood building among newly arrived workers needs to be studied from perspectives other than ethnicity. It has been suggested here that, in looking for assistance, newly arrived workers relied upon neighbors, kinsmen, or countrymen who had previously migrated to the city. Such chain migration may well have been an essential element in many developing industrial communities. To understand worker adjustment, it may be necessary to look beyond the workplace at the communal context of a variety of developing industrial cities.

It has been suggested here, too, that some caution be used in delineating what is strictly "urban" about developing industrial communities. It has been shown that, while Manchester was, to be sure, a great industrial center, it was neither exclusively urban nor exclusively industrial. The survival, within the city, of a small but inportant farming community served as an important vehicle for the transmission of information to many people who made a successful transition from farm life to industrialism. It also constituted a means by which workers who were able to afford more than their less skilled counterparts could retain a rural lifestyle within a rapidly developing urban and industrial environment. Farms that barely paid their own way, or that lost money, constituted an important choice for a small segment of the work force. The extent to which similar patterns and choices were available in other industrial communities, and the role that such patterns played in other communities, needs to be subjected to future study.

This study has concluded that, by concentrating on workers' community, family, and neighborhood context, we can, perhaps, learn more about the underlying sources of working class discontent than we can by focusing narrowly on the formation of formal unions or upon periodic episodes of labor turmoil. In the case of Manchester's working population, protest took place in the absence of formal unions and had as much to do with the deterioration of living conditions—extra-factory circumstances involving the growth of tenement housing—as with the conditions of factory labor.

It has been suggested that the relationships between a paternalistic employer and the industrial work force are more complex than has been suggested in much of the literature. In Manchester's case, the older stereotypes about a factory town, with an absolutist kind of repression of workers, do not hold up. The Manchester experience suggests that a paternalistic employer may have been able to achieve the goal of a tractable work force and an uninterrupted work schedule by "giving in" to workers' requirements, or perhaps it is more accurate to say that employers seemed to give in, rather than by exercising the kind of unbending absolutism that is the underlying assumption of much of the literature on factory towns. In view of the Manchester experience, it may be time to re-examine the experiences of other paternalistic corporate towns. In Manchester, the corporation was well served not by a capricious exercise of absolutism, but by formulating individualistic workroom policies based on the overseer-worker relationship and by modification of the design for the company town. In this fashion, workers were allowed a certain amount of leeway in finding their own places within the town and the factory. What served the workers' immediate interests may have, in the longer run, served the corporation more than the worker. The extent to which such subtle policies of worker control were utilized and succeeded in other industrial environments would seem to deserve further exploration. The subtlety of worker control, it has been suggested, is better studied in times of apparent success than by concentrating on the relatively few instances when control breaks down.

The whole process of struggle and protest—its emergence or suppression —is perhaps best understood not in the context of strikes at all, but in the context of working class culture, ethnicity, and environment. The Manchester experience has suggested that practices and institutions that assisted workers in times of arrival, adjustment, and hardship may have been a double-edged sword. While providing cultural and ethnic reference groups, they may have served the company as well as the worker. By adopting policies that fostered ethnic identity and otherwise divided group from group, employers in other "corporation towns" may have been able successfully to arrest the development of working class consciousness.

Appendices

1. The 1835 and 1845 Tax List Samples

The 1835 and 1845 tax lists, at Manchester's City Hall, were computer coded, keypunched, and analyzed using both SPSS and programs written in Fortran by the author. Both lists were complete listings of all taxpayers. The 1835 list included all adult males, even those who did not vote or own property. The 1835 list provided data for 236 individuals. The 1845 data was for 1,518 taxpayers, and the categories reported were much more extensive, requiring use of two 80-column cards. The following was the coding system utilized:

1835 Tax List   N = 236

Field	Item Encoded
1	School District
2	Voting Status
3	Name of Taxpayer
4	Value of Real Estate
5	Value of Horses, 4 years old
6	Value of Horses, 2 years old
7	Value of Oxen
8	Value of Cows
9	Value of Neats
10	Value of Sheep
11	Value of Stock in Trade
12	Value of Bank Stock
13	Value of Carriages
14	Bank Deposits
15	Total Tax Assessment (individually reported as state, county, town, and school taxes)

1845 Tax List   N = 1,518

Field	Item Encoded
CARD ONE	
1	Card Number
2	Case Number
3	Name of Taxpayer
4	District
5	Voting Status
6	Value of Land
7	Value of Buildings
8	Value of Mills and Factories
9	Value of Ferries
10	Value of Toll Bridges
11	Value of Locks and Canals
12	Bank Deposits
13	Cash on Hand
14	Stock in Trade
CARD TWO	
—	Card Number as in Field 1
—	Case Number as in Field 2
—	Name of Taxpayer as in Field 3
15	Value of Carriages
16	Number of Horses
17	Value of Horses
18	Number of Cows
19	Value of Cows
20	Number of Sheep
21	Value of Sheep
22	Total Valuation
23	Reduced Valuation
24	Tax Assessed
25	Highway Tax
26	School Tax

2.   1850 Manuscript Census Schedules of Population and Agriculture

Census of Population (Property Owners)

N = 691

Field	Item Encoded
1	Identification Number
2	Name
3	Household Status
4	Race
5	Sex
6	Age
7	Occupation Code
8	Property Valuation
9	Birthplace
10	Marital Status

Census of Agriculture

N = 132

Field	Item Encoded
1	Name
2	Cash Value of Farm
3	Value of Implements and Machinery
4	Number of Improved Acres
5	Number of Unimproved Acres
6	Value of Livestock
7	Value of Horses
8	Number of Mules
9	Number of Cows
10	Number of Working Oxen
11	Number of Other Cattle
12	Number of Sheep
13	Number of Swine

3.   1870 Manuscript Population Schedule

N = 957

Field	Item Encoded
1	Identification Number
2	Household Number as Listed by Enumerator
3	Name
4	Number of Persons in Household
5	Number of Children in Household
6	Number of Households in this Dwelling Place
7	Age
8	Sex
9	Race
10	Occupation Code
11	Value of Real Estate
12	Value of Personal Estate
13	Place of Birth
14	Father of Foreign Birth
15	Mother of Foreign Birth
16	Attended School During Year
17	Ability to Read
18	Ability to Write
19	Deaf-Dumb-Insane
20	Probable Relationship to Head of Household

4. 1880 Census of Agriculture, District 134

N = 114

Field	*Item Encoded*
1	Identification Number
2	Name of Farmer
3	Tenure (Owner, Renter, Etc.)
4	Tilled Fields (acres)
5	Meadows (acres)
6	Woodlands (acres)
7	Other Lands (acres)
8	Value of Farm
9	Value of Machinery
10	Value of Livestock
11	Year's Fence Cost
12	Year's Labor Cost
13	Number of Weeks of Hired Labor During Past Year
14	Total Value, All Farm Products
15	Value of Orchard Products
16	Value of Nursery Products
17	Value Market Garden Products
18	Value of Forest Products
19	If Linked to Census Population, Number of Person as Listed in That Coding

**5.   1880 Manuscript Census of Population, Districts 133, 134, Sample from
       District 121**

Field	Item Encoded
1	Identification Number
2	Household Number as Listed by Enumerator
3	Name
4	Number of Persons in Household
5	Number of Children in Household
6	Number of Households, This Dwelling
7	House Number
8	Encoded Street Name
9	Race
10	Sex
11	Age
12	Marital Status
13	Relationship to Head of Household
14	Occupation Code
15	Place of Birth
16	Father's Birthplace
17	Mother's Birthplace
18	Sick or Disabled Code
19	School Attendance Code
20	Literacy Code
21	Married Within the Year
22	Relationship of Boarder to Own Head of Household
23	Household Structure Code
24	Family Structure Code
25	Located in Census of Agriculture (for Dist. 134)
26	District Number
27	Number of Months Unemployed This Year
28	Works for Amoskeag/Stark Mills
29	Identified Dwelling as Company Owned Housing (District 121 Only)

District 121, N = 666
District 133, N = 2,037
District 134, N = 920

Notes

Introduction

1. This approach is evident in John R. Commons et al., *History of Labor in the United States* (New York, 1935) and in John R. Commons et al., eds., *A Documentary History of American Industrial Society*. The institutional stress of labor is evidenced clearly in the one volume treatments of labor such as Foster Rhea Dulles, *Labor in America* (New York, 1966); Henry Pelling, *American Labor* (Chicago, 1960); Thomas R. Brooks, *Toil and Trouble: A History of American Labor* (New York, 1966); and, as is obvious from the title, in Philip Taft, *Organized Labor in American History* (New York, 1964). It was also evident in the earlier issues of *Labor History*. More recently articles in *Labor History* have reflected the new stress on social history. For a discussion of the newer type of writing see Paul Faler, "Working Class Historiography," *Radical America*, 3 (1969), pp. 56-68; Robert H. Zeiger, "Workers and Scholars: Recent Trends in American Labor Historiography," *Labor History*, 12 (1972), pp. 245-266; Thomas Krueger, "American Labor Historiography: Old and New— A Review," *Journal of Social History*, 4 (1971), pp. 277-285; David Brody, "The Old Labor History and the New: In Search of an American Working Class," *Labor History*, 20 (1979), pp. 111-126. An important and well-argued plea for breaking down the artificial barriers between labor history and social history appears in Elizabeth H. Pleck, "Two Worlds in One: Work and Family," *Journal of Social History*, 10 (1976), pp. 178-195. American historians have become intensely aware of the cultural context within which workers must be treated by historians thanks to the work of E.P. Thompson, *The Making of the English Working Class* (New York, 1963).

2. Tamara K. Hareven, "Family Time and Industrial Time: Family and Work in a Planned Corporation Town, 1900-1924," *Journal of Urban History* 1 (May, 1975), pp. 365-389. Herbert G. Gutman, "Work, Culture and Society in Industrializing America, 1815-1919," *American Historical Review*, 78, no. 3 (June, 1973), pp. 531-588.

3   Caroline F. Ware, *Early New England Cotton Manufacture* (New York, 1931); Norman Ware, *The Industrial Worker, 1840-1860* (New York, 1924); Lance Davis, "The New England Textile Mills and the Capital Market: A Study in Industrial Borrowing, 1840-1860," *Journal of Economic History*, XX (March, 1960), pp. 1-30; Lance Davis, "Sources of Industrial Finance: The American Textile Industry, A Case Study," *Explorations in Entrepreneurial History*, 1st ser., IX (April, 1957), pp. 189-203; Lance Davis, "Stock Ownership in the Early New England Textile Industry," *Business History Review*, XXXII (Summer, 1958), pp. 204-222; Constance M. Green, *Holyoke, Massachusetts: A Case Study of the Industrial Revolution in America* (New Haven, 1939); David Jeremy, "Innovation in American Textile Technology During the Early 19th Century," *Technology and Culture*, vol. 14,

no. 1 (January, 1973), pp. 40-76; Hannah Josephson, *The Golden Threads: New England's Mill Girls and Magnates* (New York, 1949); Robert G. Layer, *Earnings of Cotton Mill Operatives, 1825-1914* (Cambridge, 1955); Robert G. Layer, "Wages, Earnings and Output of Four Cotton Textile Companies in New England, 1825-1860," unpublished Ph.D. dissertation, Harvard University, 1952; Robert G. LeBlanc, *Location of Manufacturing in New England in the 19th Century* (Hanover, N.H., 1969); Paul F. McGouldrick, *New England Textiles in the Nineteenth Century: Profits and Investments* (Cambridge, 1968); Vera Shlakman, *Economic History of a Factory Town: A Study of Chicopee, Mass.* (New York, 1935).

4. Hareven, "Family Time", also see Tamara K. Hareven and Randolph Langenbach, *Amoskeag: Life and Work in an American Factory-City* (New York, 1968).

5. Thomas Louis Dublin, "Women at Work: The Transformation of Work and Community in Lowell, Massachusetts, 1826-1860," Ph.D. dissertation, Columbia University, 1975.

6. Daniel J. Walkowitz, *Worker City, Company Town: Iron and Cotton Worker Protest in Troy and Cohoes, New York, 1855-84* (Urbana, 1978).

7. Hareven, "Family Time."

8. Walkowitz, *Worker City*, p. 70; p. 249.

9. See Stanley Buder, *Pullman: An Experiment in Industrial Order and Community Planning 1880-1930* (New York, 1967).

10. See John Coolidge, *Mill and Mansion: A Study of Architecture and Society in Lowell, Massachusetts, 1820-1865* (New York, 1942); also Shlakman, *Chicopee*, and Green, *Holyoke*.

11. See Gutman, "Work, Culture, and Society"; also Gutman, "Class, Status, and Community Power in Nineteenth-Century American Industrial Cities—Paterson, New Jersey: A Case Study," in Frederic Cople Jaher, ed., *The Age of Industrialism in America* (New York, 1968), pp. 263-87; William Goode, *World Revolution and Family Patterns* (New York, 1963); Tamara K. Hareven, "The Laborers of Manchester, New Hampshire, 1910-1922; Patterns of Adjustment to Industrial Life," *Labor History*, 16 (1975), pp. 249-265.

12. For recent treatment of this problem in textile towns see Dublin, "Women at Work"; also Jonathan Prude, "The Coming of Industrial Order: A Study of Town and Factory Life in Rural Massachusetts, 1813-1860," unpublished Ph.D. dissertation, Harvard University, 1976. For treatment of the general problem of population mobility see Peter R. Knights, *The Plain People of Boston, 1830-1860* (New York, 1971); Stephan Thernstrom and Peter R. Knights, "Men in Motion: Some Data and Speculations About Urban Population Mobility in Nineteenth Century America," *Journal of Interdisciplinary History* 1 (Autumn, 1970), pp. 7-35.

13. For the design of the town by the corporation see Randolph Langenbach, "An Epoch in Urban Design," *Harvard Bulletin* (April, 1968).

14. Dublin, "Women at Work," has argued that the sense of community that prevailed among native born working women in Lowell prior to the coming of the Irish was a major factor in labor protest.

15. Lowell, Holyoke and Chicopee have all been dealt with in work previously cited and in an abundance of additional literature. Lawrence has been treated in Donald Cole, *Immigrant City* (Chapel Hill, 1963).

16. Hareven and Langenbach, *Amoskeag*; Hareven, "The Laborers of Manchester;" Hareven, "Family Time."

17. Dublin, "Women at Work;" see also Thomas Louis Dublin, "Women, Work and the Family: Female Operatives in the Lowell Mills, 1830-1860," *Feminist Studies* 3 (1975), pp. 30-39, and Dublin "Women, Work, and Protest in the Early Lowell Mills," *Labor History* 16 (1975), pp. 99-116. Immigrant forms of community were undoubtedly different from those of the Yankee millgirls, but it is the case in Manchester that immigrants formed their own communities soon after arrival. These communities gave the same kind of support and assistance to their members as did the company boarding house system to the native born.

18. Prude, "Coming of Industrial Order" suggests that "leaving," out-mobility, was one of the strategies of workers in the Slater mills in Webster, Oxford, and Dudley. While this was also an alternative for workers in Manchester, a far wider range of choices was available. These included use of a sympathetic press, pressuring the overseer to overlook strict enforcement of work discipline, formation of ethnic communities and institutions, "larceny" of cloth, and appeals to the town's middle class citizenry for support. The sympathy and identification with the millworkers in Manchester extended by the town in general is not the case in all mill communities. For a contrasting view see David L. Carlton, "Mill and Town: The Cotton Mill Workers and the Middle Class in South Carolina, 1880-1920," Ph.D. dissertation, Yale University, 1977.

19. Walkowitz, *Worker City*.

20. See David Brody, "The Old Labor History" for comments on the value of quantitative materials to new approaches in labor history and social history.

21. Daniel Creamer and Charles W. Coulter, *Labor and the Shutdown of the Amoskeag Textile Mills* (Works Project Administration, 1939); George Waldo Browne, *The Amoskeag Manufacturing Company of Manchester, New Hampshire: A History* (Manchester, 1915). Recently scholars have begun to utilize the manuscript returns of the census of manufacturing to round out our knowledge of social history. While economists have long recognized the value of such materials, its use by social historians, asking new questions of the materials, holds great promise. See Bruce Laurie, et al., "Immigrants and Industry: The Philadelphia Experience, 1850-1880," *Journal of Social History,* 9 (1975), pp. 219-248; Anthony E. Broadman and Michael P. Weber, "Economic Growth and Occupational Mobility in 19th Century America," *Journal of Social History* 11 (1977), pp. 52-73.

Chapter 1

1. A listing of town office holders appears in John B. Clarke, *Manchester. A Brief Record of Its Past and a Picture of Its Present* (1875). Town Records, Old Derryfield Books No. 1 and 2 are printed in *Manchester Historic Association Collections, 1906*.

2. Old Derryfield Books, Town Records.

3. From 1830 to 1840, three men served once as selectmen, three men served twice, four men served three terms, one man served five terms, and one man served seven terms. Only 25% of the selectmen's positions were held by one-time office-holders. In the following ten years, 81% of the men who would serve as selectmen would serve for one term only.

4. Old Derryfield Books, Records of 1799, 1797, 1793.

5. Ibid., 1799.

6. Chandler E. Potter, *The History of Manchester* (1856). 1835 tax records from *Collections* of Manchester Historic Association. Clarke, *Manchester*.

7. 1851 *Address* of Rev. Cyrus W. Wallace. Rev. Wallace's impression of the moral quality of fishermen at Amoskeag Falls is confirmed by William Moore and Joseph Kidder in Vol. III Manchester Historic Association *Collections*, "Early Recollections of Manchester," pp. 65-79; "Manchester as a Village," pp. 211-214.

8. Chandler Potter's 1856 *History* gives a brief sketch of the Judge's colorful personality as well as his imprecation. Rev. Wallace, in 1851, suggested that the judge may have been upset at the coming of the factory for not altogether civic-minded reasons. The judge had been considered one of the more well-educated members of the community and had performed some accounting tasks for the Bell and Island Mills and may have served a term as interim agent for those mills. The larger corporation dispensed with the judge's services.

9. Potter, *History;* Clarke, *Manchester*.

10. "Reminiscenses of David Lane Perkins, Who Saw the City Grow from a Sandbank," presented at first meeting of the Manchester Historic Association, 1896. Manuscript, Manchester Public Library. The process described herein whereby an older agricultural community was absorbed—overwhelmed—by the new industrial settlement was not the case in all instances. Jonathan Prude, "The Coming of Industrial Order: A Study of Town and Factory Life in Rural Massachusetts, 1813-1860," unpublished Ph.D. dissertation, Harvard University, 1976, demonstrates that the town of Webster was founded after Oxford and Dudley were able successfully to resist domination by the Slater interests. It should be noted that the Slater operation in Southern New England was not undertaken on the scale of the Boston Associates' communities. Caroline Ware, Constance Green, and Vera Shlakman all illustrate the large-scale undertakings of the Boston group. By contrast, the Slater interests apparently were not prepared to take over and dominate existing communities. They apparently found it easier to move than to fight established and determined local interests.

11. U.S. Census, 1820-1890. Moses Fellows would provide an unofficial estimate of population for 1835, a non-census year, during which construction of the mills was taking place. Fellows set the 1835 population at "under 1,000."

12. Rev. Cyrus Wallace, 1851. David Lane Perkins, "Reminiscenses."

13. Town Record Book, 1839. Potter noted the pride of the older village by their fairness.

14. Joseph Kidder, "Early Recollections of Manchester."

15. Both Potter and Perkins give accounts of the disruptions of the 1840 town meeting. John Clarke's 1875 work also presents an account of that meeting.

16. In spite of the 30 constables, and the reading of the riot act, violence erupted. When one constable attempted to quell the disturbance, he was chased from the meeting by a mob and force to hide for fear of his life.

17. Old Derryfield Record Books, 1780.

18. Rev. Cyrus Wallace, 1851.

19. George W. Browne, *The Amoskeag Manufacturing Company*, pp. 20-26. Rev. Wallace gives a full account of Blodgett's life. There is additional manuscript material on Blodgett and the building of the canal in Blodgett boxes at the Manchester Historic Association Library.

20. Ibid., p. 24.

21. Ibid., pp. 20-26.

22. John Borden Armstrong, *Factory Under the Elms*. New Hampshire governors would repeatedly complain about the abandonment of the farms as a major problem for the state.

23. Rev. C. W. Wallace tells of the return of this son to Manchester as an old man, lamenting the fact that economic circumstances had forced him to abandon the family farm.

24. Joseph Kidder, "Early Recollections of Manchester." As a boy, Kidder was warned to beware of the raftsmen and taught to differentiate between raftsmen and boatsmen.

25. Ibid.

26. 1835 tax records from *Collections,* Manchester Historic Association.

27. Ibid.

28. Ibid.

29. Ibid. The Bell and Island Mills engaged in woolen as well as cotton manufacture, thus would provide a market for local wool. The original charter granted to Benjamin Pritchard and others was for "The Amoskeag Cotton and Woolen Manufactory Company."

30. Ibid.

31. Rev. C. W. Wallace, 1851.

32. Wallace would later study at Amherst for the ministry, but in his youth he participated in the home manufacturing process. He gives the account of Agent Gillis carrying yarn on the back of his saddle, and finished goods, woven into cloth, which he would pick up, tied to the front of his saddle. Wallace's notebooks are in the library of the Manchester Historic Association.

33. George W. Browne typescript in New Hampshire Collection, Manchester Public Library. Agent Dean's notebooks and papers are in the library at the Manchester Historic Association.

34. Agent Dean's notebooks and papers.

35. Ibid.

36. Ibid.

37. Ibid.

38. Ibid.

39. Agent Dean kept memoranda of oral agreements which he had reached with local farmers as well as of written agreements which he made with workers and building craftsmen.

40. Dean notebooks and papers.

41. Ibid.

42. Manchester City Directories, 1842, 1844, 1846.

43. David L. Perkins; Rev. C. W. Wallace.

44. Moses W. Fellows, *Address,* 1851.

45. 1846, Register of Residents of Manchester, New Hampshire, in library, Manchester Historic Association.

46. Ibid.

47. 1846, Register of Residents, Defense Department Tables, 1968. Dublin's findings on early Lowell confirm the local nature of migrants to early industrial cities. See Thomas Louis Dublin, "Women at Work."

48. *Daily Gleaner,* April 5, 1845. Box of Parker Murder materials at Manchester Historic Association.

49. Parker Murder material, Manchester Historic Association.

50. E. P. Thompson has dealt extensively with the culture of pre-industrial work in *The Making of the English Working Class.* Gutman has taken up this theme in his essay, "Work, Culture, and Society."

Chapter 2

1. Wirth's formulation appeared in his "Urbanism as a Way of Life," *Amer. Journal Socio-
    logy,* July, 1938, pp. 1-24. For the extent to which sociologists have accepted Wirth's hypo-
    thesis, see, for example, Nels Anderson, "Urbanism and Urbanization," *Amer. Journal
    Sociology,* Vol. 65, 1959. Anderson clearly views urbanism's influence as penetrating and
    pervasive. Similarly, Kingsley Davis argued in the mid-'50's, that such phenomenon "af-
    fect every aspect of existence." Moreover, Davis argued, this effective domination of other
    aspects of a society should have been at its height during the years of the fastest rate of ur-
    banization—in the U.S., between 1861 and 1891. See Kingsley Davis, "The Origin and
    Growth of Urbanization in the World," *Amer. Journal Sociology,* 60 (1955), pp. 429-37.
    The effect of writing since Wirth's 1938 essay has been to stress Wirth's conclusion that
    "the individual becomes effective only as he acts through organized groups." The overrid-
    ing importance of impersonal forces in shaping the character of societies versus the role
    which individuals can play in those societies was reinforced by Maurice Stein's argument in
    The Eclipse of Community (Princeton, 1960). Stein regarded industrialization, urbaniza-
    tion, and bureaucratization as the major forces shaping modern societies. This has tended,
    until very recently, to reinforce the basic outlook of the work of John R. Commons and as
    sociates. For Commons, workers reacted to the impersonal forces of the marketplace and
    the mode of production. They were acted upon. Workers acted only insofar as they opera-
    ted within the context of union organization—only insofar as they themselves became de-
    personalized. The stress is upon organization of both stimulus and response—organized re-
    sponses to impersonal forces. Workers were important to Commons and other Wisconsin
    scholars only insofar as they related to overall patterns of economic development. Workers'
    attitudes, cultures, habits, or traditions were important only insofar as they affected the
    growth and maturation of national unions. These larger groups constituted forces powerful
    enough to have some impact upon the development of industrial society, and, in turn, on
    workers' lives. This famework of the operation of impersonal forces has been taken fur-
    thest, perhaps, by Clark Kerr. See, for example, Clark Kerr et al., *Industrialism and Indus-
    trial Man* (New York, 1964). Kerr argued that industrialism's power is so overwhelming as
    to eventually force all industrial societies into a similar mold. In Kerr's "pluralistic industri-
    alism," culture, politics, economic organization, institutional background, even historical
    development and uniqueness are all, ultimately, unimportant. Kerr regards industrialism as
    so overwhelming in power as to subsume all differences to force a similar framework upon
    all industrial societies. See also, Sidney Greenfield, "Industrialization and the Family in
    Sociological Theory," *American Journal of Sociology,* 67 (1961), pp. 312-22.

2. The recent work of new labor and social historicans has tended to raise questions about the
    validity of the Commons' approach. Recent work has stressed local as opposed to national
    trends, viewing local and ethnic culture and tradition as important determinants of reac-
    tions towards the industrial system. Gutman's work stands in contrast to the Commons
    school's stress on the so-called manualist psychology, whereby workers are regarded as
    creatures concerned solely with goal-oriented, job-centered solutions to industrial problems.
    Gutman has stressed, in *AHR,* vol. 78, June, 1973, the importance of culture as a major
    factor in workers' lives and in their reactions to their total situation. See also Gutman's
    "The Worker's Search for Power in the Gilded Age," in H. Wayne Morgan, ed., *The
    Gilded Age.* Others have begun to question a framework which ignores workers' cultures,
    traditions, and family patterns. For a discussion of some of this work, and a suggestion that
    the family might be regarded as a force for social change, see Tamara Hareven's "The His-
    tory of the Family as an Interdisciplinary Field," in *Journal Interdisciplinary History,*

Autumn, 1971. This argument is strengthened in Hareven, "Family Time." American historians are heavily indebted to the work of E.P. Thompson who has illustrated the rich variety of class and cultural resources of British workers.

3.   Alan Sweezy, "The Amoskeag Manufacturing Company," in *Quarterly Journal of Economics,* vol. LII, pp. 473-512. Both the local histories of Potter and Clarke stress the importance of the early years of the Amoskeag in terms of coming to terms with a new way of life.

4.   U.S. Census of Population, manuscript and published tabulations, 1850-1880. "Town Report," 1850, at N.H. State Library, Concord.

5.   Ibid.

6.   The manuscript returns of the Census of Manufactures for 1850-1880, located at the N.H. State Library, Concord, are a particularly valuable source on the employment patterns of women and children in an era when no state agencies existed to investigate such matters. For the tables presented here, the Census Bureau's published data for 1840 and 1880 were utilized. The data for 1850, 1860, and 1870 was gathered and tabulated by the author from the manuscript returns. In all cases, tables for those years were compiled by the author and include data for *every* industrial establishment making returns, regardless of size of industry.

7.   The extent to which employment was available to women and children in non-textile areas of work in Manchester was limited throughout this period. While the Amoskeag's announced policy was not to "exploit" child labor, the Amoskeag did differentiate between employing and exploiting children. While children were employed by the Amoskeag, the number of child employees was far below the proportion anticipated by the company's size and importance, and was far fewer, in percentage and absolute terms, than the number of children employed by other companies in Manchester. The very fact that smaller companies employed far more children than did the Amoskeag may indicate that in fact the company was conservative in its employment (abuse) of child labor. It should be noted that the Amoskeag's cautiousness was not a town-wide policy, and other textile firms such as the Manchester Print Works and the Langdon Mills, for example, were free to set their own policies in this regard. For comparable data on Lowell in 1850 and 1860, see Thomas Dublin, "Women at Work," p. 512.

8.   Data compiled by the author from manuscript returns, Census of Manufactures, N.H. State Library, Concord.

9.   *Amoskeag Representative,* Jan. 10, 1840. See also *Amoskeag Memorial.* A large number of local newspapers were published in Manchester. Between 1839 and 1849, Chamberlain's bibliography of Manchester newspapers indicates at least 36 separate titles. While some of these titles remain preserved in shameful neglect at the Manchester Public Library, many more were available when Daniel Creamer's W.P.A. team undertook its study of the closing of the Amoskeag. The author is indebted to Creamer for the use of his notes on newspaper material which he located, and to Randolph Langenbach for making copies of Creamer's notes available. The best source for Manchester newspaper material today remains the Manchester Public Library and the N.H. Historic Society. Use of local materials gives a far different picture of the worker than can be obtained from relying on national and area-wide periodicals or periodicals of special interest concerns.

10. *Manchester Operative,* April 27, 1844. This periodical encountered the difficulty of many early Manchester newspapers whose chief interest was "the interests of manual labor." Within two years of its foundation, by a local printer, William Haradon, it merged with a Lowell labor periodical, and although it continued to carry a Manchester masthead and maintain a local office, its main work was done at Lowell and its main concerns were with the wider New England Workingmen's Movement, and not with Manchester's workers. This serves to illustrate one of the pitfalls of the Commons' approach. Working men and women in Manchester or in other towns for the most part operated in a local context. Their responses, their culture, their concerns, their traditions, were reactions to and influenced by local conditions or grievances. While some workers were concerned with the larger philosophical issues of a New England Workingmen's Movement, a far greater determinant of workers' perceptions of their own well-being was, for example, the cost of land and housing in Manchester. These sorts of concerns influenced the day to day lives of most workers far more than did the speculations of a New England-wide workingmen's conference. For a local man, Asa Reed, for example, a vital concern was that he be able to hold on to the plot of land on Vine Street which he, as a laborer, had purchased from the Amoskeag in 1838. By 1844, Reed would remain in the house that he built there, but between 1844 and 1848 he joined the ranks of those who took profits from a rising real estate market, and sold. Like Asa Reed, most workers were uninterested in "movements" of workers. To concentrate on state-wide or region-wide movements is to ignore the experiences of the majority of workers. Data on Asa Reed obtained from Amoskeag materials, M.H.A., Amoskeag Land Sales Books, M.H.A., city directories, 1842-48. By relying on periodical material, especially labor periodicals, Commons focused on the concerns of the leaders of the wider movements rather than on the life experiences of the majority of workers. For examples of the extent to which Commons relied on the wider circulation labor press or on phalanx literature (*The Harbinger,* for example), see his *Documentary History,* especially his treatment of the N.E. Workingmen's movement. *Manchester Representative,* Jan. 1842. George W. Browne manuscript material, Manchester Public Library.

11. *Manchester American,* Jan. 1863. See the Amoskeag Company's drawings and planbooks at M.H.A.; Land and Water Power Company—agreements and contracts, M.H.A.; *Weekly Mirror,* Sept. 29, 1855; *Dollar Weekly Mirror,* April 9, 1864.

12. *Amoskeag Representative,* Oct. 18, 1839. Newspapers often took the part of the workers, advocating workers' interests and denouncing their fellow editors as corporate lackeys. For an illustration of this kind of newspaper war see, for example, *Manchester Representative,* Sept. 3, 1841; Gleaner, Oct. 5, 1844; Aug. 31, 1844, Sept. 6, 1845; *Union Democrat,* Dec. 1, 1842; *Daily Union,* Feb. 1853; *Democrat,* Sept. 25, 1851. Even the pro-corporation *American* used this strategy. Any editor too openly or frequently favoring the Amoskeag was sure to come under attack as the *American* did frequently. The *American* maintained that it advocated "true neutrality," while other editors claiming neutrality summarized the arguments of their warring brethren.

13. *The Weekly Mirror,* Sept. 29, 1855, gave a general account of land policy and land prices in Sept., 1855. *Dollar Weekly Mirror,* April 9, 1864; *Daily Union,* April 1865. The rise in land values was also noted by Susan Blount and by David Lane Perkins in materials preserved at the Manchester Public Library. See also, *The Operative,* April 1844.

14. See following tables compiled from manuscript census returns, 1850. SPSS data analysis of 1850 manuscript census returns demonstrate age and occupation cross tabs. The author is indebted to Thor Olsen, Director of Computer Operations, Holy Cross College, and to Al Larsen, Computer Center Director of Clark University, for their technical advice and aid in debugging his programs.

15. *Dollar Weekly Mirror,* April 9, 1864.

16. Ibid., Sept. 29, 1855.

17. Lewis Mumford has been among those to take note of the Amoskeag's workers' housing, citing Manchester as a notable exception to the prevailing general foulness of workers' housing conditions. Mumford, *The Culture of Cities,* pp. 166-67. Susan Blount also mentions workers' housing in manuscript material at M.H.A.

18. Rev. Henry M. Dexter, *Address,* 1848; William Jewett Tucker, "The Spiritual Life of the Modern City," 1896. Tucker was President of Dartmouth College and had served the early years of his ministry as a clergyman in Manchester.

19. Dexter, *Address,* 1848; Tucker, "Spiritual Life," 1896; Rev. Samuel Bartlett, *Address, 1854.*

20. Stearns Papers, M.H.A. Stearns' general account is confirmed by Potter; Amoskeag Papers, directives to workers M.H.A.

21. See Alan Sweezey's account of the Amoskeag's closing years; data presented in Tables 5-7 confirm the earlier figure.

22. Potter and Clarke give an account of early mill policy. One key to the policy of non-competition was in the selling agency. All of Manchester's mills customarily marketed their production through the same agent. For many years, the agent for Manchester's mills was Gardner Brewer and Company.

23. Both Potter and Clarke give details of Straw's rise from surveyor to agent. The importance of the Straw family throughout Manchester's history is confirmed in Hareven's *Amoskeag.* She notes that many workers felt that the Straws owned the mills.

24. David Perkins, *Reminiscences.* Browne manuscript material, M.P.L.

25. Browne material and Carter Papers, M.P.L.

26. The newspapers served not only to herald good times, but to predict bad times as well. *Amoskeag Representative,* Jan. 1841; *Weekly Mirror,* Feb. 1855; Jan. 13, 1855; *The Democrat,* Dec. 21, 1848; *Gleaner,* January 7 and June 1, 1843.

27. Potter and Clarke both deal with the corporation's benevolence towards the town as does Browne's history of the company. See also Browne typescript at M.P.L. and Amoskeag material, M.H.A.

Occupation

Legend (cell contents):
- Count
- Row %
- Col %
- Tot %

Age	Profes-sional	Semi-Prof.	Farm	White Collar	Skilled	Semi-Skill	Unskill	Not Known	Total
15-19	0	0	0	0	1 33.3 1.4 .1	0	1 33.3 1.4 .1	1 33.3 1.4 .1	3
20-24	1 3.7 3.3 .1	2 7.4 1.9 .3	3 11.1 2.9 .4	1 3.7 4.3 .1	13 48.1 4.8 1.9	0	4 14.8 6.4 .6	3 11.1 4.2 .4	27
25-29	2 2.2 6.7 .3	5 5.6 4.9 .7	9 10.1 8.8 1.3	2 2.2 1.9 .3	52 58.4 19.2 7.5	8 8.9 2.7 1.1	7 7.9 11.3 1.0	4 4.5 5.6 .6	89
30-34	3 2.6 10.0 .4	23 19.8 22.3 3.3	13 11.2 12.7 1.9	4 3.4 17.4 .6	47 40.5 17.3 6.8	10 8.6 33.3 1.4	10 8.6 16.1 1.4	6 5.2 8.3 .9	116
35-39	8 5.8 26.7 1.2	32 23.4 31.1 4.6	13 9.5 12.7 1.9	3 2.2 13.0 .4	63 46.0 23.2 9.1	6 4.4 20.0 .9	5 3.6 8.1 .7	7 5.1 9.7 1.0	137
40-44	5 4.9 16.7 .7	13 12.7 12.6 1.9	16 15.7 15.7 2.3	7 6.9 30.4 1.0	37 36.3 13.7 5.3	3 2.9 10.0 .4	13 12.7 21.0 1.9	8 7.8 11.1 1.2	102

Occupation

Age	Count / Row % / Col % / Tot %	Profes-sional	Semi-Prof.	Farm	White Collar	Skilled	Semi-Skill	Unskill	Not Known	Total
45-49		5 / 6.5 / 16.7 / .7	14 / 18.2 / 13.6 / 2.0	10 / 13.0 / 9.8 / 1.4	0	26 / 33.8 / 9.6 / 3.8	1 / 1.3 / 3.3 / .1	5 / 6.5 / 8.1 / .7	16 / 20.8 / 22.2 / 2.3	77
50-54		2 / 3.4 / 6.7 / .3	4 / 6.8 / 3.9 / .6	11 / 18.6 / 10.8 / 1.6	4 / 6.8 / 17.4 / .6	17 / 28.8 / 6.3 / 2.5	1 / 1.7 / 3.1 / .1	10 / 16.9 / 16.1 / 1.4	10 / 16.9 / 13.9 / 1.4	59
55-59		2 / 5.1 / 6.7 / .3	5 / 12.8 / 4.9 / .7	12 / 30.8 / 11.0 / 1.7	2 / 5.1 / 8.7 / .3	7 / 17.9 / 2.6 / 1.0	1 / 2.6 / 3.3 / .1	5 / 12.8 / 8.1 / .7	5 / 12.8 / 6.9 / .7	39
60-64		1 / 3.7 / 3.3 / .1	3 / 11.1 / 2.9 / .4	8 / 29.6 / 7.8 / 1.2	0	6 / 22.2 / 2.2 / .9	0	1 / 3.7 / 1.6 / .1	8 / 29.6 / 11.1 / 1.2	27
over 65		1 / 5.9 / 3.3 / .1	2 / 11.8 / 1.9 / .3	7 / 41.2 / 6.9 / 1.0	0	2 / 11.8 / .7 / .3	0	1 / 5.9 / 1.6 / .1	4 / 23.5 / 5.6 / .6	17
Total		30	103	102	23	271	30	62	72	693

Source: 1850 Manuscript Census of Population

28. Workers called the benevolence of the company into question before the general public began to do so. *Gleaner,* May 11, 1844. Local histories deal with the Valley Cemetery donation as does the company history. *The Memorial and Manchester Workman,* 1841. Perhaps last openly to criticize the company were public officials. For an example of the latter, see Major Frederick Smyth's *Third Electoral Address.* Smyth stresses the importance of the town's self-determination "without dictation." Also see *Union Democrat,* April 1854.

29. The labor press was the first to pick up the theme of the Amoskeag's use of land restrictions to threaten would-be dissenters. *Manchester Operative,* June 8, 1844.

30. Town Reports, N.H. State Library. Specifically, reports of parks and cemeteries stress required improvements that were never made.

31. Some farmers would find the new towns a source of unanticipated wealth. Supplying industrial residents with wood, food, firewood, services, and building materials would play an important part in the social and the economic lives of farmers located within traveling distance of the industrial town. The extent to which farm and factory provided one another with mutual support is a question that has received little exploration. Michael Anderson's work on Lancashire textile workers has demonstrated that significant rural-urban differences and interrelationships may exist. A question that remains relatively unexplored is the relationship between farmers and factory workers living in close proximity to one another. Did farmers' sons and daughters enter the factory work force? Was farm income alone sufficient to support the family? Could industrial workers find shelter or employment on the nearby farms? The danger in regarding a town such as Manchester as the model of a factory town is that such a model ignores the very presence of a substantial farming community. Even to the time of the closing of the mills, contemporaries saw farms as an important part of the town's life. Jonathan Prude's dissertation treats the relationship between a farming and an industrial population. In a later chapter, census data from the census of agriculture will be correlated with data from the census of population and used as a basis for comparison between agricultural and industrial residents of Manchester. Another question which has been largely ignored is the co-existence of an entire category of "labor" —farm labor. In the 1855 dispute over the hours of labor, workmen would often be urged by the corporation to judge their own position in relative terms—measured against the long day worked by the shopkeeper and the still longer day of the farmer. Michael Anderson, *Family Structure in Nineteenth Century Lancashire* (Cambridge, 1971).

32. Such a system is discussed as a rationale for the founding of Manchester's Franklin Street Church. The manufacturing town, with its all-pervasive influence, was regarded by contemporaries as "a new element in the civilization of this century." Clergymen regarded the organized activity and control program of the company as an absolute necessity if "civilization" was to survive. Henry M. Dexter, *Discourse,* 1847, M.H.A.

33. See Agent Straw's memorandum on company regulations, bound with workers' signatures, at M.H.A. Official policy was very clear that only those who abided by the rules should be employed. See also Stearns' material, and company material at M.H.A. for examples of "work releases" for those employees faithfully following rules.

34. Henry M. Dexter, *Discourse,* 1847; Rev. Samuel C. Bartlett, *An Address,* 1854.

35. Amoskeag Register of Employees and Regulations, M.H.A. By 1878, workers were no longer required to accede to company policy in writing.

36. Commons' *Documentary History* views such practices as commonplace, but not for a time period so late as the 1870's. See pp. 135 ff. Rules are presented in *Documentary History* as typifying the 1840's.

37. For an example of a worker's unwillingness to accept a situation where "we the leaders manufacture public sentiment for you, and you must bow to our benefits, and woe to those who do not follow in our wake," see *Democrat,* April 15, 1852. At each election, attempts to influence workers' votes were vigorously denounced and those corporate officers guilty of such practices openly accused and named. See, for example, *Gleaner,* Dec. 16, 1843; *Union Democrat,* April 5 and 17, 1854; *The Democrat,* Aug. 23, 1842; June 1843; *Union Democrat,* Oct. 1852; March-April, 1863. The same paper deals with managers instructing overseers to persuade workers not to buy labor newspapers—June 22, 1853. The Amoskeag's rationale for discontinuing its workers' savings bank was that the need for such a bank no longer existed with the opening of banks in town. Nevertheless, at the time discontinuation was announced, there were no savings banks in town—only banks dealing with businesses. One of the reasons for discontinuance may have been worker pressure and protest over the corporation's extension into areas of their lives other than work. Such a protest, aimed specifically at the Amoskeag's savings bank, appeared in *Union Democrat,* April 6, 1853.

38. The table for 1880 should be regarded with some caution, since it was tabulated by the Census Bureau and thus its data can be misleading when viewed in the context of the 1850-1880 series presented here. It would be wrong, for example, to judge the percentage of children employed in textiles as seriously declining (strictly interpreted the tables would imply that child employment in textiles fell from 95% of the child labor force in 1870 to 50% in 1880). The 1880 figure represents cotton manufacturing mills only, whereas previous data reflected all textile industrial employment. A more accurate reading of the 1880 table in relation to the others in this series can be obtained by a careful consideration of the "cotton goods," and "other" categories combined. The "other" employed by the census, in tabulating the 1880 data, includes wool manufacturing, all dying, finishing and weaving operations— by the standards applied in compiling the other tables in this series, all of these are very clearly "textile" operations. Similar cautions apply when judging the relative employment spectrum opportunities for men and women from 1850-1880. For example, the 1880 figure indicating that around 80% of females were employed in "cotton goods" does not mean that a large number of non-textile jobs opened up for women between 1870 (when about 95% of employed women were engaged in textile operations) and 1880. Judged in this context, it seems fair to say that there was little significant widening of employment opportunities outside of textile manufacturing throughout the 1850-1880 period. Even in terms of male (non-farm) employment opportunities, the dominant fact throughout the period was the tremendous growth of textile manufacturing. While larger numbers of men, absolutely speaking, would find non-textile employment over the years, the overall percentage of males engaged in textile employment, certainly from 1850 to 1870, and probably to 1880, remained substantially the same.

Chapter 3

1. Alan Dawley, *Class and Community: The Industrial Revolution in Lynn* (Cambridge, 1976) deals with the context of the larger community within which workers found themselves but stresses political structure and response as a product of industrial capitalism. See, for example, Chapter 4, pp. 97-128. David Montgomery, "The Shuttle and the Cross: Weavers and Artisans in the Kensington Riots of 1844," *Journal Social Hist.*, 5 (1972), pp. 411-46, deals with ethnic and cultural backgrounds and traditions of workers. On the importance of the practice of boarding as an adaptive mechanism, see the insightful article by John Modell and Tamara K. Hareven, "Urbanization and the Malleable Household: An Examination of Boarding and Lodging in American Families," *Journal of Marriage and the Family*, 35 (1973), pp. 467-79.

2. Agent Dean's notebooks, M.H.A. for earlier period. Data on workers' housing obtained from samples of workers entering AMC taken by the author from 1860 and 1870 company records, M.H.A.

3. Data from Amoskeag records, M.H.A. The approach emphasizing workers' roles as members of unions, tended to overlook the impact which workers could have on the work processes outside of union actions. In 1971, writing in the *Journal of Social History*, 5, Thomas Krueger noted that until recently this had been the dominant approach to the study of labor —". . . the history of American labor has been little more than a series of extended footnotes and additional appendices to the work of the Wisconsin historians." Krueger, pp. 277-285, "American Labor Historiography, Old and New: A Review Essay," reinforces the recency of the newer approach. See also Elizabeth Pleck's article "Two Worlds in One: Work and Family," *Journal of Social History*, 10 (1976), pp. 178-95.

4. *Gleaner*, June 10, 1843.

5. Ibid. The importance of Mary's account is not that it is a colorful narrative, but that it was published. The fact that workers possessed mechanisms for warning their colleagues of bad working conditions, unfair treatment, pay shortages, unjust overseers and the like, serves to illustrate the point that workers were not helpless victims in the face of larger forces dominating their lives. They could, and did, have an effect on the factory system's discipline and working conditions. This effect was a powerful determinant of the responses of factory managers to workers. While managers may have negotiated only with unions, they responded to a wide variety of stimuli. Public opinion was a powerful force, and recognized as such by both workers and managers. Gutman has suggested that public attitudes are seriously affected by company size. Such a position regards stereotypes of labor's powerlessness in the face of an oppressive capitalism as an approach that needs to be revised. Gutman's work would suggest that workers like Mary are not atypical, and that bread and butter issues were not workers' sole concerns.

6. Ibid., June 17, 1843. Letter to the editor dated June 14.

7. Ibid. This represents a demonstration of the fact that workers were concerned with larger issues of freedom of choice in matters such as where one was to live. These matters could be paramount to workers. They were not obsessed solely with the question of wages. Perlman's manualist psychology may be out of touch with the reality of workers' everyday needs. The local battle for public opinion (which Commons overlooks) assured that com-

promise was part and parcel of the process of worker-management accommodation. In Manchester's case, bread and butter issues such as wages and hours come to our attention not only because they were the only issues, but because they were the areas where, because of the structure of the industry, local accommodation broke down.

8. *Weekly Mirror,* May 19, 1855; *Gleaner,* April 15, 1843; data compiled by the author from 1846 Register of Residents, M.H.A.

9. In a town that witnessed the tremendous growth of Manchester, demand for labor was practically constant, and was one additional factor pushing factories towards local accommodation. This was especially true in view of the tremendous turnover in labor. Henry Dexter termed Manchester a vast boarding school where operatives stayed, on the average, 4-5 years. See manuscript material at Manchester Public Library and M.H.A. *Weekly Mirror,* May 19, 1855; Agent Dean's notebooks for early employment situation. For changes, see *Manchester Democrat,* Sept. 8, 1847; *Union and Democrat,* Sept. 15, 1852; *Weekly Mirror,* June 30, 1855; *Dollar Weekly Mirror,* Feb. 13 and May 12, 1864.

10. *Dollar Weekly Mirror,* Jan. 30, 1864. This story also indicates a new camaraderie between overseers and workers as a result of the need for experienced help. See *Gleaner,* May 6, 1843, for the evil in working conditions that could result from "the gradual encroachments of one or two overseers" in relation to traditional supervisor-worker relations.

11. The number and variety of Manchester's newspapers played an important role in the battle for public opinion. The number of men in town with printing presses and pages to fill assured operatives with grievances of a public hearing. Likewise, it assured overseers that poor treatment would be made known and the supply of good workers willing to go into their rooms would diminish. The corporation's concern for public opinion is demonstrated not only in their courting of middle-class opinion makers, but also in the corporation's eagerness to answer criticism in the press. *Manchester Representative,* Nov. 19, 1841; *Gleaner,* May 6, 1843; *Manchester Memorial,* Dec. 1842; *Operative,* May and June 1844; *Amoskeag Representative,* Jan. 1841.

12. Statistical data on places of child employment from 1870 Census of Manufactures, manuscript returns, N.H. State Library; *Union Democrat,* Dec. 14, 1853; *Daily American,* May 23, 1862; *Weekly American,* Dec. 10, 1863; *Democrat and American,* Jan. 29, 1863; *Dollar Weekly Mirror,* Jan. 9 and Nov. 12, 1864; *Daily Union,* Jan. 13, June 5, Nov. 18, 23, and 30, 1865.

13. *Weekly Mirror,* Nov. 24, 1855. When almost 80% of child workers worked in large textile enterprises, and when only eight business places in town utilized child labor, the Amoskeag's policy of refusing to exploit child labor must have seemed just more futile corporation rhetoric to townsmen. The grievance of the abuse of child labor was a real one, despite the Amoskeag's policy in that regard.

14. Manuscript returns, Census of Manufactures, N.H. State Library.

15. *Weekly Mirror,* May 19, 1855 (a time when reading in the workroom might be expected to have stopped completely); *Gleaner,* Oct. 11, 1845. Once again it should be stressed that the issues involved here are not Perlman's "bread and butter" issues of the labor "movement," but the issues of custom and tradition stressed by the newer approach. See Selig Perlman

and Philip Taft, *A History of Trade Unionism in the United States, 1896-1932* (New York, 1935); Selig Perlman, *A Theory of the Labor Movement* (New York, 1928).

16. *Union Democrat,* Oct. 27, 1852. Workers clearly regarded the workroom regulations as subject to adjustment between individual overseers and their workers. Such day-to-day operating accommodations were arrived at between employers (overseers) and workers, and involved such issues as perceived dignity, traditions, and customs.

17. *Manchester Representative,* July 23, 1841. Fears of Europeanization involved anxieties regarding loss of traditional position, customs, and rights, as much as they involved wages and hours. Burial in common land, the right to live where one chose under rules of one's own making—such issues as these were part of what workers sought and obtained outside of a formal union structure.

18. Frederick Smyth, Mayoral Address, 1854, M.H.A.; *Union Democrat,* April 1855.

19. *Manchester Operative,* June 1844.

20. *Amoskeag Representative,* July 1840; *Manchester Representative,* Dec. 1841.

21. *Manchester Democrat,* May 1848; July and Sept. 1847; *Weekly Mirror,* May 1855; Feb. 1855.

22. Town Report, 1852, N.H. State Library. Speakers on temperance were frequent in Manchester An investigation by the Mass. Bureau of Labor Statistics included testimony, in 1879, from a N.H. weaver regarding the pressures of the workroom that drove him to drink.

23. *Union Democrat,* Aug. 1852; see testimony of an operative regarding the cost of credit to buy shoes for his son, since he was paid only once per month. Mass. Bureau of Labor Statistics, 1879.

24. *Gleaner,* May 1844; *Democrat,* Dec. 1848; *Manchester Operative,* May 1844; *Manchester Democrat,* May and Aug. 1847.

25. *Manchester Democrat,* May 26, 1847. See also *Manchester Operative,* June 18, 1844 for complaints about manipulation of factory time.

26. The fact that Commons stresses the Ten Hour Movement to the extent that he does reflects his sources. While there is no doubt that the hours of labor were a vital issue to Manchester's workers, it was only one of many issues of vital concern to them. Only when a grievance finds its way into the literature of a state-wide, region-wide, trade-wide, or major newspaper or movement does it tend to become incorporated into the older history. The fact that New Hampshire passed the first Ten Hour Law in the nation forced Commons to deal with it (*Documentary History,* pp. 188 ff.), but for the most part he relied on wider area press coverage. He thus overlooked other issues which were closely allied to the simple demand for ten hours. While lesser grievances go untreated (lesser in the sense of geographically or trade-wide), the mechanisms for adjusting those grievances goes likewise undealt with. *Union Democrat,* Sept. 1847; *Manchester Operative,* May 1844; *Manchester Democrat,* Aug.-Sept., 1847.

27. *Manchester Democrat,* Sept. 15, 1847.

28. Workers sought out overseers with favorable attitudes towards their workers, and much of the letter writing published in newspapers was directed towards informing fellow workers of the character of the overseer. The rapport between a sympathetic overseer and his workers was but one of the ways in which workers avoided "Europeanization." Being hired by the overseer, rather than a corporation official, the worker could retain at least the feeling of being an artisan engaged by a master. A sympathetic overseer could do much to humanize the large corporation. Good overseers were regarded as fellow workers as well as being viewed as supervisors. Hardbitten overseers were regarded as embodying the evils brought along with the corporation. *Union Democrat,* June 1853; *Democrat,* April 1852; *Dollar Weekly Mirror,* Jan. 30, 1864.

29. *Manchester Democrat,* May 26, 1847, expresses the view that in the past corporations had demonstrably "... yielded to ... the tide of public opinion ... they must yield more." An overseer's letter in *Manchester Democrat,* Aug. 23, 1847; *Union Democrat,* Oct. 1853.

30. *Weekly Mirror,* Feb. 17, 1855. For Corporation viewpoints, consult *Manchester American.*

31. *Union Democrat,* March 28, 1855.

32. Ibid.; *Manchester American,* March 1855.

33. *Weekly Mirror,* Feb. 17, 1855; *Union Democrat,* July and Aug. 1855, March 1855.

34. Stearns Papers, M.H.A.; Kidder Papers, M.H.A.; *Weekly Mirror,* Feb. 17, 1855; *Union Democrat,* March 28, 1855.

35. *Union Democrat,* March 28, 1855.

36. By 1855, to be too closely allied with "the corporation" was a dangerous matter for a politician or a newspaper's survival. To this extent, a newspaper war involving the swapping of charges of being "corporation lackeys" was conducted. In truth, the *Manchester American* seems to have been, under the disguise of taking a "fair minded" approach, the paper to present corporate views. Their balanced view, as they called it, urged workers to judge their hours of labor in relationship to those of a shopkeeper or farmer; some were won over by this argument. Joseph Kidder makes essentially the same argument in his diaries.

37. *Union Democrat,* March 28, April 4, April 11, 1855.

38. Not only the mill management, but also the workers and the middle class saw the value of public opinion. Certainly by the mid-1850's, public opinion can be safely said to have favored the worker. Thereafter, the boosterism and pride in the Amoskeag which characterized much of the earlier literature would be replaced with an attitude of wariness. Earlier workers' fears of the corporation gained widespread support, while boosterism became the narrow concern of business and commercial men in testimonials and banquets. *Union Democrat,* April 4, 1855.

39. Ibid., April 11, also see July and August 1855.

40. Utilizing local sources, Gutman's views regarding the importance of other than the bread-and-butter issues are reinforced. Workers operated within the self-perception of a spinner,

a weaver, a worker for Mr. Otterson or Mr. Pine, not with the perception of being part of a vast area-wide working class. They found that they could affect corporate policy at the level where it most directly affected them—the room where they worked.

41. Only recently has recognition been given to the fact that the answer to what workers want (as opposed to what labor wants) may be more than "more." The disruptions of General Motors' Lordstown, Ohio assembly plant clearly have been involved with other than bread-and-butter issues. See, for example, William Serrin, *The Company and the Union* (New York, 1970); *Daily Union,* Nov. 1865; *Union and Democrat,* Oct. 10, 1865.

42. *Daily Union,* Feb. 1865. The phenomenon of cloth stealing is but another example of workers' attempts to find their own informal solutions to grievances. Given the inflexibility of wage policy, the stealing of cloth represented a way in which workers could, on their own, utilize informal mechanisms of accommodation, and apply those mechanisms to a new area—the area of wages. Workers took in kind what they had been denied in cash.

43. *Daily Union,* Feb. 9 and 14, Oct. 19, Nov. 2 and 10, 1865; *Union and Democrat,* Nov. 7, 1865.

44. *Union and Democrat,* Nov. 7, 1865; *Daily Union,* Oct. 10, 1865.

45. Town records, N.H. State Library. City directories and local biographical testimonials were utilized in determining office holders' occupations.

Chapter 4

1. Margaret Byington, *Homestead: The Household of a Mill Town* (Pittsburgh, 1974), Hays' Preface, "Homestead Revisited," pp. xvii-xxxiv.

2. Hays discusses some of these factors in his preface. See also Hareven, *Amoskeag.*

3. Town Records, Tax Collector's Office, City Hall.

4. Ibid. Actual range of real value, 1835, was $20-$5,000.

5. Data for 1845 arranged by residence allows test for propinquity as does 1850 census data. In both 1845 and 1850, propertyless residents frequently will be found in propinquity to property-owning residents of the same surname.

6. Town Records, 1835.

7. Ibid. M.H.A. Collections, Potter, *History.*

8. Ibid., School District Minutes, 1830-1840.

9. Parker murder files, M.H.A. Town Records, 1845. Tax Collector's Office, City Hall; John B. Clarke, *The Parker Murder,* pamphlet, 1886, Manchester; *The Gleaner,* April 5, 1845.

10. Town Records, 1845. Published Record Collection, M.H.A.

11. Town Records, 1845. Kidder manuscript, diary collection, M.H.A. Kidder files, M.H.A.

12. Town records, 1845.

13. 1850 U.S. Census.

14. Potter, *History;* Clarke, *History;* Perkins material, Manchester Historic Association; Browne, *History Amoskeag.* Stephan Thernstrom, *Povery and Progress* (Cambridge, 1964), provided a pioneering discussion of the issue of property acquisition and social mobility among the unskilled.

15. Savings Bank Records, Amoskeag New Mills, M.H.A. Collections.

16. Savings Bank material, M.H.A. City Directories, 1840-1846. Workers listed in directories as Stark workers found with AMC savings accounts.

17. *Union Democrat,* April 6, 1853, directly challenged the Amoskeag's right to carry on what the editor called a general banking business in violation of its charter. *Union Democrat,* April 12, 1854, in a slap at corporation-sponsored newspapers, similarly challenged the Amoskeag's involvement in the newspaper business.

18. Savings Bank material, M.H.A.

19. Amoskeag New Mills Savings Bank Records, M.H.A.

20. Ibid.

21. Savings Bank Records; Kidder material.

22. Sermon material, M.H.A. Stephan Thernstrom and Peter Knight, "Men in Motion: Some Data and Speculations about Urban Population Mobility in Nineteenth-Century America," *Journal of Interdisciplinary History* 1 (1970), pp. 7-35, discusses the complexity of population mobility in detail.

23. Town Records, 1845.

24. Town Records, 1835, 1845; City Directories; Potter, *History.*

25. Town Records, 1835, 1845.

26. Ibid.

27. Ibid.

28. Town Records, 1835, 1845; Census of Agriculture, State Library, Concord.

29. Census of Agriculture, 1850; Census of Population, 1850; City Directories, 1846-1850; ANM paybooks, M.H.A.

30. Calculations of local wages based upon business records at M.H.A. and the Kidder diaries.

31. For a contrasting experience, see David Lee Carlton, "Mill and Town." Carlton found great hostility between "town people" and "mill people". Jonathan Prude has also dealt with hostility between an industrial and an established population.

32. Town Records. Data from SPSS Codebook Analysis of Aggregate Data, utilizing DEC system-10, Edition 2.

33. Ibid. Figures from SPSS Codebook Analysis of Aggregate Data.

34. Town Records, 1835.

35. Ibid.

36. Ibid., 1845.

37. Ibid., 1835, 1845.

38. Ibid.

39. Ibid.

40. Ibid., 1845.

41. Ibid.

42. Ibid., 1835, 1845.

43. Ibid., 1845.

44. Ibid., 1835.

45. U.S. Mscpt. Census, Population Schedules, 1850, State Library, Concord.

46. 1850 U.S. Census.

47. Ibid.

48. Ibid.

49. Ibid.

50. Ibid.

51. Ibid.

52. Town Records, 1835, 1845.

53. U.S. Census, 1850.

54. Ibid.; Town Records, 1845, 1835.

55. U.S. Census, 1850.

56. City Directories, 1844, 1848, 1849, 1850, 1852.

Chapter 5

1. In his work on Lowell, Dublin found that, by 1860, the native born work force was displaced by immigrants.

2. Thernstrom and Knights, "Men in Motion," discuss the problem of tracing a mobile people. Dublin encountered similar difficulties in dealing with the Lowell work force. See Dublin, "Women at Work."

3. Kidder material, M.H.A. Joseph Kidder's 36 volume manuscript of diaries provides a rich supplement to the history of Manchester in this period. While Kidder was not himself a factory worker, he was an active and prolific speaker, often speaking before workingmen's groups. A descendant of General John Stark, Kidder actually represented the old, native elite.

4. Town officeholders, newspaper editors, and factory managers reflected the Yankee background of the town. Growing numbers of immigrant workers could no longer be ignored by a company and a town that sorely needed their labor.

5. For the impact of the Irish and their role in this period, see Anonymous Sister of Mercy, *Memoir of Reverend McDonald* (Manchester, n.d.). Both Potter and Clarke clearly reflect native dominance in their contemporary histories. David Montgomery had illustrated the importance of nativist sentiment and its deleterious effect upon working class consciousness. See Montgomery, "The Shuttle and the Cross: Weavers and Artisans in the Kensington Riots of 1844," *Journal of Social History* 5 (1972), pp. 411-46.

6. See Dublin, "Women at Work," for a recent discussion of the Lowell boardinghouse system. U.S. Manuscript Census returns, 1860.

7. U.S. Manuscript Census returns, 1860.

8. Ibid.

9. The manuscript census returns of the Census of Agriculture provides details of farm income and farm life that have been widely overlooked by historians. Jonathan Prude, "Coming of Industrial Order" discusses the impact of industry in an agrarian community.

10. U.S. Census manuscript returns, 1860. Amoskeag materials, M.H.A. Amoskeag files, M.P.L.

11. The Amoskeag's company housing followed hard and fast rules in its early years. The Colton and Cotton materials, at the M.H.A., illustrate the strict moral supervision imposed on company housing residents. Young women went to great lengths to keep any improprieties from the boardinghouse superiors lest they lose home and job as well. The prevalence of the female boardinghouse keeper, though, seems not to be applicable. The company seems to have preferred to let its houses to families. Boarders were then, in turn, placed with these

families by the company. For a discussion of the importance of boarding within the family, see Hareven and Modell, "Urbanization and the Malleable Household." A discussion of residents of company owned housing follows in the next chapter.

12. Amoskeag files, M.P.L. A great variety of material on firefighting survives both at the M.P.L. and M.H.A.

13. *Memoir of Reverend McDonald.* See also sermon materials at M.H.A. Denunciations of the "large boarding house" were a direct slap at the Amoskeag which maintained one boardinghouse with 104 residents. Local clergymen repeatedly condemned such houses as being destructive of the virtues of home and family. The local revival of the YMCA came, in part, as a way to counter the large, impersonal boarding house.

14. U.S. manuscript census, 1860. See file material on the fireman's riot at M.P.L. and M.H.A. The latter institution also has a collection of material relating to the Amoskeag-built fire engines.

15. YMCA material, M.H.A. Also, charities material, M.H.A.

16. Clarke, *History of Manchester.* U.S. Census, 1860; Manchester city records, 1860.

17. Browne, *Amoskeag Company.*

18. A variety of materials on the "Scots Girls" survives at the M.H.A. including records of expenditures and advances

19. Brown, *Amoskeag Company History.* U.S. manuscript census, Census of Industry, 1870 city directories. For an authoritative discussion of the French Canadian population, see Rev. Wilfred Paradis, "The French Canadians in New Hampshire," unpublished master's thesis on file at M.P.L. The author is thankful to Monsignor Paradis for his help early in this project.

20. *Memoir of Rev. McDonald.* Wilfred Paradis, "French Canadians."

21. U.S. manuscript census, 1870.

22. Ibid.; also manuscript Census of Industry, 1870.

23. See Hareven and Modell, "Urbanization and the Malleable Household."

24. Herbert Gans, *The Urban Villagers* (New York, 1962) develops the idea of the importance of ethnic neighborhoods and discusses factors promoting their formation.

25. U.S. manuscript census, Census of Industry, 1850, 1870. Census of Population, 1870. Amoskeag New Mills materials, M.H.A.

26. Company savings bank material, M.H.A. U.S. manuscript census, 1870.

27. Clarke, *History.* Richard Alcorn, "Leadership and Stability in Mid-Nineteenth Century America: A Case Study of an Illinois Town," *Journal of American History,* 61 (1974), pp.

685-702. Alcorn argues that a small core element of a stable population—community leaders—accounted for the seeming stability of mid-nineteenth century communities marked by great population fluidity. Alcorn's argument is well made, but the core element to which he refers need not always be "leaders" in a community. A stable core element of workingmen, or of middle class businessmen, could provide a sense of social continuity in the factory as well as in industrial and working class neighborhoods.

28. U.S. Manuscript Census of Population, 1860. The original enumerators' return books are in the State Library at Concord.

29. U.S. manuscript census, Census of Industry, 1860.

30. U.S. manuscript census, 1860 and 1870.

31. Ibid.

32. U.S. manuscript census, Census of Industry, 1870.

33. U.S. manuscript census, 1870.

34. Ibid.

35. Ibid.

36. U.S. manuscript census, 1860, 1870, 1880.

37. U.S. manuscript census, 1870.

38. Ibid.

39. Ibid. Compare with Dublin, "Women at Work."

40. U.S. manuscript census, 1870.

41. Ibid.

42. Ibid. See Paradis, "French Canadians" on migration to Manchester.

43. U.S. manuscript census, 1870.

44. U.S. census, 1850, 1860, 1870.

45. U.S. Census, manuscript returns, 1850.

46. U.S. manuscript census, 1870.

47. Ibid.

48. Ibid.

Chapter 6

1. Manuscript census returns, city directories, and company records were utilized in trace efforts. Dublin encountered similar difficulties in the Lowell study and found company records invaluable.

2. A wide variety of literature continued to be directed at farmers on the local level. This included statewide and local press, speakers, and newspaper articles. The importance and persistence of the farming population in Manchester is reflected in the manuscript census of agriculture and in town records.

3. Data from the manuscript census of agriculture and the manuscript population returns was correlated by hand and electronically to provide fuller information on the farming/industrial work force.

4. Lougee material drawn from census of population and census of agriculture, manuscript returns. It is important to note that not all overseers chose to retreat to the isolation of rural life. Many chose to live in the company-owned housing district that abutted the mills. As immigrants rose in the industrial hierarchy, increasing numbers of overseers and second hands would be found in the immigrant neighborhoods, further away from the company housing/mill district. Lougee, then, may well be atypical. What is important about him, though, is that in the context of the sample taken here, there is a notable absence of supervisory personnel in the 1880 immigrant neighborhood sample. This is a sharp contrast between both the rural district sample and the sample drawn from the company owned housing district. Supervisory personnel tended to live, in 1880, in areas overwhelmingly populated by the native born of native born parents. This is most evident, perhaps, in company owned housing where 51.3% of residents were native born and 45.8% were of native born fathers. See note 52.

5. U.S. manuscript census, 1880. District 134. Early Amoskeag New Mills materials at the M.H.A. give a clear picture of local farmers begging for job opportunities for their daughters. See Agent Dean's notebooks for example.

6. U.S. manuscript census of agriculture, 1880. City directory, 1880. Clarke, *History.*

7. See the city census, 1882 and 1884. Manuscript enumerators' books survive at M.H.A.

8. U.S. manuscript census, 1880.

9. City censuses, 1882 and 1884.

10. Manchester *Daily Union,* January-June, 1878.

11. Ibid., Jan. 24, 1878.

12. Ibid., August 1878.

13. Ibid. Kearneyite notices and news items appeared sporadically from 1878 to 1880 in the daily press.

14. See, for example, the episode appearing in March 15, 1878, *Daily Union.*

15. Regular disputes over city expenditures were reported in the local press. See, for example, the *Daily Union,* April 12, 1878, February 23. For corporate officials' influence on city government, see Governor Straw's public letter, January 28. Straw reminded Manchester and its citizens of their "dependence on the corporation," and warned that municipal salaries should not rival Amoskeag salaries.

16. From 1876 onward, the evening schools took up increasing attention of local school officials. They seemed to promise an ideal way of meeting financial obligations at reduced expenditures. The local press amply documents this as do the city records.

17. City Reports, 1877, 1878, 1879. See also the lively controversy in the pages of the *Daily Union.*

18. For the Amoskeag's twentieth century paternalism, see Hareven, *Amoskeag*; Hareven, "Family Time;" Hareven, "The Dynamics of Kin in an Industrial Community," *AJS* 84 (1978), pp. S151-S182.

19. Browne, *Amoskeag Company,* Amoskeag files, M.P.L.

21. Manchester *Daily Union,* March 1880.

21. Amoskeag files, M.P.L.

22. Ibid. See particularly biographical and obituary material on Amoskeag overseers.

23. Ibid.

24. Hareven, *Amoskeag,* discusses the company's post-1886 plans.

25. U.S. manuscript census, 1870 and 1880. Manchester City Directories, 1870 and 1880.

26. U.S. manuscript census, 1880. City Directory, 1880. The patterns for immigrant and native workers differ. As has been shown, the native born did not avoid company housing, but immigrants did do so.

27. A stable group of immigrant and native born workers constituted a small core of company "loyalists." As Alcorn has suggested (Alcorn, "Leadership and Stability"), such a group could make a crucial difference in providing stability in the midst of seeming chaos. The problem facing the Amoskeag after 1886 would be to enlarge this core into the immigrant neighborhoods.

28. Amoskeag files, M.P.L.

29. Ibid. See particularly the manuscript *Memoirs* of Hannah Pope Austin.

30. Austin, *Memoirs.*

31. See Chapter 2 for a discussion of the early paternalist policies of the Amoskeag.

32. U.S. Manuscript Census of Population, 1880. Enumeration district 134 was chosen for this sample, and every resident of the entire district was included in the sample. The codebook system utilized for this district will be found in the appendix. In designing his codebook, the author is grateful to Stuart Blumin and Tamara Hareven for allowing him to examine their codebooks. Their classifications were a great assistance in developing the codebooks used for this study.

33. U.S. manuscript census, 1880. Enumeration Districts 134 and 121.

34. U.S. manuscript census, 1880, District 134. By contrast, see Table 6.17. Note that textile work has far greater numbers of each household membership category, while fewer people could afford the luxury of remaining at home, retired, or unemployed in the immigrant and company-dominated neighborhoods.

35. U.S. manuscript census, 1880, District 134.

36. Farm income is based on returns from the U.S. manuscript census of agriculture. Other wages are based on local wage rates and a computerized match of job and prevailing local wages. Note that the sample size is considerably reduced, since wage information was not available for all occupations.

37. U.S. manuscript census, 1880, Enumeration Districts 134, 133, 121. Sample sizes: District 134 = 920; District 133 = 2,037; District 121 = 666.

38. City Census, 1884.

39. U.S. manuscript census, 1880, Districts 134, 133, 121. Note that company housing was not only dominated by the native born, but also by native born of native parents. See note 52.

Company Housing District—Places of Birth

	Nativity	Father's Nativity
N.H.	50.8	41.0
Other N.E.	22.1	19.4
Other U.S.	6.8	7.5
England-Scotland-Wales	2.9	4.5
Ireland	3.0	4.8
Canada	10.8	11.9
Other Foreign	3.3	9.5
Not Known	0.5	1.5
	N = 666	N = 666

Source: U.S. manuscript census, 1880, District 121.

40. U.S. manuscript census, 1880, Districts 133, 134, and 121.

41. Ibid., 1880, Districts 133, 134, 121. Note the scarcity of older population in both immigrant and company owned housing districts. Note, too, that the immigrant industrial district has a population markedly biased towards the young. This would indicate a growing influence for these groups in the years to come, and a decline in influence of the native born who were dominant in the other two areas.

42.   Ibid., 1880, Districts 133, 134, 121.

43.   Ibid., 1880, District 133. Note the difference in District 121, company owned housing:

Size of Dwellings, Company-Owned Housing District:

	Privately Owned	Company Owned
1 Family	31.4%	43.4%
2 Family	7.7	15.6
3 Family		2.0

Note that not all housing in this district was company owned by 1880, but that company owned housing predominated. The tenement house, as such, was a phenomenon of the new immigrant neighborhoods, the product of the unique needs of a new population.

44.   Ibid., 1870 and 1880, District 133.

45.   Ibid., 1880, District 133. Hareven and Langenbach, *Amoskeag,* have pointed out the design and substantive quality of the company's housing. See also Langenbach, "Amoskeag Mill-yard."

46.   Ibid., District 133.

47.   Ibid., Districts 133 and 134. Wage data drawn from local wage rates for 52 industrial occupations.

48.   Ibid., Districts 133 and 121.

49.   Ibid., Districts 133 and 121.

50.   Ibid., Districts 133, 134, and 121. Unlike earlier years, company owned housing was not dominated by female occupants nor was the private housing market:

	Private	Company
Male	12.6	26.6
Female	26.4	34.4
N = 666		

51.   Ibid., District 133.

52.   Ibid., District 133. Neighborhoods such as this one served to ease the immigrant's plight. See Herbert Gans, *The Urban Villagers* for the uses of such neighborhoods into the twentieth century. Note the contrast of opportunity between natives and the foreign born in the company housing district:

	Native	Ireland	Canada
Semi-Prof.	3.5		1.6
White Collar	8.6		1.6
Skilled	22.0	6.5	13.1
Semi-Skilled	1.9		1.6
Unskilled	8.9	19.3	11.5
Textile	54.9	74.2	70.5

53. For a discussion of 1855, see Chapter 3. U.S. manuscript census, District 133. Compare with District 121, company owned housing:

	Non-Company Owned	Company Housing
Semi-Prof	2.9	2.1
White Collar	1.4	9.3
Skilled	16.3	22.8
Semi-Skilled	.4	2.1
Unskilled	11.5	8.2
Textile	67.3	55.4
N =	208	280

Selected Bibliography

I. Primary Sources

A. Unpublished Manuscripts

1. Amoskeag Manufacturing Company Records. For the purpose of this study, the large manuscript collection at the Manchester Historic Association was heavily utilized. These include:

Account of Goods Manufactured by Girls, Amoskeag Mills, 1 volume, 1832-1835.
Agreements Book, 1 volume, 1836-1842.
Business Letter Books, 8 volumes, 1844-1908.
Cost of Labor and Average of Wages, 2 volumes, 1867-1870; 1870-1872.
Daily Journal, 1859.
Journals, Amoskeag Industries, 16 volumes, 1826-1859.
Journal, Early Employment, n.d.
Land Sales Book, 1 volume, 1843-1919.
Leases to Boarding House Owners, 2 volumes, 1855-1860; 1860-1861.
Letterbooks, 5 volumes, 1826-1848.
Miscellaneous Papers, 6 boxes, 1850-1879.
Payroll Books, 14 volumes, 1836-1879.
Register of Workers, Amoskeag New Mills, 1859-1878.
Salaries and Wages Letterbook, 1 volume, 1870-1908.
Savings Bank Books, 2 volumes.
Scots Girls Books, 2 volumes, 1868; 1870.
Superintendent's Scrapbook, 1878.
Tenement Books, 2 volumes, 1878; 1880-1882.
Tenement House Papers, 2 boxes, 1827-1852; 1858-1886.

2. Amoskeag Materials and City Materials at the Manchester Public Library.

Amoskeag Files, 3 drawers.
Amoskeag and Stark Mills, Maps, 1850-1885.
George Calvin Carter. *Papers.*
City Hotel Register, 3 volumes, 1855-1860.
Insurance Maps of Manchester, 1897.

3. Manchester City Records.

Manchester Public Library. Manchester Annual Report, 1845-1880.

Manchester Historic Association. Manchester City Census, 2 volumes, 1882; 1884. Manuscript
    returns.
Manchester City Hall. Manchester City Clerk's Financial Records, 1850-1851.
Manchester Public Library. Manchester City Library Annual Report, 1854-1858.
Manchester Public Library. Manchester High School, Directory of Students, 1 volume,
    1846-1880.
Manchester City Hall. Manchester Tax Lists. Tax Collector's Record Books, 1835; 1845.
Manchester Historic Association. Register of Students in Two Primary Schools, 1870-1880.

4.   Federal Manuscript Censuses.

United States. Bureau of the Census. Sixth Census, 1840, *Census of Population*. Hillsborough
    County, New Hampshire. Manuscript returns.
_____. Sixth Census, 1840, *Census of Agriculture*. Hillsborough County, New Hampshire.
    Manuscript returns.
_____. Seventh Census, 1850, *Census of Population*. Hillsborough County, New Hampshire.
    Manuscript returns.
_____. Seventh Census, 1850, *Census of Agriculture*. Hillsborough County, New Hampshire.
    Manuscript returns.
_____. Eighth Census, 1860, *Census of Population*. Hillsborough County, New Hampshire.
    Manuscript returns.
_____. Ninth Census, 1870, *Census of Population*. Hillsborough County, New Hampshire.
    Manuscript returns.
_____. Ninth Census, 1870, *Census of Agriculture*. Hillsborough County, New Hampshire.
    Manuscript returns.
_____. Ninth Census, 1870, *Census of Manufactures*. Hillsborough County, New Hampshire.
    Manuscript returns.
_____. Tenth Census, 1880, *Census of Population*. Hillsborough County, New Hampshire.
    Manuscript returns.
_____. Tenth Census, 1880, *Census of Agriculture*. Hillsborough County, New Hampshire.
    Manuscript returns.
_____. Tenth Census, 1880, *Census of Manufactures*. Hillsborough County, New Hampshire.
    Manuscript returns.

5.   Diaries, Letters, and Papers.

Manchester Historic Association. Theodore Abbott, Inaugural Address, 1856, 1 box.
Manchester Historic Association. Second Baptist Society, Minutes, 1848-1852.
Manchester Public Library. Individual Biographies, Amoskeag Manufacturing Company, 1 box.
Manchester Historic Association. Miscellaneous Biographical Sketches of Manchester Men.
    Scrapbook.
Manchester Historic Association. Journal of Susan Blount, 1 volume, ca. 1830-1845.
Manchester Historic Association. Church Manuals, Reports, Programs, 1 box.
Manchester Historic Association. City Missionary Society, 1 box.
Manchester Historic Association. Elkins Letters, 1 box, 1824-ca. 1845.
Manchester Historic Association. Moses Fellows. Mayoral Address and Papers, 1 box, 1851.
Manchester Historic Association. J.C. Field Papers, 1 box, 1830-ca. 1880.
Manchester Historic Association. Fraternal Orders, Collections of Miscellaneous Papers,
    5 bound volumes, ca. 1850-1890.
Manchester Historic Association. Record Book, Justice of the Peace, July 1826-August 1849.

Manchester Historic Association. Joseph P. Kidder, Papers and Diaries, 5 boxes, 1838-1901.
Manchester Historic Association. Little Family Papers, 1 box, 1821-1853.
Manchester Historic Association. Old Residents Association, 1 box, n.d.
Manchester Historic Association. Parker Murder Materials, 1 box.
Manchester Historic Association. Byron Richardson Letters, 1 box, February 1861-January 1866.
Manchester Historic Association. Rogue's Gallery Portraits, Ledger, Manchester Police
    Department, 1880.
Manchester Historic Association. Sermons by Manchester Ministers, 1 box.
Manchester Historic Association. Miscellaneous Diaries of Sermons, 2 boxes.
Manchester Historic Association. Frederick Smyth Papers, 14 boxes, 1854-1874.
Manchester Historic Association. Voters Check Lists, 2 boxes, 1848-1870.

B.   Published Works

1.   Books, Pamphlets, Articles

Bacon, C.F. *Manchester and Its Leading Business Men.* Manchester, N.H. 1891.
Bibliography of Books, Pamphlets, Magazines for Manchester (Nutfield, Londonderry, Chester,
    Harrytown, and Deerfield), New Hampshire, 1843-1885. Manchester, New Hampshire, 1894.
Browne, George W., ed. "Early Records of the Town of Derryfield, Now Manchester, New
    Hampshire, 1751-1800." Manchester Historic Association *Collections,* Volumes 8 and 9.
_____. "Early Records of the Town of Manchester, 1801-1835." Manchester Historic Associa-
    tion *Collections,* Volumes 10, 11, and 12.
Centennial Celebration Pamphlet. Manchester, New Hampshire, 1851.
Clarke, John B. *Manchester. A Brief Record of Its Past and a Picture of Its Present.* Manchester,
    New Hampshire, 1875.
Disappointed Love! A Story, Drawn from Incidents in the Lives of Miss Clara C. Cochran and
    Miss Catherine B. Cotton, Who Committed Suicide by Drowning in the Canal at Manchester,
    N.H., August 14, 1853. Manchester, Weekly Mirror Printing Establishment, 1853.
Eastman, H.W., ed. *Semi-Centennial of Manchester.* Manchester, New Hampshire. 1897.
Manchester Historic Association. *Collections.* 12 volumes. Manchester, New Hampshire.
A Sister of Mercy. *Memoir of Reverend William McDonald.* Manchester, New Hampshire:
    Saint Anne's Convent, ca. 1890.
Potter, Chandler E. *The History of Manchester.* Manchester, New Hampshire, 1856.

2.   Directories, Alamanacs, Guides

Manchester Directory. 1844-1880.
Pocket Business Directory and Industrial and Social Statistics of the City of Mancheser. Man-
    chester, New Hampshire: Temple and Farrington Publishers, 1879.
Ryder's Real Estate Guide. Manchester, New Hampshire, 1879.
Van Slyck, J.D. *Representatives of New England Manufacturers.* Volume 2. Manchester, New
    Hampshire, 1890.
Wetmore, S.F. *Manchester Almanac, Directory and Annual Advertiser.* Manchester, New
    Hampshire, 1845.

3.   Newspapers

Barrett's Capillary Journal, September 1868-September 1869.
Business Advertiser, July 1869-May 1870.

Business Monitor, 1867.

Clark's Advertiser, May 1875.

Colt's Illustrated Scientific Commercial Advertiser, December 1868-March 1869.

Echo des Canadiens, November 1880-March 1883.

Every Month, December 1867-November 1868.

French's Journal, November 1867-February 1869.

Gleaner, October 1842-March 1846.

Granite Farmer, December 1850-January 1851; December 1853-January 1854; December 1856-January 1858.

Granite State, September-November 1878.

Greenback Lever, June-September 1878.

Greenback Press, January-May 1880.

Holiday News, December 1873.

Independent Democrat, May 1845-June 1845.

Iris and Literary Repository, April 1842-April 1843.

Little Live Daily, September 1869.

Manchester Allodium, January-April 1843.

Manchester American and Messenger, September 1844-February 1858.

Manchester American, September 1845-April 1846.

Manchester Daily American, April 5, 1856-December 31, 1863; January 1875-May 1880.

Manchester Business Index, February-April 1869.

Manchester Courier, November 1874.

Manchester Democrat, April 1842-January 1843; January 1847-June 1852; June 1856-April 1863.

Manchester Enterprise, October 1882.

Manchester (Weekly) Guardian, July 1883-May 1884.

Manchester Illustrated Bulletin, May 1873.

Manchester Daily Item, December 1877-January 1878.

Manchester Itemizer, May 1879-July 1880.

Manchester Magazine, December 1839-March 1840.

Manchester Massabesic, June-September 1878.

Manchester Memorial, January 1840-August 1844.

Manchester Mirror and Farmer, January 1851-December 1852.

Manchester Daily News, January-May 1869.

Manchester Palladium, March 1846-February 1947.

Manchester Record, December 1883-April 1884.

Manchester Representative, December 1841-February 1842.

Manchester Republican Volunteer, August-October 1880.

Manchester Spy, August 1850-November 1851.

Manchester Telescope, September 1848-April 1850.

Manchester Times, August 1878-May 1882.

Manchester Transcript, April 21-August 4, 1843.

Manchester Workman, November 7, 1840.

New Hampshire Journal of Agriculture, April 1859; April 1861.

New Hampshire Magazine, August 1843-July 1846.

New Year's Call, January 1870.

Old City Hall Drug Store and the Manchester Advertiser, October 1874-May 1875; December 1878-January 1880.

Operative, February 1843-November 1844.

Our Horn, February 1874.

Our Mutual Friend, May 1874; December 1886.

Phonograph, October 1878.
Pioneer, September 1879-February 1880.
Saturday Messenger, January 1845-November 1848.

4. Government Reports, Published Papers, Documents

Massachusetts. Bureau of Labor Statistics. "The Canadian French." *Third Annual Report, 1880.* Boston, 1882.
New Hampshire. *Governor's Messages.* 1817; 1821-23; 1835; 1858; 1865; 1867; 1869; 1871; 1887. Concord, New Hampshire.
_____. *Legislative Report on the Shortening of Hours of Child Labor.* Concord, New Hampshire, 1847.
_____. *Report of the State Board of Agriculture.* Concord, New Hampshire, 1873.
United States. Bureau of Labor Statistics. *Reports 1886-1890.* Washington, 1887-1891.
_____. Bureau of the Census. Tenth Census, 1880. *Census Reports, Tenth Census. June 1, 1880.* Vol. 1, pt. 2. *Statistics of the Population, embracing extended tables of population of states, counties and minor civil divisions.* Ed. Francis A. Walker and Henry Gammett. Washington, 1883.
_____. Tenth Census, 1880. *Census Reports, Tenth Census. June 1, 1880.* Vol. 18. *Social Statistics of Cities.* Comp. George E. Warring, Jr. Washington, 1887.
_____. Tenth Census, 1880. *Census Reports, Tenth Census. June 1, 1880.* Vol. 20. *Statistics of Wages in Manufacturing Industries.* Comp. Joseph E. Weeks. Washington, 1888

II. Secondary Sources

Alcorn, Richard S. "Leadership and Stability in Mid-Nineteenth century America: A Case Study of An Illinois Town." *Journal of American History,* 61 (December 1974), 685-702.
Anderson, Michael. *Family Structure in Nineteenth Century Lancashire.* London: Cambridge University Press, 1971.
Armstrong, John B. *Factory Under the Elms: A History of Harrisville, New Hampshire, 1774-1969.* Cambridge: M.I.T. Press, 1969.
Berthoff, Rowland T. *British Immigrants in Industrial America, 1790-1950.* Cambridge: Harvard University Press, 1953.
Blauner, Robert. *Alienation and Freedom: The Factory Workers and His Industry.* Chicago: University of Chicago Press, 1964.
Blood, Grace Holbrook. *Manchester on the Merrimack.* Manchester, New Hampshire: Lew Cummings Co., 1948.
Brody, David. "The Old Labor History and the New: In Search of an American Working Class." *Labor History,* 20 (Winter, 1979), 111-126.
Brooks, Thomas R. *Toil and Trouble: A History of American Labor.* New York: Delta Books, 1964.
Browne, George Waldo. *The Amoskeag Manufacturing Company of Manchester, New Hampshire: A History.* Manchester, New Hampshire: The Amoskeag Manufacturing Company, 1915.
Buder, Stanley. *Pullman: An Experiment in Industrial Order and Community Planning 1880-1930.* New York: Oxford University Press, 1967.
Byington, Margaret. *Homestead: The Household of a Mill Town.* Pittsburgh, Pennsylvania: University Center for International Studies, 1974.
Carlton, David Lee. "Mill and Town: The Cotton Mill Workers and the Middle Class in South Carolina, 1880-1920." Unpublished Ph.D. dissertation, Yale University, 1977.

Clark, Victor S. *History of Manufactures in the United States, I.* New York: Peter Smith, 1949.

Clarke, John B. *The Parker Murder.* Manchester, New Hampshire: John B. Clarke Co., 1886.

Cole, Donald B. *Immigrant City: Lawrence, Massachusetts, 1845-1921.* Chapel Hill: The University of North Carolina Press, 1963.

Commons, John R. et al. *A Documentary History of American Industrial Society.* VII, VIII. Cleveland: Arthur H. Clark Co., 1910.

_____. *History of Labour in the United States,* 4 vols. New York: The Macmillan Company, 1918-1935.

Coolidge, John. *Mill and Mansion: A Study of Architecture and Society in Lowell, Massachusetts, 1820-1865.* New York: Columbia University Press, 1942.

Creamer, Daniel B. and Coulter, Charles W. *Labor and the Shut-Down of the Amoskeag Textile Mills.* Philadelphia: Works Progress Administration, 1939.

Cumbler, John T. *Working Class Community in Industrial America: Work, Leisure and Struggle in Two Industrial Cities, 1880-1930.* Westport, CT: Greenwood Press, 1979.

Davis, Kingsley. "The Origin and Growth of Urbanization in the World." *American Journal of Sociology.* 60 (1955), 429-437.

Davis, Lance. "The New England Textile Mills and the Capital Market: A Study in Industrial Borrowing, 1840-1860." *Journal of Economic History.* XX (March 1960), 1-30.

_____. "Sources of Industrial Finance: The American Textile Industry, A Case Study." *Explorations in Entrepreneurial History.* 1st ser., IX (April 1957), 189-203.

_____. "Stock Ownership in the Early New England Textile Industry." *Business History Review,* XXXII (Summer 1958), 204-22.

Dawley, Alan. *Class and Community: The Industrial Revolution in Lynn.* Cambridge, Mass.: Harvard University Press, 1976.

Dollar, Charles M. and Jensen, Richard J. *Historian's Guide to Statistics: Quantitative Analysis and Historical Research.* New York: Holt, Rinehart and Winston, Inc., 1971.

Dublin, Thomas Louis. "Women at Work: The Transformation of Work and Community in Lowell, Massachusetts, 1826-1860." Unpublished Ph.D. dissertation, Columbia University, 1975.

_____. *Women at Work: The Transformation of Work and Community in Lowell, Massachusetts, 1826-1860.* New York: Columbia University Press, 1979.

_____. "Women, Work, and the Family: Female Operatives in the Lowell Mills, 1830-1860." *Feminist Studies,* 3 (Fall 1975), 30-39.

_____. "Women, Work and Protest in the Early Lowell Mills: 'The Oppressing Hand of Avarice Would Enslave Us'." *Labor History,* 16, 99-116.

Dulles, Foster Rhea. *Labor in America: A History.* New York: Thomas Y. Crowell Co., 1966.

English, Walter. *The Textile Industry: An Account of the Early Inventions of Spinning, Weaving, and Knitting Machines.* London: Longmans, Green and Co., 1969.

Erickson, Charlotte. *Invisible Immigrants: The Adaption of English and Scottish Immigrants in Nineteenth Century America.* Coral Gables, Florida: University of Miami Press, 1972.

Ewing, John S. and Norton, Nancy P. *A History of the Bigelow-Sanford Carpet Company: Broadlooms and Businessmen.* Cambridge: Harvard University Press, 1955.

Faler, Paul. "Working Class Historiography." '*Radical America,* 3 (1969), 56-68.

Floud, Roderick. *An Introduction to Quantitative Methods for Historians.* Princeton, New Jersey: Princeton University Press, 1973.

Gibb, George Sweet. *The Saco-Lowell Shops: Textile Machinery Building in New England, 1813-1949.* Cambridge: Harvard University Press, 1950.

Ginger, Ray. "Labor in a Massachusetts Cotton Mill, 1853-1860." *Business History Review,* XXVIII (1954), 67-91.

Gitelman, Howard M. 'No Irish Need Apply: Patterns and Responses to Ethnic Discrimination in the Labor Market." *Labor History,* XIV (Winter 1973), 56-68.

_____. "The Waltham System and the Coming of the Irish." *Labor History,* VIII (Fall 1967), 227-253.

Green, Constance McLaughlin. *Holyoke, Massachusetts: A Case History of the Industrial Revolution in America.* New Haven: Yale University Press, 1939.

Greenfield, Sidney M. "Industrialization and the Family in Sociological Theory." *American Journal of Sociology,* 67 (November 1961), 312-22.

Gutman, Herbert. "Work, Culture and Society in Industrializing America, 1819-1918." *American Historical Review,* 78 (1973), 531-88.

_____. *Work, Culture and Society in Industrializing America: Essays in America's Working Class and Social History.* New York: Random House, 1977.

Hareven, Tamara K. and Langenbach, Randolph. *Amoskeag: Life and Work in an American Factory City.* New York: Pantheon Books, 1978.

Hareven, Tamara K., ed. *Anonymous Americans: Explorations in Nineteenth Century Social History.* Englewood Cliffs, N.J.: Prentice-Hall, 1971.

_____. "The Dynamics of Kin in an Industrial Community." *American Journal of Sociology,* 84 (1978), *Supplement,* S151-S182.

_____. *Family and Kin in Urban Communities, 1700-1930.* New York: New Viewpoints, 1977.

_____. "The Family as Process: The Historical Study of the Family Cycle." *Journal of Social History,* 7 (1974), 322-39.

_____. "Family Time and Industrial Time: Family and Work in a Planned Corporation Town, 1900-1924." *Journal of Urban History,* I (1975), 365-89.

_____. "The Laborers of Manchester, New Hampshire, 1910-1922: Patterns of Adjustment to Industrial Life." *Labor History,* 16 (1975), 249-65.

Josephson, Hannah. *The Golden Threads: New England's Mill Girls and Magnates.* New York: Duell, Sloan, and Pearce, 1949.

Katz, Michael B. *The People of Hamilton, Canada West: Family and Class in a Mid-Nineteenth Century City.* Cambridge, Massachusetts: Harvard University Press, 1975.

Kerr, Clark et al. *Industrialism and Industrial Man: The Problems of Labor and Management in Economic Growth.* New York: Oxford University Press, 1964.

Kingsbury, Susan M., ed. *Labor Laws and Their Enforcement, With Special Reference to Massachusetts.* New York: Longmans, Green and Co., 1911.

Kirkland, Edward C. *A History of American Economic Life.* New York: Appleton-Century-Crofts, 1951.

Knights, Peter. *The Plain People of Boston, 1830-1860: A Study in City Growth.* New York: Oxford University Press, 1971.

Knowlton, Evelyn H. *Pepperell's Progress: History of a Cotton Textile Company, 1844-1945.* Cambridge, Massachusetts: Harvard University Press, 1948.

Krueger, Thomas A. "American Labor Historiography, Old and New: A Review Essay." *Journal of Social History,* 3 (Spring 1971), 277-85.

Kulik, Gary and Bonham, Julia C. *Rhode Island: An Inventory of Historic Engineering and Industrial Sites.* Washington: 1977.

Langenbach, Randolph. "The Amoskeag Millyard: An Epic in Urban Design." *Harvard Alumni Bulletin,* (April 15, 1968).

Laurie, Bruce, et al. "Immigrants and Industry: The Philadelphia Experience, 1850-1880." *Journal of Social History,* 9 (1975), 219-48.

Layer, Robert G. *Earnings of Cotton Mill Operatives, 1825-1914.* Cambridge: Harvard University Press, 1955.

_____. "Wages, Earnings and Output of Four Cotton Textile Companies in New England, 1825-1860." Unpublished Ph.D. dissertation, Harvard University, 1952.

LeBlanc, Robert G. *Location of Manufacturing in New England in the 19th Century.* Hanover, New Hampshire: Geography Publications at Dartmouth, 1969.

Lynd, Alice and Lynd, Staughton. *Rank and File: Personal Histories by Working Class Organizers.* Boston: Beacon Press, 1973.

McGouldrick, Paul F. *New England Textiles in the Nineteenth Century: Profits and Investments.* Cambridge: Harvard University Press, 1968.

McLaughlin, Virginia Lans. "Patterns of Work and Family Organization Among Buffalo's Italians." *Journal of Interdisciplinary History,* II (Autumn 1971), 299-314.

Mailloux, Kenneth. "Boston Manufacturing Company of Waltham, Massachusetts, 1813-1848: The First Modern Factory in America." Unpublished Ph.D. dissertation, Boston University, 1957.

Modell, John. "The Peopling of a Working Class Ward: Reading, Pennsylvania, 1850." *Journal of Social History,* V (Fall 1971), 71-95.

Mumford, Lewis. *The Culture of Cities.* New York: Harcourt Brace, 1938.

Navin, Thomas R. *The Whitin Machine Works Since 1831.* Cambridge: Harvard University Press, 1950.

Paradis, Wilfred H. "French Canadian Influence in Manchester, New Hampshire, Before 1891." Unpublished M.A. thesis, St. Mary's Seminary, Baltimore, Maryland, 1949.

Pelling, Henry. *American Labor.* Chicago: University of Chicago Press, 1960.

Pleck, Elizabeth. "Two Worlds in One: Work and Family." *Journal of Social History.* 10 (1976), 178-95.

Prude, Jonathan. "The Coming of Industrial Order: A Study of Town and Factory Life in Rural Massachusetts, 1813-1860." Unpublished Ph.D. dissertation, Harvard University, 1976.

Sennett, Richard. *Families Against the City: Middle Class Homes of Industrial Chicago, 1872-1890.* Cambridge: Harvard University Press, 1970.

Serrin, William. *The Company and the Union.* New York: Alfred A. Knopf, 1973.

Shlakman, Vera. *Economic History of a Factory Town: A Study of Chicopee, Mass.* Smith College Studies in History, 1934-35.

Silvia, Philip T. *Spindle City: Labor, Politics, and Religion in Fall River, Massachusetts, 1870-1905.* Unpublished Ph.D. dissertation, Fordham University, 1973.

Smelser, Neil. *Social Change and the Industrial Revolution.* Chicago: Universitay of Chicago Press, 1959.

Straw, William Parker. *Amoskeag in New Hampshire: An Epic in American Industry.* New York: Newcomen Society of England, American Branch, 1948.

Swanson, Dorothy. "Annual Bibliography on American Labor History." *Labor History,* vol. 18 (Fall 1977), S45-S69.

Sweezy, Alan R. "The Amoskeag Manufacturing Company." *Quarterly Journal of Economics* 52, 1937-1938, 473-512.

Thernstrom, Stephan. *The Other Bostonians: Poverty and Progress in the American Metropolis, 1880-1970.* Cambridge: Harvard University Press, 1973.

_____. *Poverty and Progress: Social Mobility in a Nineteenth Century City.* Cambridge: Harvard University Press, 1964.

_____, and Knights, Peter R. "Men in Motion: Some Data and Speculations about Urban Population Mobility in Nineteenth-Century America." *Journal of Interdisciplinary History,* 1 (Autumn 1970), 7-35.

_____, and Sennett, Richard, eds. *Nineteenth Century Cities: Essays in the New Urban History.* New Haven: Yale University Press, 1969.

Thompson, E.P. *The Making of the English Working Class.* New York: Random House, 1963.

Tymeson, Mildred McClary. *The Norton Story.* Worcester, Massachusetts: The Norton Company, 1953.

United States. Bureau of the Census. *Historical Statistics of the United States: Colonial Times to 1957.* Washington: Government Printing Office, 1960.

_____. *Report on the Condition of Women and Child-Earners in the United States, I, Cotton Textile Industry.* Washington, Senate Document 65, 61st Congress, 2nd Session.

Walkowitz, Daniel J. *Worker City, Company Town: Iron and Cotton-Worker Protest in Troy and Cohoes, New York, 1855-84.* Urbana, Illinois: University of Illinois Press, 1978.

Wallace, Anthony F. D. *Rockdale: The Growth of an American Village in the Early Industrial Revolution.* New York: Knopf, 1978.

Ware, Caroline F. *Early New England Cotton Manufacture.* New York: Russell and Russell, 1966.

Ware, Norman. *The Industrial Worker, 1840-1860: The Reaction of American Industrial Society to the Advance of the Industrial Revolution.* Boston: Houghton, Mifflin Co., 1924.

Wiebe, Robert. *The Search for Order, 1877-1920.* New York: Hill and Wang, 1967.

Winchester, Jan. "The Linkage of Historical Records by Man and Computer: Techniques and Problems." *Journal of Interdisciplinary History,* I (Autumn 1970), 107-124.

Wright, Carroll D. *The History and Growth of the United States Census.* Washington: Government Printing Office, 1900.

Zeiger, Robert H. "Workers and Scholars: Recent Trends in American Labor Hitoriography." *Labor History,* 13 (1972), 245-66.

Index